A TASTE OF HISTORY

Photography By Bill Touchberry,
Raleigh, North Carolina

The North Carolina Museum Of History Associates, Inc.

ISBN: 0-961-01180-7

Printed by Edwards & Broughton Company
Raleigh, North Carolina

The North Carolina Museum of History Associates, Inc.
109 E. Jones Street
Raleigh, North Carolina 27611

The North Carolina Museum Of History Associates, Inc.

Since 1898 the North Carolina Museum of History has had the official responsibility of preserving North Carolina's social, economic and political history for millions of visitors and school children who come not only to the Museum in Raleigh, but to historic sites all over the state. In 1976, the North Carolina Museum of History Associates was organized as a statewide support group for the Museum and 23 state historic sites.

A primary concern of the Museum Associates is that antiques and artifacts which tell North Carolina history are often lost or sold outside the state. Because the Museum receives only $4,500 annually from the state for acquisitions, the Associates raise funds through membership dues and projects like this cookbook to purchase significant North Carolina artifacts.

Associate funds are also used to take the Museum to the people of the state through hundreds of educational programs in communities all over North Carolina. In addition, the Associates provide lectures, tours, assistance to local history museums and programs within the Tar Heel Junior Historian Association. The Associates' Blue Ribbon Committee to Save the Flags raised more than $160,000 from individuals, businesses, foundations and the General Assembly to restore and display the state's collection of historic flags.

Continuing financial and volunteer support by the Associates will enable the Museum to preserve North Carolina's heritage and make it accessible to more people.

Cookbook Committee

Mrs. Charles Merrill
Co-Chairman

Mrs. Edwina Hardy Shaw
Co-Chairman

Mrs. Thomas Alexander
Hors d'oeuvres

Mrs. Frank Bridger
Co-Chairman, Parties

Mrs. Charles P. Bugg
Salads

Mrs. Frank J. Butler
Typing

Mrs. Donnell B. Cobb, Jr.
Co-Chairman, Menus

Mrs. David W. Cox
Indexing

Mrs. T. Barker Dameron III
Design

Mrs. J. Roger Edwards
Co-Chairman, Marketing

Mrs. Robert W. Estill
Soups

Mrs. Jill Flink
Bread

Mrs. Richard Haar
Proofreading

Mrs. Ira Hardy
Seafood

Mrs. Carl Hiller
Co-Chairman, Vegetables

Mrs. Tad Iredale
Illustrator

Mrs. Walton Joyner
Co-Chairman, Brunches

Mrs. William D. Lease
Cakes/Pastry

Mrs. Frank R. Liggett III
Poultry/Game

Mrs. Lynn McIver
Desserts
Co-Chairman, Soups

Mrs. Betsy Miller
Co-Chairman, Vegetables

Mrs. Kenneth Morris
Co-Chairman, Vegetables

Mrs. John C. Palmer
Co-Chairman, Marketing

Mrs. James Peden, Jr.
Photography

Mrs. Ward Purrington
Co-Chairman, Menus

Mrs. William G. Rand
Credits

Mrs. Emerson Scarborough
Meats

Mrs. Richard Simmons
Co-Chairman, Brunches

Mrs. Natalie Talyor
Co-Chairman, Marketing

Mrs. Robert Turner
Co-Chairman, Parties

Mrs. Robert S. Warren
Microwave

Mrs. Charles Winston
Sauces

4

MENUS

St. Thomas Church, Bath

BRUNCHES

Kir Royal
or
German Sekt

Eggs Hussard with
Marchand de vin sauce
Garlic Grits Souffle
Curried Hot Fruit Compote
Cheese biscuits
Praline Creme Caramel

Blanc de Noir
Champagne

Grapefruit Halves
Dove and Sausage Gumbo
Tomatoes Parmesan
Corn Light Bread with Fresh Strawberry Jam
Individual Prune Souffles

Asti Spumante

Melon Compote
Orange Glazed Ham
Zucchini Rounds
Easy Oven Omelette
Original Pecan Pralines

Mimosa's
(Champagne &
O.J.)

Make Ahead Scrambled Eggs
Apple Sausage Bake
Coffee Cake
Garlic Grits

German Riesling
   Kabinett
or
Spritzer (white wine
   & soda)

Curried Eggs
Cranberry Chutney
Asparagus Fried Rice
Baked Apricots
Croissants *
Toffee Bars

LUNCHEONS

Fino sherry
Medium dry rose
Medium dry German
White Zinfendel

Crabmeat Asparagus Soup
Ham Mousse
Peach Salad
Herbal Popovers

Caroline's Brownies
Pecan Caramel Bars

Macon

Oyster Soup
Crustless Ham and Asparagus Quiche
Raw Spinach Salad
Whole Wheat Biscuits

Orange Custard

Rhinegau
Gewurztraminer

New Orleans Crabmeat
Suzanne's Tomatoes Florentine
Zucchini Sticks
Sourdough English muffins
Lemon Custard in Meringue Tarts

*Recipe not included in book.

Soave or dry German	Cold Cucumber Soup
	Garibaldi Salad
	Croissants *
	White Chocolate Mousse

Medium dry Rose or Medium dry Loire Valley wine, such as Bonray	Cream of Fresh Tomato Soup
	Ham & Swiss Sandwiches
	Broccoli Salad
	Lemon Chess Tarts

SUNDAY NIGHT SUPPERS

Chardonnay or St. Veran	Tomato Soup Gratinee
	Chicken Pie with Oysters
	English Peas *
	Derby House Green Salad
	Frozen Lemon Chiffon

California Zinfandel or Chianti	Beef Patties Parmesan
	Tomatoes Provencale
	Black Eyed Peas
	Pickled Onions
	Sally Lunn Bread
	Brown Sugar Pie

COCKTAIL BUFFETS

California Gamay	*Marinated Eye of Round*
Beaujolais or	*Mustard **
Pinot Noir Blanc	*Mayonnaise **
	Cheese Ring with Melon Ball Melange
	Lime Sauce on Broccoli
	Whiskey Chute Tomatoes
	Marinated Shrimp
	Swedish Rye Bread
	Moravian Love Feast Buns

fruity white such	*Smokey Pecans*
as Chenin Blanc or	*Mushroom Pastries*
medium dry blanc	*Molded Avocado Pinwheel*
de noir	*Country Ham*
	Feta Cheese Ball
	Perfect Party Pate
	Crudites with Artichoke Dip
	Onion Rye Bread

California Savignon	*Shrimp Salad Spread*
Blanc or	*Roquefort Pate*
Italian Gavidegavi	*Crab Mousse*
	Artichoke Squares
	Edwina's Scallop Skewers
	Pappy's Famous Half Shells
	small toasts, crackers and wafers

FORMAL DINNERS

Dry Chenin Blanc

Individual Blue Cheese Souffles
Chicken with Asparagus and
    Lemon Sabayou
Tomatoes Parmesan
Salad Vinaigrette*
Yeast Rolls*

Frozen Cognac Cream
Almond Crescents

White Burgandy or
Pinot Blanc

Cream of Celery Soup I
Fish Fillets with Nantua Sauce
Spinach Timbales
Pear Salad
French Bread*

Kahlua Souffle
Pound Cake Wafers

California Cabernet
or
French Bordeaux

Shrimp with Dilled Mustard Sauce
Filet Mignon in Foil
Esther's Celery with Almonds
Bean Bundles
Charleston Salad

Judy's Easy Italian Bread

Swiss Chocolate Almond Pie

ALFRESCO

Beaujolais Village
or
Zinfandel

Artichoke Cheese Appetizers
Lamb Shish Kabobs
Suzanne's Rice Octavie
Day Ahead Green Salad
Oat Sesame Bread

Frozen Grand Marnier
Souffle in Orange Cups

Full bodied red
such as Cabernet or
Bordeaux

Butterflied Leg of Lamb
Ratatouille
German Mushrooms
Citrus Salad
Parmesan Casserole Bread
Ice Creamed Grasshoppers

California Petite
Sirah or
Zinfandel

Tyrolean Beef
Zucchini Casserole
Sour Cream Cornbread
Bavarian Fruit Torte

California
Pinot Noir Blanc
or a good beer

Deep Fried Cheese
Spare Ribs
Asparagus Salad
Batter Bread

Fresh Peach Sherbet
Pound Cake Wafers

DINNERS

California Gamay	Hot Apple Soup
	Elegant Pork Loin
	Sweet Potato Pudding
	Freezer Slaw
	Onion Rye Bread
	Lemon Trifle with Strawberry Melba Sauce

Torre di Giano	Veal Aucitron
	Steamed Asparagus with Lemon Butter*
	Spinach Salad
	Italian Rolls
	Raspberry and Strawberries Romanoff

MICROWAVE

Old State House, Raleigh

BASIC COOKING TIMES
FOR 600-700 WATT OVENS

The amount of wattage microwave ovens have varies. One should be aware of the cooking power of the particular model to be used. Generally, 600-700 watt ovens are the highest powered on the market. Many older models have considerably less wattage, and will require greater cooking time than the more highly powered models.

POULTRY: Cook 5 minutes per pound on full power for whole birds or pieces which are prepared plain or with a light glaze. Six minutes per pound for birds which are stuffed or pieces cooked in extra sauce. Whole birds should be tied and turned 1 - 2 times while cooking.

SEAFOOD: Cook 3½ minutes per pound on full power for plain fish or seafood in a light sauce; 4½ minutes if seafood is stuffed, in extra sauce, or on a bed of rice. Shellfish: Cook 3½ - 4 minutes on full power for 12 medium size clams or oysters cooked in the shell.

BEEF: Use the time guides in the cookbook accompanying your microwave oven and/or also use a thermometer or probe as directed for the particular cut of meat you are cooking. For rare cuts: 130°; for medium cuts: 140°; for well done: 150°.
To use the probe, position it in the center of cuts under 3½ pounds; over 3½ pounds place the probe halfway to the center. Be sure that the probe is out of a fat layer and not directly alongside bone. Use the 3rd to the 8th cooking levels to cook the beef. The tougher the cut, the lower the cooking level. Ground beef products should be cooked on full power. An average time guide for a medium-done roast cooked on cooking level 5 would be about 10 minutes per pound.

PORK: Cook pork to 170° to ensure that the pork is well done, or go by the time guides in the cookbook. Ground pork and sausage should be cooked on full power.
Use between the 3rd and the 8th cooking levels for pork. The tougher the cut, the lower the setting should be. An average time for a pork product cooked on cooking level 5 would be 13 - 15 minutes per pound.

BROWNING MEATS: Larger cuts of meat will brown on their own in some microwave ovens by the surface fats getting hot enough to sear the surface of the meat product. To add to this browning, start the meat on a higher cooking level for about 3 minutes per pound, then lower the cooking level to slow down the cooking so that the product will be more tender.
Smaller cuts may be browned using any of the many shapes of browning skillets. Their special coating of tin oxide will get very hot when preheated

empty. That will sear the surface of the meat coming into contact with it like a frying pan.

TENDERIZING MEATS: When using the temperature control system, holding meats at their final temperature for 45 minutes to 1 hour after that temperature has been reached will produce a more tender product even from "bargain" cuts. *Do not hold meats at or below 130°*, due to bacterial growth. Holding at higher temperatures even for prolonged periods is safe and will produce excellent results.

FRESH VEGETABLES: Cook most fresh vegetables covered, on full power, and allow 6 - 8 minutes per pound; 2 - 4 tablespoons of liquid should be added. The liquid can be water, butter, margarine, broth, bouillon, etc.
EXCEPTIONS: Butterbeans, field peas, garden peas, collards and turnip greens should be covered with liquid and will therefore require longer cooking times. Allow at least 12 - 15 minutes per pound.

FROZEN VEGETABLES: Cook most frozen vegetables covered, on full power and allow 6 - 8 minutes for a 10 ounce package. 2 - 4 tablespoons of liquid may be added if there is not enough moisture from the ice crystals frozen in the vegetable. For a 1 pound bag, allow 8 - 10 minutes. The same exceptions listed above apply here. The 12-15 minute time guide would be for a 10 ounce package.
Vegetables in the boil-safe bags can be cooked in microwave ovens directly in their bags. The bags should be pierced and placed on a plate to catch any spills.

SAUCES, PUDDINGS, CUSTARDS, ETC.: Cook those thickened with flour on cooking level 8 until thickened. Those thickened with cornstarch will cook nicely on full power. Egg thickened sauces are more easily done on cooking level 5. All sauces should be stirred after a minute or so, then periodically stirred during the cooking time.

YEAST BREADS: Let the dough rise in the microwave on cooking level 1 for 10-15 minutes for a normal loaf, having first covered the dough with a thoroughly moistened towel. If any cooking should occur, place a glass of water in the unit with the dough the next time. Cook yeast breads on cooking level 7 for an average of 7-9 minutes per loaf, or until loaf springs back when touched lightly. Remove loaf to a rack to cool. Since the bread will not brown in the microwave, run the cooked loaf under a preheated broiler for 3-5 minutes after glazing the bread with a whole egg blended well with a drop or two of Kitchen Bouquet.

CAKES: Cook bundt or tube cakes for 7-11 minutes on full power (7 minutes for a plain box mix; more time is usually required for scratch recipes). Each layer of a cake takes 3½ - 4½ minutes; for 6-7 cupcakes, allow 2½ - 3½ minutes.

Cakes' surfaces should be slightly moist when removed from the microwave. The surface moisture will often cook off with carry-over cooking. To test for doneness, touch the top of the cake with your finger. If the moist layer comes off on your finger, but reveals cooked cake below it, the cake is done.

The toothpick test should work after allowing the cake to carry-over cook for a few minutes. A cake that contains raw batter in the bottom means that there was too much liquid in the batter. *Remember* that the *TOTAL* liquid volume (egg, oil, water and anything else that makes the batter looser) should be reduced *by* ¼th. A tough textured cake indicates overcooking...and that can't be corrected!

OTHER TRICKS THE MICROWAVE OVEN CAN DO INCLUDE: Drying herbs, making croutons, roasting nuts, cooking perfect candies, frostings, and syrups, not to mention making fondue. During the summer months, use your microwave for blanching vegetables, making jams, jellies, preserves and pickles! No changes are required for these recipes except in the time!

On the decorative side, bread dough ornaments can be made in the microwave unit easily and flowers may be dried in your unit (with the aid of silica gel).

TIPS FOR MICROWAVE COOKING

CARDINAL RULE OF MICROWAVE COOKING: Always *UNDER*estimate your cooking time. You can always go back and add extra time, but you can't take any time when your product is already overcooked!

HOW MICROWAVES COOK: Microwaves cook from the outside through to the center of the food product. They are attracted to the moisture in the food and create vibrations between the water molecules which result in friction and heat. There are no molecular changes, no ionization, nothing dangerous, *just friction!*

CARRY-OVER COOKING: The water molecules slowing down after the microwave cuts off still generate heat and therefore cook. Carry-over cooking (standing time or resting time are the same thing) can finish off the cooking to perfection or can ruin a product by overcooking. Compensate for this by leaving a little cooking to be done when the food comes out. Most microwave recipes have allowed for this and recommend a standing time. Minimize carry-over cooking by uncovering the product after cooking and stirring. Maximize carry-over cooking by leaving the dish covered and placing it out of a draft for several minutes.

DEFROSTING: The defrost setting on most microwave ovens is comparable to about 30% cooking power. This setting is often too fast for defrosting and some cooking results around the edges. Depending upon your own microwave oven, to avoid too rapid defrosting, change to a lower cook cycle for a few moments. This is especially helpful when defrosting large, hard-frozen foods as well as frozen ground meats.

COVERING PRODUCTS: Although foods need not always be covered, it is generally the rule to cover the product if you want to hold in moisture or prevent splattering, or absorb moisture. Saran Wrap (other wraps will melt) or glass lids hold the moisture in best as well as preventing splatters. Waxed paper will hold in some moisture and works well to prevent splatters.

Paper towels will prevent splattering and will absorb excess moisture. Do not cover, or cover only with a paper towel when a crisper product is desired.

DOUBLING VOLUMES: When doubling the volume of a food to be cooked in a microwave oven, do not double the time. Add approximately ⅔ additional time.

COVERTING CONVENTIONAL RECIPES: This conversion involves 2 steps: (1) time and (2) moisture content. Liquids should be reduced *by* ¼ when they will not be entirely absorbed by the food. This is generally necessary in cakes and in some casseroles. Liquids include eggs, oil, water, broth, bouillon, etc. Time is usually reduced *to* ¼, or if uncertain refer to another microwave recipe that is similar to the one being prepared and use that as a guide. *REMEMBER* to undercook!

BLANCHING VEGETABLES

The easiest method for blanching vegetables in the microwave involves Ziploc freezer bags or any boil-safe bag.

Use fresh unblemished vegetables for the best results. Wash the vegetables thoroughly. Put freshly washed, not drained, vegetables directly into the bags. (You can measure them out into a 2 or 4 cup measure, then just pour them into the bags. That way you are assured of equal volumes in each bag.) Add 2 to 3 teaspoons of water to each bag if the vegetables have air dried before bagging them.

Seal the bags *halfway* — not all the way — so that some steam is able to escape and so that the bag is easier to seal when the time comes.

Place the bags in boxes to maintain upright positions, except in the case of corn-on-the-cob which should be placed flat on the glass tray. Fold the tops of the bags over if possible so that the steam does not have a direct outlet.

Heat the vegetables on full power for about ¼ the microwave cooking time. (You may want to use the guide in the cookbook.) The vegetables should heighten in color, but little if any texture change should occur. Don't forget that when you double the volume of product to be cooked or blanched in the microwave, you only increase the time by ⅔. Doubling it will be too much.

Do not stack the vegetables in the microwave for blanching, but do feel free to cover the entire glass tray with a single layer of product. Up to 14 pints may be blanched at a time by arranging the bags loosely, in an upright position, in shoe boxes or some other box that will fit in the unit.

Lower the blanched vegetables in the bag into ice water up to the level of the seal. Then seal the bags completely.

STUFFED MUSHROOMS   *Serves 6*

8 ounces large fresh
   mushrooms

¼ cup unsalted butter

4 large green onions, with
   bulbs and greens chopped
   separately

½ teaspoon garlic salt

¼ teaspoon dry mustard

1 teaspoon soy sauce

⅛ teaspoon oregano

1½ tablespoons Parmesan
   cheese, grated

1½ tablespoons Romano
cheese,
   grated

3 tablespoons Italian bread
   crumbs

Grated Parmesan for sprinkling

Rinse mushrooms and remove stems. Chop ½ of the stems finely. Melt butter in a 1 quart bowl, or measuring cup. Add and saute the next 3 ingredients on full power for 2 minutes.

Stir in remaining ingredients, except cheese for sprinkling. Microwave on full power for 1 minute. Stuff mushroom caps with mixture and place in a buttered 9 inch glass pie plate. Sprinkle with grated cheese. Cover with Saran Wrap. When ready to serve, microwave on full power for 3 minutes. Rotate 1 time.

YAKITORI

½ pound raw chicken breast
   meat, thinly sliced

2 tablespoons soy sauce

3 tablespoons sake or sherry

1 tablespoon brown sugar

¼ teaspoon ginger

Marinate chicken in mixture of remaining ingredients for 20 minutes. Thread on 6 wooden skewers. Arrange skewers on serving plate. Cover with waxed paper, cook 2 minutes. Turn skewers, cook 1 minute longer.

ARTICHOKE NIBBLES

2 (6 ounce) jars marinated
  artichoke hearts

½ cup onion, minced

2 cloves garlic, minced

4 eggs

¼ cup seasoned bread crumbs

¼ teaspoon salt

⅛ teaspoon red pepper

⅛ teaspoon oregano

⅛ teaspoon Tabasco

2 tablespoons parsley, minced

½ pound Cheddar cheese,
  grated

Drain liquid from 1 jar of artichokes into a 2 cup measure. Add onions and garlic. Saute on full power for 2 - 3 minutes. Chop artichokes.

Beat eggs; add all remaining ingredients. Pour into greased 7 x 11 inch baking dish. Elevate on inverted saucer in microwave oven. Microwave on full power for 7-8 minutes. Rotate half way through cooking time. Let stand 5 minutes before slicing into 1 inch squares. Serve hot or cold.

BEEF JERKY

1½ pounds flank steak

1 teaspoon seasoned salt

½ teaspoon liquid smoke

⅓ teaspoon garlic powder

⅓ teaspoon black pepper

1 teaspoon onion powder

¼ cup Worcestershire sauce

¼ cup soy sauce

Have butcher butterfly the flank steak. Cut with the grain into 1 inch wide strips. Marinate overnight in the refrigerator with above ingredients, which have been combined and well mixed.

Lay strips on paper towel on oven floor (about ¼ of the strips). Set control on defrost or 40% power and cook for 5 minutes. Cover with paper towel and cook on defrost or 40% power for 5 minutes more. Turn and cook on defrost for an additional 3 minutes. Remove from oven and let cool on paper towel. Cook the remaining beef strips and let cool. Taste cooled jerky. If crisper jerky is desired return all strips to oven on paper towel (in a single layer), cover with another paper towel and cook on defrost for 3 minutes.

Let jerky cool thoroughly and store in a covered jar in the cupboard or brown paper bag. It will keep for weeks without refrigeration, but may be frozen for longer storage.

TEMPTING APPETIZER PIE
Yield: 8 inch pie

1 (8 ounce) package Cream
  cheese
2 tablespoons milk
1 (2½ ounce) jar sliced dried
  beef, finely snipped
2 tablespoons onion, minced
2 tablespoons green pepper,
  finely chopped

⅛ teaspoon pepper
½ cup dairy sour cream
¼ cup pecans, coarsely chopped
Assorted crackers

Place Cream cheese in 1½ quart glass dish. Heat in microwave on 30% power for 3 to 4 minutes, or until cheese is softened. Add milk to Cream cheese and blend well. Stir in beef, onion, green pepper and sour cream. Mix well. Spoon into 8 inch glass pie plate. Sprinkle pecans over top. Heat in microwave, uncovered on full power for 2½ to 3½ minutes, or until heated through. Serve with assorted crackers.

HOT CRAB ANTOJITO
Serves: 45

1 pound white crabmeat,
  flaked
¾ cup Monterey Jack cheese
  with hot peppers, grated
¼ cup sour cream
½ cup mayonnaise
1 tablespoon green onion,
  minced

1 tablespoon fresh lemon juice
1 tablespoon white wine
½ teaspoon salt
¼ teaspoon cayenne pepper
¼ teaspoon Tabasco
Melba rounds

Mix all ingredients, except Melba rounds, and toss lightly. Spoon mixture on Melba rounds. Place 15 rounds on a paper plate. Microwave on full power for 45 seconds. Repeat with remaining rounds. Serve hot.

CLAMS CASINO

2 dozen clams, opened

3 slices bacon, cooked and
crumbled

2 tablespoons onion, minced

2 tablespoons green pepper,
minced

2 tablespoons parsley, minced

2 tablespoons celery, minced

1 tablespoon butter, melted

1 teaspoon Worcestershire
sauce

Dash Tabasco

Place opened shells on tray or paper plate. Combine remaining
ingredients. Spoon over clams. Microwave on full power for 4 minutes.
Serve hot.

BEER-CHEESE
CAULIFLOWER SOUP

Serves 5 to 6

¼ cup butter

1 small onion, finely chopped

⅔ cup all purpose flour

1 (13½ ounce) can chicken
broth

Milk

1 jar (8 ounce) pasteurized
processed cheese spread

1 cup shredded Cheddar cheese
(about 4 ounces)

1 cup beer

1 (10 ounce) package frozen
cauliflower

Place butter and onion in 3 quart casserole. Cover and microwave until
onion is tender, 2 to 3 minutes. Stir in flour. Pour broth into 4 cup
measure and add enough milk to make 3 cups. Add to flour mixture.
Cover and microwave for 6 minutes; stir. Cover and microwave to boiling,
3 to 5 minutes.

Stir in cheese spread, cheese and beer. Cover and microwave until hot
and cheese is melted, 3 to 4 minutes; stir. Place cauliflower, in its box, on a
paper towel or paper plate. Pierce several times with a fork. Cook in the
microwave for 5 minutes. Open box, divide cauliflower into serving size
pieces and add to soup. Stir and serve.

CRAB FLORENTINE SOUP

Yield: 2½ quarts

4 cups chicken broth

⅔ cup celery, finely chopped

½ cup onion, finely chopped

1 (10 ounce) package frozen chopped spinach, cooked

½ pound crabmeat, rinsed and well drained

3 tablespoons cornstarch

¼ teaspoon Fines Herbes

3 to 4 gratings of fresh nutmeg

Pepper to taste

Pierce spinach package with tines of fork, place on paper plate and cook in microwave for 6 minutes on full power. Remove spinach from package and drain.

In a 3 quart casserole, combine chicken broth, celery, onion and Fines Herbes. Cook covered on full power for 8 minutes. Add spinach, well squeezed, and crabmeat. Dissolve cornstarch in small amount of cool liquid (broth or water) and add to other ingredients. Cook, covered, on full power for 12 to 15 minutes until thickened. Ladle into soup bowls.

SPINACH CHEESE CUSTARD

Serves 6

2 (10 ounce) packages frozen chopped spinach

1 clove garlic, minced

⅛ teaspoon pepper

1½ cups Cheddar cheese, shredded

¼ cup Bisquick

4 eggs

1 cup milk

1 tablespoon butter

Place spinach in 1½ quart casserole. (Do not add water.) Microwave, covered for 5 minutes on full power. Stir spinach and return to oven, covered; cook 3 to 4 minutes more on full power. Remove and drain well. Squeeze dry to remove all liquid. Combine spinach, garlic, pepper, 1 cup of cheese and Bisquick. Stir in eggs and milk until well blended. In an 8 inch glass baking dish, melt butter in microwave. Tilt dish to coat bottom and sides of the dish. Pour in spinach mixture. Cover. Cook in microwave for 3 minutes on full power; stir mixture; cook 1 minute more. Stir again; cook 3 minutes more on full power. Remove from oven, top with remaining ½ cup cheese; cook, uncovered, for 1 minute on 50 percent power.

NOTE: May also be made with broccoli, corn or cauliflower.

FISH FILLETS
WITH NANTUA SAUCE

Serves 4

2 pounds fish fillets (flounder, sea bass, snapper, etc.)
1 tablespoon lemon juice
2 tablespoons butter, melted
Pepper

Place fish in flat glass baking dish. Top with lemon juice, butter and pepper. Cover with Saran Wrap. Cook in microwave on full power 7 to 8 minutes or until fish flakes easily with a fork. While fish stands, make the following sauce:

Nantua Sauce:

4 tablespoons butter, melted   **¼ cup chicken broth**
4 ounces small cooked shrimp   **¼ cup clam juice**
2 tablespoons butter   **¼ cup dry white wine**
2 tablespoons flour   **½ cup half and half**
¼ teaspoon salt   **¼ teaspoon lemon juice**
Dash white pepper

Combine melted butter and shrimp in food processor and puree until smooth; set aside. In a 4-cup measure melt 2 tablespoons butter in microwave on full power for 40 seconds. Add flour and cook on full power for 1 minute. Stir in chicken broth, clam juice, and wine. Return to microwave and cook on full power for 2½ to 3 minutes. Stir after 1½ minutes and again after 2½ minutes. Stir in half and half and return to microwave for 1½ to 2 minutes, stirring occasionally. Remove and stir in lemon juice and shrimp butter. Transfer fish to platter, pour sauce over all and serve.

CHICKEN IN WINE

1 (3 pound) chicken, cut up   **½ teaspoon oregano**
1 cup Rose' wine   **½ teaspoon ginger**
¼ cup soy sauce   **2 tablespoons brown sugar**
1 teaspoon oil   **2 tablespoons water**

Mix all ingredients and pour in glass casserole dish and cover. Cook for 15 to 20 minutes on full power, rearranging and turning once or twice during cooking.

CHICKEN WITH FORTY CLOVES OF GARLIC

8 leg quarters

2 to 3 large heads of garlic peeled (up to sixty cloves)

⅔ cup olive oil

4 ribs of celery, thinly sliced on the bias

Handful of parsley sprigs, minced

1 generous tablespoon salt

Freshly ground pepper

Freshly ground nutmeg

Drop the garlic into rapidly boiling water for 10 seconds or so. Drain. Run under cold water. Trim off tops and bottoms and slip off the outside skin. Sliver. Set aside. (Garlic cloves may be left whole if you are serving to garlic lovers.)

Pour oil into 3 to 4 quart Corning Ware or similar casserole with a lid. Turn all the chicken pieces over in the oil so they are well coated. Lift out of the casserole. Add the garlic to the oil. Arrange half the chicken pieces in the bottom of the casserole. Scatter half the celery and parsley on top, then half the salt and a generous amount of pepper and nutmeg. Place the remaining chicken pieces on top. Add the remainder of the celery, parsley and salt; sprinkle generously with pepper and nutmeg. Cover with kitchen parchment, then add the casserole cover.

Cook in the microwave for 25 minutes, giving the casserole a half-turn once. Rest 10 minutes before serving. DO NOT OPEN THE CASSEROLE DURING BAKING PERIOD.

BEST MEAT LOAF   *Serves: 4 to 6*

1½ pounds lean ground beef

½ cup Pepperidge Farm Dressing, finely ground

¼ cup onion, chopped (optional)

1 egg

1½ tablespoons catsup

1 cup milk

1 teaspoon salt

Dash pepper

2 tablespoons catsup

Mix ground beef with all other ingredients. Shape into a 9 inch pie plate. Spread 2 extra tablespoons catsup over top. Cover with Saran Wrap. Microwave at high for 14 to 16 minutes. If microwave has a probe, insert probe under Saran Wrap in center of meat mixture, set temperature for 170°. Let stand about 5 minutes before serving. Use of probe makes for a firmer meat loaf, although it still remains moist if the recipe contains a suitable amount of liquid, as this one does.

Try your favorite meat loaf recipe, increasing the liquid to 1 cup per 1½ pounds ground meat, use the probe to cook it.

OLD FASHIONED TURKEY PIE

2 cups cooked turkey, cubed

4 tablespoons butter or margarine

5 tablespoons all purpose flour

2 cups turkey broth (or 2 cups hot water plus 6 chicken bouillon cubes)

1 cup milk

6 small white onions

1 cup potatoes, diced

10 ounces frozen peas and carrots

Cook potatoes, onions, peas and carrots in a mixing bowl with 4 tablespoons water, covered, for 10 to 12 minutes on full power. Drain and reserve. Melt butter for 30 to 45 seconds on full power. Stir in flour. Gradually add milk and broth, stirring until smooth. Cook on medium power for 5 to 6 minutes or until thickened. Add turkey, vegetables and salt and pepper to taste. Turn into a 13 x 9 inch casserole dish. Cover with biscuit dough and cook on full power for 6 to 8 minutes or until crust is firm. Run under a broiler element to brown crust that has been brushed with butter. (Add a little Kitchen Bouquet for additional color.)

Biscuit Dough:

1½ cups all purpose flour

1½ teaspoons baking powder

½ teaspoon salt

5 tablespoons shortening

½ cup milk

Mix flour, salt and baking powder together. Cut in shortening. Add milk, stirring until soft dough is formed. Knead 30 seconds. Roll out and place on top of casserole dish. Vent crust.

VENISON, MOOSE OR ELK ROAST

Serves: 6 to 8

2 tablespoons plain flour

1 cup dry red wine

3 to 4 pounds venison roast

Salt

1 bay leaf

8 whole cloves

1 medium onion, diced

1 tablespoon thyme

Preheat oven to 325°. Place flour in small (10 x 16 inch) oven cooking bag and shake until bag is well coated.

Place bag in 2 inch deep roasting pan. Pour wine into bag and stir until well-mixed with flour. Rub roast with salt. Put meat into bag. Add bay leaf, cloves, onion and thyme around meat. Close bag with string.

Cook two hours or longer until tender. Liquid in bag is ready to use as gravy, or you may thicken with flour as you desire.

This may be cooked in the microwave on low for 1 hour. Be sure to use a tender cut.

COMPANY DINNER OR BRUNCH   *Serves: 6*

2 chicken breast halves (about 1 pound)

1 box broccoli florets

¼ pound cooked ham, sliced (preferably smoked)

3 English muffins, split and toasted

Hollandaise sauce

Arrange chicken breasts skin side up with thickest part to outside in 8 inch pie plate. Cover with Saran Wrap. Microwave on full power for 3 minutes. Rotate plate ½ turn. Microwave 3 minutes longer until chicken is done. Cool breasts and slice.

Pierce box of broccoli with fork. Place box on paper plate and microwave on full power for 6 minutes. Allow standing time while making Hollandaise sauce.

Assemble ingredients in the following manner: English muffin, smoked ham, sliced chicken and broccoli. Place in baking dish and top with Hollandaise. Reheat at 50 percent power for 1 to 2 minutes.

Poached egg may be added to each half.

Can be increased to serve as many as 12. Double or triple recipe, allowing for extra microwave time.

DATE NUT BARS

Yield: 36 bars

1 cup pecans, chopped
1 cup raisins
¾ cups dates (can use already chopped dates)
1 cup sugar
¼ cup butter or margarine

2 eggs
1 cup flour
¼ teaspoon baking powder
½ teaspoon salt
Powdered sugar

Sift flour, salt and baking powder together. Process pecans, raisins and dates in food processor or chop by hand. Can use apples in place of dates. After chopping, if using food processor, remove dates, nuts and raisins. Add eggs, sugar and cream and beat until light. Add sifted dry ingredients to creamed mixture along with fruit and nuts. Give the steel blade 1 or 2 turns.

Pour mixture into buttered 12 x 9 x 2 inch or equivalent baking dish. Microwave on 70% power or medium if your microwave has only high, medium and low, for 11 to 13 minutes. When the batter pulls away from the sides of the dish, the bars are done.

Cut into 2 inch bars and sprinkle with powdered sugar. Store in tightly closed, preferably plastic or glass, container. Reroll in powdered sugar if necessary. Keeps well.

GINGERBREAD APPLE COBBLER

Serves: 6 to 8

4 medium apples, peeled and sliced (4 cups)
½ cup packed brown sugar
1 teaspoon cornstarch

2 tablespoons water
1 tablespoon lemon juice
½ teaspoon cinnamon

Gingerbread Topping:

1 egg
½ cup buttermilk or sour milk
¼ cup molasses
2 tablespoons cooking oil
1 cup unsifted all purpose flour
¼ cup sugar

½ teaspoon soda
½ teaspoon ginger
¼ teaspoon salt
¼ teaspoon baking powder
¼ teaspoon nutmeg

Combine apples, brown sugar, cornstarch, water, lemon juice and cinnamon in an 8 inch round glass cake dish. Microwave, covered, 4 to 5 minutes or until apples are tender-crisp, stirring once. Beat together egg, buttermilk, molasses and oil in mixing bowl. Add remaining ingredients; beat until smooth. Pour over apples. Microwave, uncovered, 6 to 7 minutes or until toothpick inserted near center comes out clean, rotating dish once or twice. Serve warm or cold, plain or with whipped cream.

CHILLED LEMON SOUFFLE   *Yield: 5 to 6 servings*

½ cup sugar

1 tablespoon (1 envelope) unflavored gelatin

¼ teaspoon salt

1 cup water

3 eggs, separated

1 tablespoon lemon peel, grated

3 to 4 tablespoons lemon juice

⅓ cup sugar

1 cup whipping cream

Prepare a 3 to 4 cup souffle dish by forming a collar of waxed paper to extend about 3 inches above dish. (Greasing inside upper edge of dish holds paper in place.)

In 4 cup measure, combine ½ cup sugar, gelatin, salt and water. Separate eggs, placing whites in small mixer bowl and adding yolks to gelatin mixture. Beat in yolks until **well mixed**. Cook, uncovered, on full power, 3 minutes, 15 seconds or until mixture just begins to boil, stirring occasionally during last half of cooking time. Stir in lemon peel and juice. Cool until mixture is thickened, but not set. Beat egg whites until frothy. Beat in ⅓ cup sugar until mixture forms stiff peaks. Whip cream. Fold lemon mixture and whipped cream into whipped egg whites. Pour into prepared dish. Refrigerate 6 hours or longer. Remove waxed paper before serving from souffle dish.

Garnish with lemon slices and whipped cream.

GINGERBREAD WITH LEMON SAUCE

1¼ cups flour

¾ teaspoon baking soda

¼ teaspoon salt

½ teaspoon cinnamon

1 teaspoon ginger

¼ teaspoon cloves, ground

¼ cup brown sugar

¼ cup butter

1 egg

½ cup molasses

½ cup buttermilk

Measure all ingredients into mixing bowl. Beat well. Turn batter into 8 inch round glass cake dish lined with brown or waxed paper. Cook 6 minutes, rotating ½ turn halfway through the cooking. For variable power ovens: Cook on bake for 6 minutes and turn up to full power for 2 minutes. Allow to stand for 1 minute and turn out onto rack or serving dish. Serve with Lemon Sauce.

Lemon Sauce:

½ cup butter

1 cup sugar

¼ cup water

1 egg, well beaten

Grated peel of 1 lemon

6 tablespoons lemon juice

Melt butter in 4 cup saucemaker for 1 minute. Mix the remaining ingredients, *beating well.* Slowly add the melted butter to the lemon and egg mixture, stirring all the while. Return the mixture to the saucemaker, cover and cook on full power for 2 minutes, 30 seconds; stopping to stir every 30 seconds. For variable power ovens: Cook on medium for 3½ to 4 minutes, stirring every minute.

MINCEMEAT STEAMED PUDDING

Serves: 8 to 10

2 tablespoons butter

½ cup dark brown sugar

2 eggs

1 cup prepared mincemeat

⅓ cup milk

1¼ cups all purpose flour

1½ teaspoons baking powder

½ cup chopped nuts

Rum Sauce (follows)

Grease a 5 cup ring dish. Mix butter, brown sugar and eggs. Stir in mincemeat and milk. Mix in flour, baking powder and nuts. Spoon batter into 5 cup dish. Cover tightly with Saran Wrap and microwave for 5½ to 6 minutes, rotating dish if necessary. Cool for 5 minutes. Invert pudding onto serving plate. Serve warm with Rum sauce.

30

Rum Sauce:

¾ cup whipping cream plus
  ¼ cup milk
        or
1 cup half and half

¾ cup sugar

1 tablespoon cornstarch

½ cup butter

1 teaspoon rum flavoring or
  1 tablespoon rum

Combine sugar and cornstarch in 4 cup measure. Add whipping cream and milk. Mix. Add butter. Microwave 3 minutes on full power; stir. Microwave to boiling, 1 to 2 minutes. Stir in rum.

TOASTED ALMOND CAKE ROLL

2 cups slivered blanched
  almonds

¾ teaspoon baking powder

4 egg whites

4 egg yolks

½ cup powdered sugar

1 teaspoon vanilla extract

¼ teaspoon almond extract

Cocoa Fluff Filling or
  powdered sugar (follows)

Spread almonds in a 12 inch square baker. Microwave at full power for 4 - 5 minutes or until toasted, stirring twice. Grind almonds or process in food processor using steel blade. Measure 1½ cups. Stir in baking powder; set aside. Line same baking pan with waxed paper cut long enough to extend over ends of pan. Butter top side of waxed paper where it touches the bottom of the dish. Do not butter the extensions. In a small bowl beat egg whites with electric mixer on high speed until stiff peaks form.

In a large bowl, combine egg yolks, ½ cup powdered sugar, vanilla and almond extract. With electric mixer on high speed, beat mixture until thick and lemon colored 3 to 5 minutes. Stir nut mixture into yolk mixture. Fold in egg whites. Spread batter evenly in prepared pan. Microwave at full power for 6 minutes or until a wooden toothpick inserted in center comes out clean. Let stand 1 minute. Using extended ends of waxed paper, lift cake out of pan. Place on wire rack and cover with Saran Wrap. Cool 50-60 minutes. Prepare Cocoa Fluff Filling. Remove Saran Wrap. Spread filling on cake. Roll up jelly-roll fashion, peeling off waxed paper as you go. Be careful not to roll too tightly. Cover roll with remaining filling.

Cocoa Fluff Filling:

1 pint whipping cream

*¼ cup sweetened cocoa
  powder

Beat both ingredients until smooth and fluffy.
*Variation: Suisse-Mocha powdered coffee may be used instead.

LEBKUCHEN

2 cups molasses
1½ teaspoons baking soda
1¼ cups packed brown sugar
3 eggs
2 egg whites
¼ pound citron
½ pound dates
½ pound figs
1 cup seedless raisins
1½ cups flour

1½ teaspoons ground cloves
1½ teaspoons ground ginger
1½ teaspoons ground cinnamon
1½ teaspoons ground allspice
3 cups flour
1 cup almonds, finely chopped
1 cup pecans, finely chopped
½ lemon, juice and chopped zest
¼ cup peach brandy

Mix molasses and soda. Add sugar and lightly beaten eggs and egg whites. Grind fruits. Dredge fruit in 1½ cups flour. Mix spices with 3 cups flour, combine with fruit mixture. Add molasses mixture and remaining ingredients. Blend well. Drop mixture by scant teaspoonfuls onto greased *cookie sheets. Cook a dozen at a time on full power for 2 to 2½ minutes. Remove to wire rack to cool. Frost when cool with the following:

1 cup confectioners sugar
2 egg whites

Combine and beat until smooth. Add extra sugar if needed to achieve a spreading consistency.

*A cookie sheet can be easily made by cutting cardboard to fit bottom of oven. Cover with waxed paper.

PEANUT BRITTLE

2 cups sugar
1 cup light corn syrup
⅓ cup water
1 (16 ounce) package raw peanuts, shelled

1 teaspoon salt
1 tablespoon butter or margarine
1 tablespoon baking soda

Grease 2, 5½ x 12 inch baking sheets. Keep warm. Place sugar, corn syrup and water in 3 quart casserole. Cook in the microwave oven on full power for 10-12 minutes, or until soft ball stage is reached. Stir occasionally during cooking time. Stir in peanuts. Cook in the microwave on medium high (if you have a variable power oven) for 14 - 16 minutes or on full power for 12 - 14 minutes, or until temperature of 300°on candy thermometer or hard crack stage is reached. Stir in butter and baking soda. Pour half of candy onto each sheet, spreading to ¼ inch thickness. Cool. Break in pieces.

BAKED WINTER FRUITS WITH SPICED WINE
Yield: *10 to 12 servings*

1½ cups dry white wine

1 cup dark brown sugar, firmly packed

1 teaspoon candied ginger, minced

1 teaspoon vanilla

¼ teaspoon each ground cinnamon, allspice and ginger

Grated peel and juice of 1 large lemon

2 pounds mixed dried fruits, chopped*

4 tablespoons butter (½ stick) broken into small pieces

1 cup pecans, chopped

1½ cups plain yogurt

Butter shallow 2 quart baking dish. Combine first 6 ingredients in medium bowl and blend well. Mix chopped fruits in another bowl. Transfer half of fruit to prepared dish. Dot with 2 tablespoons butter. Spread remaining fruit over first layer and dot with remaining butter. Sprinkle with nuts. Pour wine mixture over fruit. Cover and refrigerate overnight. Let mixture stand at room temperature for 1 hour before baking. Bake, covered, at 50% power (or use defrost cycle) for 30 minutes, stirring once, until fruit is plumped and liquid is carmelized. Uncover and let cool. Whisk yogurt until liquified. Transfer to sauceboat and pass separately. (May be prepared 2 days in advance and refrigerated.)

*Suggestions for fruit: Apricots, apples, prunes, raisins, peaches.

FRESH STRAWBERRY JAM
Yield: *8 (8 ounce) jars*

4½ cups fresh strawberries, crushed

7 cups sugar

1 (1¾ ounce) box fruit pectin

In a 4 quart casserole dish, combine the fruit and the pectin. Stir to blend thoroughly. Cook on full power for 10 to 12 minutes, stirring once. The mixture should be at a rolling boil. Add the sugar all at once. Again stir well. Continue heating on full power for 10 to 12 minutes more or until a hard rolling boil is reached. Stir once during cooking. After the mixture has reached a hard rolling boil, continue cooking for 1 additional minute.

Remove mixture from the microwave and stir for 5 minutes. Skim. Spoon hot preserves into hot canning jars. Seal with parafin or Mason jar lids.

CRANBERRY CHUTNEY

Yield: 4½ cups

1 pound fresh cranberries

1 cup water

2 teaspoons ground cinnamon

½ teaspoon allspice

⅛ teaspoon ground cloves

1½ teaspoon ground ginger

½ teaspoon salt

1 large unpeeled apple, cubed

½ cup pecans, chopped

1 cup dried apricots, cut in quarters

4 thin slices lemon, seeded and quartered

1 cup granulated sugar

½ cup packed brown sugar

1 cup seedless grapes

1 cup celery, chopped

½ cup bottled cocktail onions (or 1 cup chopped onions)

Wash cranberries and place in a bowl. Set aside. In a 2 quart casserole combine sugars, spices, water and onion (if using fresh chopped). Microwave, uncovered, on full power for 3½ to 4½ minutes, or until mixture is bubbly. Stir. Let stand covered, 10 minutes. Add cranberries, apple, apricots, lemon, grapes, celery and onions (if using bottled). Microwave, covered, on full power for 10½ to 13 minutes, or until mixture boils. Let stand, covered, for 30 minutes. Stir in chopped nuts. Chill before serving. Refrigerate leftovers.

EASY DILL AND MUSTARD PICKLED VEGETABLES

1 pound carrot sticks, cauliflower or celery (or mixture of vegetables)

3 tablespoons vinegar

1 cup hot water

1 teaspoon dried dill

4 cloves garlic

1 teaspoon pickling spice

1 tablespoon salt

1 teaspoon dry mustard powder

1 teaspoon sugar or sugar substitute

Combine all ingredients in a 2 quart covered casserole. Cook until vegetables are tender-crisp. Pack vegetables into hot, sterilized jars. Cover with the boiling cooking liquid. Seal. Refrigerate and let stand several days or a week before using. Makes 1 quart.

HORS D'OEUVRES

Bennett Place, Durham

MOLDED AVOCADO PINWHEEL   *Yield: 3 cups*

1 envelope unflavored gelatin

¼ cup cold water

1 cup mashed avocado (2 to
  3 avocados)

1 tablespoon lemon juice

1 (0.6 ounce) package dry
  Italian salad dressing mix

1 pint dairy sour cream
  (2 cups)

3 tablespoons chopped parsley

Dash Tabasco sauce

2 or 3 drops green food
  coloring, if desired

Bread rounds or crackers

Assorted garnishes such as
  cooked baby shrimp, chopped
  green onions, chopped
  cucumbers, chopped ripe
  olives, red or black caviar,
  chopped tomatoes or a
  tomato rose.

Oil a 9½ inch porcelain quiche dish, glass pie dish or a flan tin with
indented bottom. In a small saucepan, sprinkle gelatin over cold water. Let
stand 5 minutes to soften. Cook over medium heat until mixture just
comes to a boil and gelatin is dissolved. In a large bowl or food processor
fitted with the metal blade, blend avocado, lemon juice, salad dressing mix,
sour cream, parsley and Tabasco sauce. Add dissolved gelatin. Mix
thoroughly. Stir in 2 or 3 drops of green food coloring, if desired. Pour
mixture into prepared mold. Cover with plastic wrap. Refrigerate until
firm. May be refrigerated up to 2 days. Do not freeze.

If using a quiche dish or pie dish, it is not necessary to unmold spread. If
using a flan tin, unmold before serving. Run the tip of a table knife around
the edges, dip bottom of mold in warm water and invert onto platter.
Decorate with 4 or 5 suggested garnishes. Serve with bread rounds or
crackers.

PICKLED SHRIMP   *Serves: 10*

*1 quart shrimp, cooked and
  cleaned (about 2½ pounds
  in the shell, uncooked)

1 pint of sliced white onions

7 whole bay leaves

1¼ cups oil

¾ cup white vinegar

1½ teaspoons salt (less if
  desired)

2½ teaspoons celery seed

1 jar capers, with juice

Dash of Tabasco

Place shrimp, onions and bay leaves in a bowl. Mix all other ingredients
and pour over the mixture. Cover and allow to marinate 24 hours, or
overnight, in the refrigerator, turning occasionally. Drain off most of
marinade before serving. Serve with picks.

*Note on cooking shrimp: Be sure to undercook the shrimp in order to
prevent toughness after marinating.

CAVIAR-CROWNED MOLD

Serves 35 to 40

1 cup Cottage cheese

1 cup dairy sour cream

1 teaspoon lemon juice or more to taste

1 teaspoon Worcestershire sauce

¼ teaspoon seasoned salt

1 (.25 ounce) envelope unflavored gelatin

¼ cup chilled dry white wine

3 hard-cooked eggs

1 (2 ounce) jar red or black caviar (red has stronger flavor)

3 green onions, finely chopped

3 slices lemon

Pumpernickel bread or rye bread, thinly sliced

In blender or food processor, combine Cottage cheese, sour cream, lemon juice, Worcestershire sauce and seasoned salt. Process until smooth, 10 to 20 seconds. In a small saucepan, sprinkle gelatin over wine; let stand 3 to 4 minutes to soften. Stir over low heat until gelatin dissolves. Gradually stir dissolved gelatin mixture into Cottage cheese mixture. Pour into 9 or 10 inch quiche pan or springform pan. Refrigerate until firm, 4 to 6 hours. Finely chop hard-cooked eggs; set aside. Invert firmly set mold onto a large round platter; remove pan. Spoon caviar in a 1 inch ring around outer edge on top of mold. Spoon chopped eggs in a 1½ inch ring inside caviar ring. Cover remaining surface with chopped onions. Garnish center with lemon slices. Serve as spread with pumpernickel bread or rye bread.

ARTICHOKE DIP

Serves 20 to 25

1 (8 ounce) package Cream cheese, softened to room temperature

2 cups sour cream

5 tablespoons white wine

½ teaspoon garlic salt

½ teaspoon salt

2 jars (6 ounces each) marinated artichoke hearts, drained completely of oil

Freshly ground pepper to taste

Mix together thoroughly the Cream cheese, sour cream, wine and seasonings. Chop artichoke hearts. (A food processor or a blender may be used. However, if using a blender, be careful not to puree). Stir into sour cream mixture. Chill thoroughly. Serve with fresh vegetable dippers, such as cucumbers, cauliflower, carrots, celery, zucchini, squash and radishes. May be done the day before.

JALAPENO MEAT DIP

Serves 40

1½ pounds ground beef
½ pound sausage, bulk style

2 large onions, chopped
2 pounds Velveeta cheese

2 (medium) ripe but firm tomatoes, chopped or a 1 pound can, drained and chopped
3 large or 4 small Jalapeno peppers, chopped (remainder freezes well)

Brown meat and drain. Add onion and cook until glossy. Melt the cut up cheese in a double boiler. Add meat and onion mixture, tomatoes and peppers. Cook slowly for 30 minutes. Serve hot with Taco-style chips. May be frozen.

SOUR CREAM-CURRY DIP FOR FRUIT

2 cups sour cream
3 tablespoons brown sugar

¼ to ½ teaspoon curry powder (to taste)

Combine all ingredients and beat until smooth. Adjust amounts of brown sugar and curry, depending on sweetness and strength of curry flavor desired.

EGGPLANT WITH CAPERS

1 medium eggplant
    (1½ pounds)
¼ cup olive oil
1 (8 ounce) can tomato sauce
12 ripe/black olives, pitted and sliced

12 capers
1 clove garlic, crushed
½ teaspoon oregano
Salt and pepper to taste

Cut eggplant into 1 inch cubes, peeled and rubbed with a bit of lemon juice to prevent discoloration. Heat oil in skillet over medium heat. Add eggplant and cook, turning pieces often, until browned and tender but not soft, about 10 minutes. Add more oil if necessary. Mix remaining ingredients in a small bowl and pour over eggplant in skillet. Cover and cook 5 minutes. Uncover and cook 5 minutes if necessary. More sauce may be added if preferred, but dish should be dry. Serve hot or cold with table crackers. Freeze slightly undercooked, about 3 minutes covered and 3 minutes uncovered.

CHEESE PUFFS

1 cup all purpose flour	6 tablespoons (¾ stick) unsalted butter
⅛ teaspoon pepper, freshly ground	1 teaspoon salt
Dash of red pepper, ground	8 dashes Tabasco sauce
Dash of nutmeg	4 eggs
1 cup water	½ cup Parmesan cheese (freshly grated if possible)

Preheat oven to 425°. Grease baking sheets and set aside. Combine flour, peppers and nutmeg in a small bowl. Mix water, butter and salt in a heavy medium saucepan. Bring to boil, stirring occasionally until butter is melted. Reduce heat, add flour mixture all at once and stir vigorously until mixture is smooth and pulls away from sides of the pan. Remove from heat and allow to cool for 5 minutes.

Using electric hand mixer (or processor), beat Tabasco sauce into batter. Add eggs one at a time, beating well after each addition until mixture is smooth and shiny. Beat in Parmesan cheese. Fit pastry bag with ½ inch round tip and fill with dough. Squeeze onto baking sheet in 1 inch mounds. Bake until puffed and golden, about 20 minutes. Turn off oven. Remove baking sheet and slit side of each puff with sharp knife. Return to oven, leaving door ajar, until puffs are dry, about 10 minutes. Let cool on racks in draft-free area. May be frozen at this point.

Use filled with duxelles — and reheated at 300° — or serve cold with other fillings such as shrimp salad, chicken salad, or crabmeat filling.

NOTE: These puffs are not difficult as the batter is easy to work with. The pastry bag and tube simplify shaping, but they could also be shaped by scooping out mounds with a spoon and using a spatula to push them off the end of the spoon. Be careful not to make them too large.

CROUSTADES

1 loaf of cheapest, fattest and freshest white bread

Cut into rounds with cookie or biscuit cutter. Flatten circles with rolling pin and fit into buttered muffin tins. Bake at 400° for 10 minutes. (8 minutes if freezing) Cool. Fill with duxelles or other fillings of your choice.

MUSHROOM DUXELLES

Duxelles (duke sel) originally created in 17th century France by the chef of the Marquis D'Uxelles. A versatile mixture of chopped mushrooms sauteed with various seasonings which can be used for filling pastries, in sauces, gravies, as a spread or countless other uses.

4 tablespoons butter

3 tablespoons spring onion, finely minced

½ pound mushrooms, finely minced

2 tablespoons flour

1 cup heavy (whipping) cream

Dash cayenne

½ teaspoon salt

1 tablespoon finely chopped parsley

1½ tablespoons finely chopped chives or freeze dried

½ teaspoon lemon juice

Saute onions and mushrooms in melted butter over low heat about 8 to 10 minutes. Add flour and stir well. Add cream, bring to a boil, stirring to thicken and then simmer about 5 minutes. Add remaining ingredients. If using to fill croustades, sprinkle with parmesan cheese and top with dot of butter. Bake at 350° for 10 to 12 minutes.

If using to fill cheese puff pastries, fill pastries, replace tops and place on cookie sheet in 300° oven. Bake for about 5 minutes or until just hot.

WALNUT DUXELLES

4 cups fresh mushrooms, chopped

4 tablespoons butter

½ cup chopped green onions (whites only)

¼ teaspoon dried thyme

1 teaspoon salt

⅓ cup sherry

8 ounces Cream cheese, softened

1 cup finely chopped walnuts, toasted

¼ cup chopped fresh parsley

Dash Tabasco sauce

¼ cup chopped fresh chives

In a heavy 10 to 12 inch skillet melt the butter over moderate heat. Add the mushrooms, green onions and thyme. Cook, stirring, until onions are transparent, about 5 to 8 minutes. Add the salt and sherry and cook until the liquid is almost evaporated. Remove from heat and cool. Mix the softened cream cheese and the mushroom mixture in a large bowl. Stir and blend thoroughly. Stir in the walnuts, parsley and Tabasco. Use to fill croustades, cheese puffs or hollowed out cherry tomatoes, cucumbers, etc. or may be chilled, (covered) in a serving dish or crock, sprinkled with the chives and served as a spread with crackers.

BLEU CHEESE SOUFFLE

Serves 12

1 envelope unflavored gelatin

2 tablespoons cool water

4 tablespoons sweet butter, softened

4 ounces Cream cheese, softened

4 ounces Bleu cheese, softened

1 egg, separated

1 teaspoon Dijon mustard

½ cup heavy cream, whipped

Soften gelatin in cool water, then gently stir over low heat to dissolve. Using a food processor or electric mixer, beat together butter and cheeses, adding egg yolk, mustard and gelatin. Beat egg white until stiff but not dry, and gently fold into mixture. Then fold in whipped cream.

Prepare a 1 cup souffle dish with a collar of oiled waxed paper or foil. Tie to the dish with string. Spoon mixture into the dish so that it comes up over the sides and up to the top of the collar. Chill for several hours or overnight. Remove the collar and serve with crackers or raw vegetables.

CHEESE LOG

Serves 10-12

½ pound sharp Cheddar cheese, grated

3 ounces Cream cheese, softened

1 tablespoon butter, softened

2 teaspoons chopped fresh parsley

1 tablespoon grated onion

½ teaspoon salt

1 teaspoon Worcestershire sauce

Dash Tabasco sauce

In the large bowl of your electric mixer, beat together until well blended (it will be quite soft) the Cheddar, Cream cheese, butter, parsley, onion, salt, Worcestershire and Tabasco. Place mixture on a large sheet of waxed paper and roll to form a log approximately 8 inches long and 2 inches in diameter. Close the ends of the waxed paper. Place in the freezer for 30 minutes.

Blue Cheese Frosting:

2 ounces Bleu cheese (or Roquefort)

3 ounces Cream cheese

2 tablespoons heavy cream

Dash Tabasco sauce

½ cup chopped pistachio nuts

Beat together in a small bowl the Bleu cheese, Cream cheese, heavy cream and Tabasco until light and fluffy. Remove the cheese log from the freezer. (It should be stone hard.) Coat evenly with the Bleu Cheese Frosting. Place in the freezer for 5 minutes. Remove and roll the log in the pistachio nuts, making sure to cover all sides and ends evenly. Roll in plastic wrap and refrigerate for at least 4 hours. Place on a serving plate with a sprig of parsley for color. Serve with assorted crackers.

ROQUEFORT PATE

1 cup Roquefort cheese

1 cup butter

½ cup heavy cream, whipped to medium-stiff peak

1½ tablespoons brandy

Chopped pistachio nuts (unsalted)

Cream together butter and Roquefort cheese. Add brandy and gently fold whipped cream into cheese mixture. Line a 16 ounce mold with a layer of cheesecloth. Place mixture into mold, cover and refrigerate until firm. When ready to serve, unmold onto serving dish, remove cheesecloth and sprinkle with chopped pistachio nuts. Garnish with watercress and serve with crackers as an appetizer.

SMOKY PECANS

2 cups pecan halves

¼ cup liquid smoke

3 tablespoons butter, melted

1 teaspoon salt

Combine pecan halves and liquid smoke, stirring until pecans are coated with liquid, let stand 20 minutes. Drain well. Spread on ungreased baking sheet. Toast in oven 250° for 1 hour or until crisp. Brush with butter and sprinkle with salt. Drain on paper toweling.

FONDUE CHOCOLATE FOR FRUIT

9 ounces Tobler's Chocolate 3 (3 ounce) bars or equivalent amount of Toblerone Chocolate for nutty consistency

½ cup heavy cream

2 tablespoons Kirsch, Cognac or orange liqueur

Heat chocolate and cream together over low heat until chocolate is melted. Blend well and stir in liqueur. Keep warm over very low flame in fondue pot on serving table, accompanied by assorted fruits. Good with any fruits or pound cake squares, lady fingers, etc.

HAM MOUSSE

Serves: 15 to 20

½ cup unsweetened pineapple juice

1 envelope unflavored gelatin

Generous dash ground cloves

1 tablespoon Dijon mustard

½ pound cooked ham, finely ground*

1 egg white at room temperature

½ cup very cold heavy or whipping cream

In saucepan combine pineapple juice, gelatin and cloves. Let stand 2 minutes, then stir over low heat until gelatin is dissolved. Stir in mustard; set aside. Stir finely ground ham into gelatin mixture, and set aside. Beat egg white until stiff but not dry. Fold into ham mixture. Whip cream until it holds a peak, and fold into the above. Spoon into a 3 cup mold. Cover and refrigerate until set, at least 3 or up to 24 hours. Unmold and sprinkle with chopped parsley. Serve with crackers or cocktail bread (such as party rye). May be served with additional mustard if desired.

*Note on ham. Smithfield-style ham is excellent and gives a sharper flavor; however, good quality precooked buffet style will substitute.

CRAB MOUSSE

Serves: 12 or more

2 envelopes unflavored gelatin

½ cup cold water

1 (10¾ ounce) can cream of mushroom soup

1 (3 ounce package) Cream cheese (room temperature)

1 pound of fresh (or frozen) crabmeat, flaked

1 cup mayonnaise

1 green pepper, diced

1 (4 ounce) jar chopped pimentos, drained

½ cup celery, diced

½ cup cucumber, diced

¼ cup green onions, chopped

1 tablespoon Worcestershire sauce

½ teaspoon salt

⅛ teaspoon white pepper

Lemon wedges

Lightly oil a 6 cup mold.

Soften gelatin in the cold water. In top of a double boiler, heat soup to boiling, add Cream cheese and stir to blend. Add softened gelatin and mix well. Remove from heat and refrigerate until mixture begins to thicken.

In a large bowl, combine remaining ingredients (except lemon wedges). Add thickened gelatin mixture and blend gently. Pour into prepared mold and refrigerate over night or until firm. Unmold on serving platter and garnish with lemon wedges.

Serve with crackers.

TUNA (OR SALMON) MOUSSE
Serves: 20

1 envelope unflavored gelatin

½ cup cold water

2 cans (6½ to 7 ounces each) tuna, drained or 1 can (15½ ounce) salmon, drained

½ cup mayonnaise

2 tablespoons green onions, chopped

2 tablespoons dry sherry

2 tablespoons lemon juice

2 teaspoons fresh dill, chopped, or ¾ teaspoon dried dill weed

½ teaspoon salt

½ teaspoon bottled hot pepper sauce

1 cup heavy or whipping cream

In small saucepan sprinkle gelatin evenly over water; let stand 1 minute. Cook over low heat, stirring constantly, until gelatin is completely dissolved. Remove saucepan from heat; set aside.

In blender container or in food processor with steel blade attached, blend gelatin mixture with next 8 ingredients until smooth.

Beat cream until soft peaks form. Gently fold whipped cream into tuna mixture. Pour into 6 cup mold; cover and refrigerate 4 to 5 hours or overnight.

To serve, unmold mousse onto chilled plate. Garnish with cucumber, lemon slices and fresh dill. Serve with crackers.

May also be served as a first course or as a light luncheon entree which serves 6 in this manner.

PERFECT PARTY PATE
Yield: 3 cups

½ pound crabmeat or 1 (7½ ounce) can

½ cup butter

2 tablespoons lemon juice

½ cup mayonnaise

⅓ cup grated Parmesan cheese

3 hard-cooked eggs

1½ teaspoons horseradish

½ teaspoon salt

¼ teaspoon garlic powder

¼ teaspoon white pepper

¼ cup minced onion

¼ cup chopped parsley

Flake crabmeat and remove any cartilage. Whip butter and lemon juice until light and fluffy. Beat in mayonnaise, Parmesan cheese, chopped egg yolks and seasonings. Finely chop egg whites and add along with crab, onion and parsley. Pack into small serving bowl or crock. Chill several hours or overnight. Garnish with sprigs of parsley. Serve with crackers.

SHRIMP — WELL SAUCED

Cook about 1 pound of medium shrimp using any preferred method of seasoning while cooking. Shell, devein and chill. Use either of the following sauces, combing it with the chilled shrimp early in the day it will be served or as far ahead as the night before. Fold the shrimp into the sauce, and refrigerate until serving time. Serve with picks.

Dilled Mustard Sauce:

¼ cup Dijon-style mustard

2 teaspoons dried dill weed

3 tablespoons heavy cream

3 tablespoons red wine vinegar

1 tablespoon light brown sugar (or to taste)

½ cup vegetable oil

In a food processor (with steel blade) or in a blender, combine all ingredients except oil. Blend until the mixture is well combined. With the motor running, add the ½ cup oil in a stream and blend until the mixture is thick and smooth. Makes about ¾ cup. Combine with the shrimp and store covered in refrigerator.

Celery Marinade For Shrimp:

½ cup celery, finely minced

1 cup mayonnaise

¼ cup scallions, minced

2 tablespoons plus 2 teaspoons Dijon-style mustard

2 tablespoons plus 2 teaspoons red wine vinegar

4 teaspoons fresh parsley leaves, minced

4 teaspoons lemon juice

Cayenne, salt and pepper to taste

Combine all ingredients, folding in shrimp as above and store in refrigerator. (This should be more than enough sauce for 1 pound of shrimp.)

CURRY DIP

1 cup mayonnaise

1 tablespoon chili sauce

1 tablespoon chutney

1 tablespoon Worcestershire

2 tablespoons onion, grated

1 teaspoon curry powder

1 teaspoon Tabasco

Garlic salt to taste

Chill and serve with cold shrimp, raw vegetables, or fried chicken breast tidbits.

CRAB-STUFFED MUSHROOMS

Serves: 8

About 25 medium mushrooms

2 tablespoons salad oil

1 (6 ounce) package frozen crabmeat, thawed and drained well (or equivalent amount of fresh)

1 egg, lightly beaten

2 tablespoons mayonnaise

2 tablespoons onion, chopped

1 teaspoon lemon juice

½ cup soft breadcrumbs, divided

2 tablespoons butter or margarine, melted

Clean mushrooms and pat dry. Remove stems. Brush caps with salad oil, and place in a buttered baking dish. Combine crabmeat, egg, mayonnaise, onion, lemon juice and ¼ cup breadcrumbs. Stuff caps with crabmeat mixture. Combine remaining ¼ cup breadcrumbs with butter; sprinkle over crab mixture. Bake at 375° for 15 minutes. Serve immediately while warm.

EDWINA'S SCALLOP SKEWERS

Serves 12 to 14

1½ pounds small scallops or larger sea scallops, cut in half

Bacon strips, cut into ½ inch pieces

Bottled (pickled) cocktail onions

Button mushrooms (small fresh ones if possible, canned button mushrooms will do)

Marinade:

2 tablespoons red wine vinegar

6 tablespoons olive oil (or half olive, half vegetable if you prefer)

1 tablespoon Grey Poupon mustard

1 teaspoon salt

Mix marinade ingredients in food processor or by hand. Marinate scallops in this mixture for at least 3 hours or overnight.

Use bamboo skewers which are found in good grocery stores or specialty stores which will be about 10 inches in length and should be broken in half. Other skewers, cocktail length, may be substituted.

On each skewer, place one of each; scallop, bacon strip, mushroom and onion. Place 8 inches from broiler and cook, turning once, until done. (Be careful not to overcook.) Place in chafing dish to keep warm. Remaining marinade may be poured over cooked scallops. Salt to taste may be added in the chafing dish.

SHRIMP SALAD SPREAD
Yield: 1½ cups

1 pound shrimp, cooked, shelled, finely chopped

2 stalks celery, finely minced

3 green onions, finely chopped

2 ounces canned pimentos, finely chopped

2 tablespoons chopped parsley

2 tablespoons mayonnaise

Mix all ingredients together with a spoon, blending well. Chill for several hours to allow flavors to blend. Especially good served spread on crisp cucumber or zucchini slices. May also be served on rye bread, crackers, or as a filling for raw mushroom caps.

CHICKEN DELIGHTS
Serves 27

Marinade:

1 tablespoon Hoisin sauce

1 tablespoon soy sauce

1 teaspoon sugar

2 green onions, finely chopped

½ teaspoon sesame oil

2 chicken breasts, skinned, boned, cut into small pieces

½ pound sliced bacon

In shallow dish combine all marinade ingredients. Add chicken, cover and refrigerate for 3 to 4 hours. Cut bacon strips into thirds. Wrap a strip of bacon around each chicken piece and secure with toothpick. Place chicken on rack in broiler pan. Broil until bacon is crisp, about 5 minutes. Turn, broil on other side until crisp.

CHICKEN L'ORANGE
Makes 24 to 30 balls

Chicken Balls:

2 cups ground cooked chicken

½ cup fine soft bread crumbs

¼ teaspoon pepper

1 teaspoon salt

1 teaspoon minced onion

1 egg

1 tablespoon chicken broth

Combine all ingredients in a medium bowl. Form into balls ¾ to 1 inch in diameter. Place on greased baking sheet. Bake in hot over (400°) for 15 minutes. Place in small chafing dish, add orange sauce and keep warm. Serve with cocktail picks.

Orange Sauce:

½ cup currant jelly

½ teaspoon minced onion

¼ teaspoon Tabasco sauce

¾ teaspoon salt

½ teaspoon dry mustard

¼ teaspoon ginger

1 tablespoon chopped dill or
  1 teaspoon dried dill weed

1½ cups orange juice

2 tablespoons cornstarch

2 tablespoons cold water

In small saucepan, heat currant jelly, onion, Tabasco sauce, salt, dry mustard, ginger, dill and orange juice until boiling.

Blend cornstarch with cold water and stir into mixture in saucepan. Cook until thickened, stirring constantly.

BUTTER—HONEY CHICKEN TIDBITS *Serves 12*

6 large broiler-fryer chicken
  thighs, boned

¼ cup melted butter or
  margarine

¼ cup honey

1 teaspoon teriyaki sauce

1 teaspoon seasoned salt

½ teaspoon garlic salt

¼ teaspoon pepper

½ cup sesame seeds, toasted

Rinse chicken thighs and pat dry. Cut each thigh into 6 to 8 pieces. Refrigerate 8 hours.

Combine butter, honey and teriyaki sauce in a small saucepan; stir well. Bring to a boil; remove from heat and set aside. Sprinkle chicken pieces with seasoned salt, garlic salt and pepper. Dip each chicken piece into honey mixture, and coat with sesame seeds. Place chicken pieces on a cookie sheet. Bake at 350° for 30 minutes, turning once to brown evenly. Reheat remaining honey mixture and serve with chicken tidbits.

TROPICAL FRUIT DIP

2 tablespoons apricot preserves

1 cup sour cream

¼ cup flaked coconut

2 tablespoons chopped walnuts

Milk

Cut up any large pieces of apricot in the preserves. In a small bowl, combine the preserves, the sour cream, coconut and walnuts. Mix well. Stir in enough milk to achieve the proper dipping consistency. Chill. Turn into a serving bowl, and garnish with walnut halves and additional coconut.

ORANGE DRUMMETTES
Serves 25 to 30

3 pounds chicken (wing) drummettes

2 eggs

⅓ cup orange juice concentrate, thawed

1 cup dry bread crumbs (fine)

1 cup pecans, finely ground

1 teaspoon salt

¼ teaspoon pepper

½ cup butter

Beat egg and orange concentrate together in small bowl. Let sit 15 minutes. Mix pecans, bread crumbs, salt and pepper in another bowl. Dip chicken pieces in egg mixture then into pecan-crumb mixture. The chicken has a better flavor if this is done several hours ahead. Refrigerate the chicken until shortly before cooking. Melt butter in a baking pan large enough to hold chicken in one layer. Place chicken in pan and bake for 45 minutes at 350° turning once. Serve hot.

TOASTED BLEU CHEESE ROUNDS
Serves: 15 to 20

1 stick butter

1 cup Bleu cheese, crumbled

½ cup chopped walnuts

Small loaf of bread

Cut bread into rounds (smaller silver dollar size toast better). Mix butter, cheese and walnuts, letting it soften enough to spread. Spread mixture on bread rounds and run under broiler until bubbling.

Cheese mixture may be made ahead and keeps nicely refrigerated for a week or longer.

BLEU CHEESE STUFFED GRAPES
Serves 40

½ pound large white seedless grapes

2 tablespoons unsalted butter, softened

¼ pound Bleu cheese, crumbled and at room temperature

Cut each grape ¾ through from stem end. Pat dry with paper towels. Beat butter in processor or small bowl until creamy. Add cheese and beat until thoroughly blended. Spoon mixture into pastry bag fitted with small star tip and refrigerate until a good consistency to press through tip. Pipe some of the mixture into center of each grape, carefully pressing sides together. Chill until firm. These can be prepared a day ahead. The grapes also make a lovely and tasty garnish for other dishes.

FETA CHEESE BALL

1 small garlic clove, pressed or finely minced

2 medium green onions, white only, finely minced

1 (8 ounce) package Cream cheese, room temperature

4 to 6 ounces Feta cheese, rinsed (the larger amount for a more distinct Feta taste)

1 tablespoon sour cream

1 teaspoon dried dillweed

½ teaspoon dried oregano

¼ teaspoon freshly ground pepper

5 large radishes, shredded

2 tablespoons minced parsley leaves

Line 1½ cup bowl with plastic wrap. Blend together the softened Cream cheese, the Feta cheese, sour cream, dill, oregano and pepper, mixing well until it is smooth and creamy. Blend in the minced garlic and onion. Taste and adjust seasoning. (Add salt if necessary, but with caution as feta can be salty.) Spoon into prepared bowl, cover and chill thoroughly.

Just before serving, remove cheese ball and while still wrapped in plastic wrap shape it into a ball by molding with hands. Remove plastic and roll in shredded radishes. Press radishes into place, and garnish with minced parsley. Serve surrounded with wheat crackers, toasted pita bread or crudites.

DEEP FRIED CHEESE   *Yield: 30 hors d'oeuvres*

1 pound Swiss, Gruyere, Fontina or Port du Salut cheese

4 eggs (may need more)

2 cups fine dried bread crumbs

Oil for deep frying

Beat eggs with ½ cup bread crumbs in a medium bowl. Place remaining breadcrumbs in another bowl. Pour oil into small skillet to depth of 2 inches and heat to 380°. Cut cheese into 1 inch cubes. Dip cheese cubes into the egg mixture and then into breadcrumbs, coating well. (May be repeated if not sufficiently coated.) Fry in batches until crisp and golden, about 1 minute. Watch closely to avoid over browning. Remove with slotted spoon or small strainer, transfer to paper towels and drain well. (You may wish to transfer to paper towel lined oven-safe plate and keep warm in 200° oven while you fry more batches.) If needed, lightly sprinkle cheese cubes with salt. Serve immediately on toothpicks while they are soft and creamy inside.

COCKTAIL MEATBALLS

Yield: 85 meatballs

3 pounds lean ground beef

½ cup seasoned bread crumbs
(your own or purchased
Italian seasoned are good)

2 onions, minced

4 teaspoons prepared
horseradish

4 garlic cloves, crushed

1½ cups tomato juice

4 teaspoons salt

Pepper to taste

Preheat oven to 450°. Combine all ingredients for meatballs and shape into 1 inch balls. Place in a jelly roll pan or a cookie sheet with sides and brown in the oven for 10 minutes. Remove from the oven and drain.

Sauce:

¼ cup butter

2 onions, chopped

¼ cup flour

3 cups beef broth

1 cup red wine (dry)

¼ cup catsup

¼ cup brown sugar

2 tablespoons lemon juice

6 ginger snaps, crumbled
(optional)

2 teaspoons salt

Pepper to taste

In a large skillet, melt butter. Add onions and saute until golden. Blend in flour. Add broth, stirring until smooth. Stir in remaining ingredients and simmer over low heat for 15 minutes. Add meatballs; simmer 5 more minutes or longer. (Meatballs wait nicely in the sauce but do not let boil.)

To serve, place in chafing dish.

NOTE: May be prepared in advance. Place in refrigerator up to 24 hours, or spoon into freezer proof container with sauce; freeze up to one month. To serve, heat thawed or frozen, covered, in 300° oven until hot.

SHERRIED SAUSAGE BALLS

Serves 20

2 pounds bulk sausage ("hot" is best)

Form into small bite-size balls and fry lightly in skillet or bake on cookie sheet in hot oven (450°) for about 10 minutes. The sausage balls may be frozen at this point if desired.

Sauce:

1 (8 ounce) jar Major Grey's Chutney (chopped lightly in food
   processor)
1 (8 ounce) carton sour cream
½ cup sherry

Mix the above together in sauce pan and heat. Serve the sausage balls in
the sauce in a chafing dish.

"OH, SO GOOD!"   *Yield: 40 canapes*

1 pound very lean bacon
½ pound sharp Cheddar cheese

1 medium onion, cut up
Triscuits or party rye bread

Combine bacon, cheese and onion. Put through food grinder (with
medium plate) twice or use food processor with steel blade to chop all
ingredients until very finely chopped. If using food processor, cut bacon
and cheese into small hunks before processing with onion. Spread on
Triscuits or party rye bread. Place under broiler, with tops of canapes
about 6 or 7 inches from heat. Broil until brown. Serve immediately.
    The uncooked spread can be kept for weeks in freezer.

GOOSE AND DUCK LIVER PATE

Livers from 6 ducks and 2 to 3
   geese
2 teaspoons Vermouth
1 teaspoon instant minced
   onion
1 hard cooked egg

1 to 2 tablespoons mayonnaise
   or soft butter
1 teaspoon sugar
Salt and pepper to taste

Boil livers in small amount of water and onion. Cook until tender. Drain
water and place livers in blender or processor with hard cooked egg. After
blending, remove to small bowl and add Vermouth, mayonnaise or butter,
sugar and seasonings. Blend together well. Chill pate in refrigerator and
serve with crackers or bread.

MIDDLE EASTERN LAMB (OR BEEF) & RATATOUILLE QUICHE

2 tablespoons unsalted butter

4 ounces grated Parmesan cheese, room temperature

4 ounces Mozzarella cheese, finely shredded and well chilled

¼ cup fresh parsley leaves, lightly packed — minced after measuring

6 large scallions, thinly sliced

2 garlic cloves, minced

1 small onion, chopped

1 tablespoon vegetable oil

8 ounces leftover cooked lamb or raw lamb coarsely chopped (may use beef)

1½ teaspoons dried oregano

1 teaspoon cinnamon

4 large eggs

1 cup heavy cream

½ teaspoon salt

⅓ cup plain yogurt

*3 cups Ratatouille — well drained (See vegetables)

Preheat oven to 375°. Use the butter to grease heavily the inside of a 9 x 13 inch baking pan.

Toss the shredded cheeses together to mix well, and press the mixture against the bottom and sides of the buttered baking dish to form a crust.

In an 8 inch skillet saute the garlic and onion in the vegetable oil over moderate heat until soft, about 3 minutes. Combine the chopped lamb or beef with the oregano and cinnamon and add to the skillet. Cook together with the garlic and onions for 10 minutes, stirring frequently to prevent sticking.

Beat the eggs with the cream and salt, and mix the yogurt, combining well.

Carefully spread the Ratatouille over the cheese in the baking dish. Sprinkle the lamb and onion mixture evenly over the Ratatouille. Pour the egg, cream and yogurt mixture on top. Sprinkle with the minced parsley and sliced scallions.

Bake in the middle of the preheated oven for 40 minutes, until the top is lightly browned. Let cool for at least 15 minutes before cutting into squares to serve.

ARTICHOKE — CHEESE APPETIZERS

Serves 16

4 baked puff pastry shells (frozen Pepperidge Farm style)

2 (3 ounce) packages Cream cheese with chives, softened

1 egg

4 canned artichoke hearts

2 tablespoons softened butter

3 drops Tabasco

6 drops Worcestershire sauce

Lemon juice to taste

Place patty shells in oven-proof serving dish. Beat cheese with egg and the seasonings. Just before baking, place spoonful of cheese mixture in each shell, top with artichoke and cover with remaining cheese mixture. Bake about 20 to 30 minutes at 400° or until filling has puffed and browned.

If appetizer size servings are desired, quarter the artichokes and place in Croustades (see index) or other individual piecrust type shells.

MUSHROOM-BACON SPREAD

Yield: 2½ cups

6 slices bacon

8 ounces fresh mushrooms, chopped (3 cups) (May increase to 4 cups)

1 medium onion, finely chopped (½ cup)

½ clove garlic, minced

2 tablespoons all purpose flour

¼ teaspoon salt

⅛ teaspoon pepper

1 (8 ounce) package Cream cheese, cubed and softened

2 teaspoons Worcestershire sauce

1 teaspoon soy sauce

½ cup dairy sour cream

Cook bacon until crisp; drain, reserving 2 tablespoons drippings. Crumble bacon; set aside. Cook mushrooms, onion and garlic in reserved drippings until tender and most of the liquid has evaporated. Stir in flour, salt and pepper. Add Cream cheese, Worcestershire sauce, and soy sauce. Heat and stir until cheese is melted. Stir in sour cream and crumbled bacon. Heat through. Do not boil. Serve warm on rye bread rounds, crackers, or rusks.

NOTE: This may be prepared the day before. Do not reheat after the sour cream and bacon are added. Reheat just before serving time.

TOLEDO CHEESE STACKS

1 long loaf Pepperidge Farm thin-sliced white bread

2 sticks margarine, softened

¾ pound sharp Cheddar cheese, grated and melted in double boiler

2 egg whites, stiffly beaten

Add soft margarine to melted cheese in double boiler. Blend well until margarine is melted. If mixture separates, cool until it can be combined. Fold in beaten egg whites.

Remove crusts from 3 slices of bread. Spread mixture on each slice and stack, one on top of the other. "Frost" top and sides. Repeat procedure, using three slices of bread at a time until all bread is used. Freeze stacks on cookie sheet, then cut into nine squares. Bag and return frozen squares to freezer for future use or bake at 450° for 8 minutes until golden and bubbly.

WHISKEY CHUTE TOMATOES

White bread slices

Cocktail tomatoes

Hellmann's mayonnaise, or homemade

Salt and pepper to taste

Parmesan cheese

Cut bread into 1½ inch circles. Spread with mayonnaise. Cut stem and top ends of tomatoes (to flatten) and then cut in half crosswise. Put ½ tomato, larger side up, on bread round. Sprinkle with salt, pepper and cover with cheese. Bake at 350° until bubbly and bread is lightly toasted on bottom.

Serve hot. May be used as a brunch dish using 2 inch rounds of bread with tomatoes to fit.

Easily adapted to any number of servings.

RAW RADISH DIP

Yield: 2 cups

1 (8 ounce) package Cream cheese, softened

1 tablespoon lemon juice

¼ teaspoon dill weed

1 teaspoon salt

1 garlic clove, mashed

1 cup radishes, chopped

Blend together Cream cheese, lemon juice, dill weed, salt and garlic. Add chopped radishes and stir until blended. Cover and refrigerate for at least 2 hours. Garnish with radish rose and parsley. Serve on bland crackers or as finger sandwich spread.

MEXICAN RELISH DIP
Serves: 10 to 12

1 (4 ounce) can chopped green chilies, including liquid

1 (4 ounce) can chopped ripe olives, drained

2 tomatoes, finely chopped

4 green onions with tops or 1 onion, finely chopped

1 teaspoon garlic salt

3 tablespoons salad oil

1 tablespoon white vinegar

Salt and pepper to taste

3 dashes Tabasco sauce (optional)

Combine all ingredients; marinate overnight and serve with Taco flavored chips.

LYNN'S CLAM DIP
Serves: 8 to 10

1 (7 ounce) can minced clams

3 tablespoons butter

1 medium onion, chopped

1 medium bell pepper, chopped

¼ cup catsup

⅛ teaspoon cayenne

1 tablespoon Worcestershire

1 tablespoon sherry

¼ pound sharp Cheddar cheese, grated

Drain clams, but reserve juice to add if dip appears thicker than desired. Saute onions and bell pepper in butter. Add remaining ingredients and heat until cheese is melted. (May be prepared the night before and refrigerated. If this is done, remove from heat before cheese melts, cool, and refrigerate in oven-proof serving dish. Reheat in medium oven about 350° until cheese is bubbly.)

Serve warm with crackers or chips. May need a spreader for serving.

FILLED PHYLLO DOUGH
SPINACH ROLLS (Spanakopetes)   *Yield: 45 pieces*

**1 pound frozen spinach,
drained thoroughly**

1 onion, finely chopped

**1 cup Feta cheese, finely
crumbled**

3 eggs, beaten

½ pound phyllo

½ pound melted butter

Let spinach thaw and drain thoroughly. Beat eggs. Add eggs, onion, salt and pepper to spinach and mix well. Add Feta and mix slightly. Salt and pepper to taste. Cut phyllo pastry into three equal parts. Refrigerate unused portion until needed. Cover remaining phyllo with a slightly dampened towel. Place 1 tablespoon of the spinach mixture at end of pastry (butter pastry before filling); fold up once, and turn in sides and roll. Brush with butter on all sides and place on a cookie sheet. Bake at 425° for 12 to 15 minutes until lightly browned. Cool slightly; serve warm.
   Can be frozen before baking.

CHEESE ROLLS (Tiropeta)

1 pound Feta cheese

4 eggs, well-beaten

1½ cups Cottage cheese

½ cup grated Romano cheese

Dash mint

Mix and roll in phyllo as indicated above.

GROUND BEEF OR GROUND LAMB

1 pound ground beef or lamb

1 onion, sauted

Salt and pepper

Dash basil

Mix and roll in phyllo as indicated above.
   NOTE: To freeze, place unbaked buttered rolls in plastic container, separating layers with wax paper, and place in freezer. When ready to serve, place frozen rolls on ungreased pan and bake. May be frozen for at least 2 months.

ARTICHOKE SQUARES

Serves 10 or 12

3 (6 ounce) jars marinated
  artichoke hearts in oil

1 clove garlic, crushed

½ cup chopped onion

4 eggs

¼ cup seasoned bread crumbs

½ pound extra sharp Cheddar
  cheese, grated

2 tablespoons minced fresh
  parsley

¼ teaspoon salt

⅛ teaspoon dried oregano

⅛ teaspoon pepper

⅛ teaspoon Tabasco sauce

Drain the oil from 1 jar of the artichoke hearts into a 12 inch skillet and, using moderate heat, gently heat the oil. Saute the garlic and onion in the oil for 5 minutes and set aside. Drain and discard the oil from the remaining artichoke hearts. Chop the hearts finely (food processor works well for this) and set aside.

In a medium-size bowl, beat the eggs until foamy and blend in the bread crumbs, cheese, parsley, oregano, salt, pepper, and Tabasco. Add the finely chopped artichoke hearts to the egg mixture and stir gently to blend. Add the onion and garlic. Again mix well and spoon into a greased 9 x 9 inch pan. Bake in a preheated 325° oven for 30 minutes. Cool well before cutting into small squares. Before serving, place in a 325° oven for 10 to 12 minutes to reheat.

NOTE: This recipe freezes beautifully. Cook and cut into squares, wrap airtight and freeze. Thaw, and reheat as above before serving.

LIME SAUCE

Serves: 25

2 cups mayonnaise

2 cups sour cream

⅓ cup fresh lime juice

1 tablespoon lime peel,
  finely grated

2 teaspoons white horseradish

2 teaspoons Dijon mustard

1 teaspoon salt

Combine all ingredients in large bowl. Cover and refrigerate. Adjust seasonings before serving. Broccoli or other vegetables may be cleaned, prepared and refrigerated the night before. From 30 minutes to 1 hour before serving, sprinkle the vegetables lightly with Italian salad dressing. Arrange on platter around a bowl of Lime Sauce for dipping.

CRAB-CHEESE ROLLS

Serves 80

½ pound Cheddar cheese, grated

1 (7½ ounce) can crab, or equivalent fresh crab

½ cup pimento stuffed green olives, chopped

¼ cup olive oil

4 ounces tomato sauce

3 green onions including tops, chopped

Salt to taste

40 party rolls (Pepperidge Farm), halved, or make your own small rolls

Mix first seven ingredients thoroughly. Spread on halved rolls, about 1½ to 2 teaspoons each. Broil until cheese melts and bubbles.

This filling is also suitable for larger rolls as a meal. If using larger rolls, pick out some bread to create a well for more filling.

Eight slices of cooked, crumbled bacon may be substituted for crab to make a more economical filling.

This recipe adapts to both food processor and microwave.

Preparation time: 1 hour. Mix may be frozen; rolls may be spread hours in advance, covered, and refrigerated.

WALNUT CHEESE ROUNDS

Yield: 3 dozen

½ cup English walnuts, finely ground

¾ cup unbleached flour

½ teaspoon baking powder

¼ teaspoon salt

¼ teaspoon dry mustard

½ cup (1 stick) butter or margarine, softened

½ cup sharp Cheddar cheese, grated

½ cup Swiss cheese, grated

1 egg, well beaten

Combine flour, nuts, baking powder, salt and mustard in medium bowl and blend well. Cut in butter or margarine with knives or pastry blender until mixture resembles very coarse meal. Add cheeses and half of the egg. Blend well until dough is stiff. With hands, shape dough into a log about 1¼ inches in diameter. Wrap carefully in waxed paper and refrigerate several hours.

Preheat oven to 350°. Slice dough into very thin wafers and place on ungreased baking sheet. Bake 18 to 20 minutes or until crackers are just lightly browned around edges. Watch closely to make sure you do not overcook.

LA GOUGERE *Serves 6 to 8*

(Cheese pastry from the Burgundian region of France. Traditionally served
at the end of the day with a glass of Burgundy.)

1 cup milk	4 eggs
¼ cup (½ stick) butter, cut into pieces	5 ounces Swiss or Gruyere cheese, grated
1 cup all purpose flour	1 teaspoon Dijon mustard
1 scant teaspoon salt	½ teaspoon dry mustard
⅛ teaspoon freshly ground pepper	

Combine milk and butter in 2 quart saucepan and bring to boil over
medium heat. Reduce heat to low, add flour, salt and pepper all at once
and stir vigorously with wooden spoon until mixture is smooth and leaves
sides of pan, forming a ball, about 1 minute. Remove the mixture from the
heat, cool slightly and add eggs one at a time, beating well after each
addition. Continue beating, using spoon or hand mixer, until dough is
shiny and smooth. Add Swiss or Gruyere cheese and mustards and blend
well. Allow the mixture to cool.

On a greased cookie sheet, using an ice cream scoop or large spoon,
make 7 equal mounds, arranged in a circle and touching each other. This
should use about ¾ of the dough. With the remaining dough, make a small
ball on top of each of the larger ones. Sprinkle the top with a little
additional cheese, finely grated. Bake in the middle of a preheated 375°
oven for about 45 minutes or until puffs are crisp, puffed and brown. (DO
NOT OPEN THE OVEN DOOR WHILE RING IS RISING.) Let cool 5
minutes before transferring to serving board or platter. The ring is served
whole (hot, warm or cold) and pieces are broken off.

NOTE: After pastry is shaped on the baking sheet, it may be refrigerated
for several hours or overnight before cooking. Remove from refrigerator
and bake in preheated 400° oven for 30 to 45 minutes.

POTTED CRAB *Serves 8 to 10*

8 ounces cooked crabmeat, finely shredded (fresh, well picked crabmeat is best — good quality canned will substitute)	2 tablespoons heavy (whipping) cream
	1 tablespoon sherry
	1 tablespoon lemon juice
6 tablespoons butter or margarine	Salt and pepper to taste
	Cayenne to taste
3 egg yolks, carefully separated from whites	1 tablespoon grated Parmesan cheese

In saucepan combine the first six ingredients and cook over low heat, stirring constantly, until smooth and thick. Be careful not to overcook as the mixture will become more firm when chilled. When mixture begins to thicken, remove from heat and add salt, pepper, cayenne and cheese. Stir well until smooth and blended. Add more sherry and lemon juice if you desire.

Pack tightly into a non-metallic cocktail dish or other serving dish. Chill until serving time. May be done the day before. Serve with wheat crackers, squares of crisp toast or crusty French bread torn into bite size pieces. May be frozen.

SOUFFLE CRACKERS

Saltine crackers (16 or multiples of 16)

Melted butter or margarine

9 x 13 inch pan filled with ice cubes covered with water (Be sure cubes are covered completely so that crackers will lie evenly on surface.)

IMPORTANT: Only work with 16 crackers at a time to insure proper timing.

Preheat oven to 400°. Place the 16 crackers one at a time on the surface of the ice water taking notice of the order in which they are placed. Immediately after placing the 16th cracker, return to the first one and begin turning them over. After you have finished turning the last cracker, return again to the first one and begin placing them on a greased cookie sheet. If your timing has been correct, the crackers should be getting slightly soft from water absorption.

At this point, if you are preparing more than 16 crackers, you may begin working with the next group and add them to the cookie sheet. NOTE: It is important not to crowd the crackers so that they are touching, as they will puff up and change shape slightly.

When the sheet is filled with crackers, brush them generously with melted butter. Place them in the oven which has been preheated to 400°, but immediately reduce the heat to 300°. Bake until golden brown, approximately 30 minutes. During the baking period, if you desire a richer flavor, brush again with melted butter. Cool and store in airtight container

This interesting technique produces a *different* kind of cracker with a *superb* flavor. Good alone or as a base for other hors d'oeuvres.

SOUPS

Moravian Church, Old Salem

STRAWBERRY SOUP
Serves: 6

1½ cups water
¾ cup light bodied red wine
½ cup sugar
2 tablespoons fresh lemon juice
Cinnamon to taste

1 quart strawberries, washed and capped
½ cup whipping cream
¼ cup sour cream
Garnish with chopped strawberries

Combine water, wine, sugar, lemon juice and cinnamon. Boil, uncovered, 15 minutes, stirring occasionally. Puree strawberries and add to soup. Boil 10 minutes. Cool and refrigerate. Whip cream and add sour cream. Fold into soup just before serving. Garnish with strawberries.

COLD PINEAPPLE SOUP
Serves: 8

1 fresh pineapple
1½ cups unsweetened pineapple juice
⅔ cup dry white wine

Sugar to taste (1 to 4 tablespoons)
Garnish with chopped pineapple

Cut both ends off pineapple. Slice down the middle. Quarter each half. Cut core out of top part. Cut shell off. Keep 2 spears to chop for garnish. Puree rest of fresh pineapple. Add juice, wine and sugar to taste. Add extra pineapple for garnish. Chill. Garnish with sour cream and bits of mint, if desired.

HOT APPLE SOUP
Serves: 6 to 8

1 tablespoon butter
1 large onion, chopped
4 cups chicken stock
4 large apples, peeled and cored
¾ teaspoon curry, or to taste

Juice of ½ lemon
3 tablespoons butter
¼ cup flour
½ cup half and half

Melt butter and saute onions until tender. Chop 2 of the apples and shred the other 2 for garnish. Stir in the 2 chopped apples, chicken broth, curry and lemon juice. Bring to a boil, reduce heat and simmer 10 minutes. Melt the rest of the butter in a large saucepan. Blend in the flour cooking 1 minute. Gradually stir the hot chicken broth mixture into the flour and butter. When broth boils and thickens, remove from heat. Cool slightly and puree in processor or blender. Stir in half and half and the shredded apples. Heat and serve.

GAZPACHO

Serves: 6 to 8

1 or 2 cloves garlic, crushed

2 tablespoons olive oil

3 tablespoons wine vinegar

1 teaspoon salt

1 teaspoon Worcestershire sauce

¼ teaspoon pepper

6 drops Tabasco

2 cups tomato juice

2 tomatoes, diced

1½ ribs celery, finely chopped

½ cucumber, peeled and finely diced

⅓ cup green onion, finely chopped

½ green pepper, finely chopped

⅓ container frozen chives

⅓ cup parsley

Optional garnish with croutons and grated cheddar cheese

Mix all ingredients and chill overnight. Garnish when served, if desired.

COLD CUCUMBER SOUP

Serves: 6

2 medium cucumbers, peeled and sliced

3 cups chicken broth

⅓ cup onion, chopped

1 tablespoon flour

1 medium bay leaf

½ teaspoon salt

1 medium cucumber, peeled and sliced

1 cup half and half

⅓ cup sour cream

2 tablespoons fresh lemon juice

Garnish with parsley and cucumber slices

Combine 2 cucumbers, chicken broth, onions, flour, bay leaf and salt. Simmer 20 minutes. Puree in blender or food processor. Chill 1 hour. Puree the other cucumber with the first mixture. Stir in half and half, sour cream and lemon juice. Chill.

CAULIFLOWER SOUP

Serves: 6 to 8

5 cups chicken stock

1½ large heads cauliflower, broken up

Salt and white pepper to taste

⅓ to ⅔ cup half and half (optional for thinning)

Chives for garnish

Cook cauliflower in stock until tender. Cool slightly and puree in processor or blender. Put back into pot and season with salt and pepper and thin, if desired, with half and half. To serve, garnish with chives. This will hold several days in the refrigerator or will freeze. Serve warm or cold.

VICHYSSOISE
Serves: 6

⅓ cup butter

6 onions, sliced

2 cups potatoes, thinly sliced

Dry sherry, to taste, if desired

4 cups chicken stock

1 cup heavy cream

Salt and white pepper to taste

Minced parsley and chives

Melt butter, add onions and saute 5 minutes over low heat. Add the potatoes and chicken stock and cook until potatoes are tender. Puree in processor or blender and return to pot. Add cream and a bit of sherry if desired. Season with salt and pepper. Heat and serve garnished with parsley and chives. Serve hot or cold.

ASPARAGUS SOUP
Serves: 6

1 pound asparagus

½ cup onions, chopped

¼ cup unsalted butter, softened

2 tablespoons flour

4 cups chicken broth, heated

2 large egg yolks

½ cup heavy cream

Lemon juice, salt, white pepper to taste

1 to 2 tablespoons dry sherry

Garnish with fresh chives

Break off and discard tough ends of asparagus. Peel lower ⅓ of stalks and cut into 1 inch pieces. Reserve tips. Cook onions in butter until soft. Add the 1 inch stalk pieces and sprinkle with flour. Cook, stirring 3 minutes. Pour in hot chicken broth. Bring to a boil, whisking. Simmer 15 minutes until asparagus is tender. Puree in food processor; return to pan; add tips and simmer 5 minutes. Beat yolks with cream. Add 1 cup hot asparagus broth to yolks and cream and mix. Add back to saucepan slowly whisking the entire time. Simmer 3 minutes but do not boil. Season with lemon juice, salt, pepper and sherry. Garnish with chives.

COLD AVOCADO YOGURT SOUP

⅔ cup plain yogurt

⅔ cup avocado, sieved or 1 whole avocado, peeled

½ cup beef bouillon

½ teaspoon salt

1 teaspoon chili powder

½ teaspoon onion juice

1 tablespoon lime juice

Put all in blender or food processor and blend well. Chill well. Can serve plain in bowls or with dollops of sour cream with twist of lime in center.

MUSHROOM SOUP

Serves: 4 to 6

¾ to 1 pound fresh
 mushrooms, wiped clean
Juice of ½ lemon
1 tablespoon butter
2 tablespoons shallots, minced
½ bay leaf

¼ teaspoon thyme
2 cups whipping cream
1½ cups chicken stock
¼ teaspoon salt, or to taste
½ teaspoon pepper
Garnish with minced parsley

Chop mushrooms with lemon juice in food processor. Melt butter and saute shallots lightly. Add mushrooms, bay leaf and thyme. Cook until liquid is completely evaporated (about 10 minutes). Blend in cream, chicken stock, salt and pepper. Bring to a boil, reduce heat and simmer 20 minutes. To serve, garnish with parsley.

TOMATO SOUP GRATINEE

Serves: 8

1 stick butter
2 tablespoons olive oil
1 large onion, thinly sliced
½ teaspoon dill weed, dried
½ teaspoon thyme, dried
½ teaspoon basil, dried
8 medium tomatoes, peeled and
 chopped or 1 (28 ounce) plus
 1 (15 ounce) can Italian
 tomatoes, drained, reserving
 juice

3 tablespoons tomato paste
3¾ cups chicken stock
¼ cup flour
Salt and pepper to taste
1 teaspoon sugar
Garnish with thick slices of
 toasted French bread or
 homemade croutons topped
 with fresh grated Parmesan
 cheese

Melt butter adding olive oil. Add the onions and dried seasonings. Cook until onions are soft. Chop tomatoes and add to soup along with tomato paste and 3 cups of chicken stock. Simmer 10 minutes. Mix the remaining chicken stock with the flour to make a paste. Add this to the soup stirring to thicken. Bring to a simmer and simmer 30 minutes. Puree in processor or blender. Add sugar, salt and pepper to taste. Garnish and serve.

CREAM OF FRESH TOMATO SOUP   *Serves: 4*

4 tablespoons olive oil
(preferably French)

2 onions, chopped

4 garlic cloves, chopped

5 tomatoes, sliced

2 tablespoons tomato paste

2 tablespoons whole wheat
flour

1 cup chicken stock

¾ cup half and half

Season to taste with garlic salt,
sugar, dill and Italian
seasoning

Garnish with croutons

Cook onions and garlic in olive oil until soft. Add tomatoes and cook 5 minutes. Puree in blender or food processor. Mix the tomato paste with the flour and add to above along with chicken stock, half and half and seasonings. Simmer 15 minutes. To serve, garnish with seasoned croutons.

FISH STOCK

2 pounds flounder skeltons
with tails but no heads

1 stick butter

2 quarts water

1 cup leeks, coarsely chopped

2 small onions, coarsely
chopped

1 rib celery, cut in half

1 whole carrot, peeled and cut
small

10 black peppercorns

2 large bay leaves

1 tablespoon salt

2 teaspoons thyme leaves

4 cloves garlic, unpeeled

Rinse, then rerinse flounder skeltons. Melt butter in large pot and add the rest of the ingredients including fish skeltons. Bring to a boil; reduce heat, cover and simmer 30 minutes. Let cool and strain. Freezes well.

OYSTER SOUP   *Serves: 6*

4 tablespoons butter

4 green onions, minced

2 tablespoons flour

1 (24 ounce) bottle clam juice

1 pint (2 cups) oysters and
liquid

2 cups half and half

1 tablespoon dry sherry

Salt and pepper to taste

Melt butter. Add onions and saute until tender. Push onions aside and sprinkle flour over. Let cook a minute. Slowly blend in the clam juice, oysters, half and half and dry sherry. Salt and pepper to taste. Bring to a boil and serve.

CLAM AND OYSTER BISQUE

Serves: 6

1 pound clams or 2 (6½ ounce) cans clams, drained

2 cups oysters, drained

½ cup butter

2 strips bacon, chopped

½ cup onion, chopped

⅓ cup green pepper, chopped

1 medium potato, peeled and diced

¼ cup celery, chopped

2 small carrots, chopped

1 teaspoon salt

¼ teaspoon pepper

Thyme to taste

6 dashes Tabasco

½ teaspoon Worcestershire sauce

2 cups half and half

In a saucepan, combine all ingredients except half and half. Cook 50 minutes. Add half and half and heat.

CELERY AND OYSTER SOUP

Serves: 8

6 cups celery, chopped

1 cup onion, chopped

6 tablespoons unsalted butter

6 cups chicken broth

1 cup whipping cream

2 (8 ounce) cans fresh oysters and liquid

Salt and pepper

Melt butter. Add vegetables and saute until tender (10 minutes). Add chicken broth and bring to boil. Reduce heat and simmer 45 minutes. Let cool a bit and puree in processor or blender. Add whipping cream and bring to a simmer. Add oysters and their liquid and cook until oysters curl a bit (3 to 5 minutes). Season with salt and pepper, if needed.

CREAM OF CRAB SOUP

Serves: 8

1 pound fresh backfin crabmeat, picked over

¼ cup butter

¼ cup flour

1¼ cups chicken broth

1 quart plus 1 cup half and half

½ cup dry sherry

1 teaspoon salt

¼ teaspoon white pepper

Melt butter and add the flour. Stir until smooth. Cook 1 minute. Gradually add broth. Cook over medium heat until sauce is thickened. Add crabmeat, half and half, sherry, salt and pepper. Heat over low heat for 10 to 15 minutes until soup is hot. Do not boil.

SCALLOP CHOWDER

Serves: 4 to 5

¼ cup firmly packed parsley, minced

1 large garlic, minced

¼ cup butter

½ cup dry white wine

¾ pound scallops, halved if large

1 cup half and half

½ cup heavy cream

1 cup freshly grated Parmesan cheese

¼ cup firmly packed parsley, minced

Fresh nutmeg, grated to taste

Salt and pepper to taste

3½ ounces frozen peas, thawed

½ pound zucchini, diced

2 tablespoons butter

Melt 2 tablespoons butter. Saute zucchini covered until tender and drain. Meanwhile in separate pan, melt ¼ cup butter. Add parsley and garlic and saute 5 minutes. Add wine and reduce over medium high heat to 6 tablespoons. Add scallops and cook 1 minute. Add half and half and cream and cook 2 minutes. Once the mixture is good and hot, remove from heat and add Parmesan, parsley, peas, zucchini, nutmeg, salt and pepper. Return back to heat and heat thoroughly to serve.

CLAM AND TOMATO BISQUE

Serves: 8

⅓ cup butter

⅓ cup flour

2 (6 ounce) cans chopped clams, drained and liquid reserved

2 cups whipping cream

1 (8 ounce) can tomato sauce

1 (16 ounce) can tomatoes, undrained and diced

Pinch of sugar

1 bay leaf

½ teaspoon thyme

Salt and white pepper to taste

Melt butter in 4 quart pan. Stir in flour and cook 2 to 3 minutes on low. Slowly add 1 cup clam liquid to the roux, increase heat and cook 3 to 4 minutes. Slowly add cream and stir until heated. Add tomato sauce, tomatoes, sugar, bay leaf, thyme, salt and pepper. Simmer uncovered 30 minutes. Remove bay leaf and add clam and adjust seasonings. Heat 1 to 2 minutes.

CRABMEAT AND ASPARAGUS SOUP

6 cups chicken stock

1 teaspoon salt (less if canned stock is used)

1 teaspoon minced ginger

1 pound fresh asparagus, cut into 1 inch size pieces

1 cup of claw meat

1 tablespoon sherry (pale dry)

1 tablespoon light soy sauce

2 tablespoons cornstarch dissolved in 4 tablespoons water

2 eggs, slightly beaten

1 or 2 scallions, finely chopped

Pepper to taste

Bring stock to boil. Add salt and ginger. Blanch asparagus until color changes. Add asparagus and crabmeat to chicken stock and bring to boil. Add sherry and soy sauce and simmer 2 minutes. Stir in dissolved cornstarch and cook 30 seconds. Add eggs, stirring constantly, in circular motion. Remove to tureen. Sprinkle chopped scallion and pepper on top.

SCANDINAVIAN SEAFOOD STEW *Serves: 8 to 10*

6 tablespoons butter

2 cloves garlic, minced

1 pound onions, coarsely chopped

6 carrots, chopped

1 teaspoon dried thyme

1 teaspoon dried dillweed

Generous pinch cardamom

1½ pounds new potatoes, peeled and cubed

8 cups fish stock

1½ pounds flounder, cut in 2 inch cubes

1 pound scallops

1 pound shrimp

Salt and pepper to taste

Melt butter and saute garlic and onions until soft. Add carrots, thyme, dillweed, cardamom and potatoes with 4 cups of the fish stock. Cook until vegetables are tender. (Don't overcook and let vegetables get mushy.) Can do ahead to this point and refrigerate. Add the rest of the stock and flounder and cook 5 minutes or until flounder is tender. Add scallops and shrimp and cook 5 to 8 minutes. Serve immediately. Don't overcook.

CREAM OF ALMOND SOUP
Serves: 4

3 cups chicken stock

1 small onion stuck with
  1 whole clove

½ bay leaf

2 tablespoons butter

2 tablespoons flour

½ tube almond paste

1 cup half and half

Dash salt

1 to 3 teaspoons Amaretto

Garnish with roasted slivered
  almonds

Simmer chicken stock with onion and bay leaf for 30 minutes. Remove onion and bay leaf. Melt butter and add flour cooking for 1 minute. Slowly mix in hot chicken stock. Add almond paste by pieces, stirring constantly to melt the almond paste. Remove from heat and add half and half, salt and Amaretto to taste. Carefully heat again being careful not to boil. Garnish heavily with roasted almonds.

CHEDDAR CHEESE SOUP
Serves: 6 to 8

2½ cups (20 ounces) beer,
  room temperature

2½ tablespoons chicken stock
  base

1 large onion, thinly sliced

3 cups milk, divided

⅓ cup flour

1 pound sharp Cheddar
  cheese, shredded

½ to 1 cup chicken broth

Salt and pepper to taste

Combine beer and chicken stock base in 3 quart saucepan. Stir over medium heat until stock base is dissolved. Add onions, cover and simmer until onions are tender (10 to 12 minutes). Blend 1½ cups of stock with flour. Stir slowly into soup. Add remaining milk and cook, stirring occasionally until soup thickens (15 minutes). Blend in cheese a little at a time. Stir until melted. Season with salt and pepper to taste and dilute to taste with ½ to 1 cup chicken broth.

ITALIAN CHEESE CHOWDER
Serves: 6 to 8

16 ounces stewed tomatoes, undrained

1 (15½ ounce) can garbanzo beans, drained (or white beans)

½ pound zucchini, sliced

2 carrots, thinly sliced

2 onions, chopped

1½ cups dry white wine

¼ cup butter

2 teaspons salt

2 teaspoons instant garlic

1 teaspoon basil

1 bay leaf

¾ cup Monterey Jack cheese, shredded

¾ cup Parmesan cheese

1 cup whipping cream

Combine all ingredients except the cheeses and whipping cream and put in a Dutch oven. Cook, covered, 1 hour at 400°, stirring occasionally. Add cheeses and cream and heat until cheeses are melted (about 10 minutes).

CREAM OF CELERY SOUP I
Serves: 6

5 tablespoons unsalted butter

4 cups chopped celery including inner leaves

2 medium onions, chopped

2 cloves of garlic, chopped

1 bay leaf

¾ cup dry white wine

4 cups chicken stock

2 teaspoons salt

Dash pepper

½ teaspoon dried basil leaves

1 cup half and half

2 tablespoons flour

Melt 3 tablespoons butter. Add celery, onions and garlic; cook 10 minutes. Add bay leaf, ½ cup wine and chicken stock. Bring to boil, reduce heat and let simmer 20 minutes. Remove bay leaf and puree mixture in processor or blender. Return to pot and add remainder of the wine, salt, pepper, basil and half and half. Melt remainder of the butter, add flour and cook a minute. Slowly add 1 cup soup to the roux and cook until thick. Add this to the soup and let soup simmer until it thickens slightly.

CREAM OF CELERY SOUP II

Serves: 10

⅓ cup butter, melted

1 cup coarsely chopped green
    onions, stem and bulb

3 cups celery, finely chopped

4 medium red potatoes, peeled
    and diced

⅓ cup butter

2 cups chicken stock

1 large bay leaf

Salt and white pepper to taste

2 cups half and half

4 tablespoons fresh parsley,
    minced

Saute the onions in ⅓ cup butter until soft. Push onions to the side and add celery. Cook 2 to 3 minutes. Remove 1 cup for garnish. Add potatoes and other ⅓ cup butter to pan. Add chicken stock and seasonings. Bring to a boil; reduce to a simmer and cook until potatoes are tender. Puree in processor or blender until smooth. Stir in half and half and parsley. Heat but do not boil. To serve, garnish with reserved celery. This will keep refrigerated 3 days or may be frozen.

SENEGALESE SOUP

Serves: 6

¼ cup butter

1½ cups onions

1 clove garlic, minced

1 teaspoon curry powder

½ teaspoon salt

¼ teaspoon white pepper

1 (10 ounce) package frozen
    peas, thawed

1 tablespoon vegetable oil

¼ teaspoon cardamom

2 tablespoons flour

2½ cups chicken broth

1 cup heavy cream

6 tablespoons diced chicken,
    garnish

Melt butter. Saute onions until soft. Add garlic, curry, salt and pepper. Add peas, breaking up. Stir. Add oil and cardamom. Cover and cook until peas are done. Add flour and chicken broth. Bring to a boil and boil 2 minutes. Cool. Blend in blender. Add heavy cream and heat and serve. Add chicken as garnish.

CREAM OF SPINACH SOUP

Serves: 4

1 (10 ounce) package frozen,
chopped spinach, cooked
and squeezed dry

¾ cup chicken stock

1 cup sour cream

1 teaspoon cornstarch

½ cup half and half

1 teaspoon salt

½ teaspoon pepper

¼ teaspoon nutmeg

¼ cup heavy cream, whipped

Shredded Swiss or Gruyere
cheese folded into whipped
cream (optional)

Mix chicken stock with cornstarch. Add spinach, sour cream, half and half, salt, pepper and nutmeg. Simmer 10 to 15 minutes to thicken soup. Serve with whipped cream and cheese.

If soup is too thick, thin with more chicken broth. May be pureed.

FRENCH ONION SOUP

Serves: 4 to 6

2 medium onions, thinly sliced

2 tablespoons butter, melted

3 cups beef broth

Salt to taste

2 to 4 tablespoons cream sherry

Parmesan croutons, topping of
2 to 3 slices French bread
halved, buttered, sprinkled
heavily with Parmesan
cheese and toasted

Melt the butter and cook the onions, covered, until tender (about 5 minutes). Uncover and stir in beef broth, salt and cream sherry. Let simmer 30 minutes. Top with Parmesan croutons to serve.

SALADS

Harper House, Bentonville Battleground

CURRIED SALMON SALAD
Serves: 6

¾ cup mayonnaise
6 tablespoons lemon juice
6 tablespoons chopped chutney
½ to 1 teaspoon curry
Salt and pepper to taste

2 cups flaked red salmon, drained
1 medium cucumber, chopped
1 green onion, chopped
4 to 6 tomatoes, optional

Combine the first five ingredients. In another bowl, mix salmon, cucumber and onion. Toss gently ⅓ mayonnaise mixture or to taste. You can stuff the salad in large tomatoes or serve on lettuce leaves.

SHRIMP SALAD
Serves: 2 to 3

1 pound cooked shrimp
1 teaspoon lemon juice
½ cup olives, chopped and well drained
2 hard cooked eggs

½ small onion, grated
Salt and pepper to taste
Mayonnaise mixed with French dressing

Moisten shrimp with lemon juice. Add all ingredients and mix well. Add mayonnaise/French dressing to taste.

STAR OF SEA SALAD
Serves: 4

½ cup mayonnaise
¼ cup milk
2 tablespoons golden raisins
1 tablespoon sugar
1 scant teaspoon curry powder

1 teaspoon lemon juice
1 teaspoon white wine vinegar
1 teaspoon catsup
1 pound cooked shrimp, scallops, crab or combination

Combine all dressing ingredients. Blend well. Chill. Spoon over chilled seafood on bed of lettuce.

RAW SPINACH SALAD

Serves: 6

1 bag raw spinach, chopped
½ cup celery, minced
½ cup onion, minced

¾ cup Old English cheese, cubed
3 hard boiled eggs, chopped

Mix together and toss with dressing.

Dressing:

½ teaspoon salt
½ teaspoon Tabasco
1½ teaspoons vinegar

1 cup mayonnaise
3 tablespoons horseradish

SPINACH SALAD

Serves: 8

1 large package fresh spinach
1 can water chestnuts
5 pieces cooked bacon, crumbled
1 can bean sprouts

2 hard cooked eggs, sliced
Artichoke hearts, halved
Mushrooms, sliced

Dressing:

1 cup oil
¾ cup sugar
⅓ cup catsup
1 grated onion

¼ cup vinegar
1 tablespoon Worcestershire sauce
Dash of salt

Mix together in a bowl with a whisk. Pour into a jar.
Preparation time: 30 minutes.

DELICIOUS FRENCH DRESSING

⅓ cup sugar
1 teaspoon salt
1 teaspoon dry mustard
1 teaspoon celery seed
1 teaspoon paprika

1 teaspoon grated onion
4 tablespoons vinegar
1 cup salad oil
3 cloves garlic

Combine sugar, salt, mustard, celery seed, paprika and grated onion.
Blend with a fork the vinegar and salad oil. Add to the above. When
mixture is blended, add garlic (optional). Let stand 1 hour. Remove garlic
before storing. Great on fruit salads and vegetable salad.

80

FRUIT SALAD DRESSING

4 eggs
1 cup sugar
2 cups pineapple juice
¼ cup lemon juice
2 tablespoons flour

1 tablespoon butter
½ teaspoon salt
1 to 2 cups whipping cream

Beat eggs lightly. Add this slowly to a heavy saucepan containing sugar, flour and salt. Turn heat to medium and slowly add pineapple and lemon juice. Stir over medium heat (constantly) until thick, approximately 10 minutes. Remove from heat and add butter. Stir. When cool cover and chill in refrigerator.

When ready to use, whip chilled cream (do not add sugar). Mix *one* part dressing with two parts whipped cream. *Do not* mix dressing with whipped cream until ready to serve. The dressing will keep in the refrigerator for a week.

This is an old family recipe. It can be used as a fruit salad dressing but in many other ways also. It gives a sweet taste but adds the subtle pineapple-lemon flavor.

APRICOT SALAD

Serves: 12

1 can (29 ounce) apricots, save all liquid
1 can (29 ounce) crushed pineapple, drained
2 packages orange gelatin

2 cups hot water
1 cup apricot juice (rest goes in topping)
¾ cup miniature marshmallows
¾ cup chopped pecans (optional)

Dissolve gelatin in hot water and juice. Add marshmallows and melt.
Put in refrigerator until syrupy. Add fruits. Pour into mold and chill until firm.

Topping:

½ cup sugar
3 tablespoons flour
1 cup apricot juice

1 egg, beaten
3 tablespoons butter
1 cup cream, whipped

Mix and cook first 5 ingredients until thick. Cool and add whipped cream. Spread over gelatin when set. Sprinkle with Parmesan cheese.

PEAR SALAD
Serves: 8

4 pears, barely ripe
Leaf lettuce
Romaine lettuce
2 tablespoons raspberry wine
  vinegar

6 tablespoons French olive oil
3 tablespoons raspberry juice
1 cup fresh raspberries
  (optional)

Peel pears, core, cut in half lengthwise. Rub lightly with lemon juice. Cut long thin slices into a bowl. Mix together the vinegar and olive oil. Add raspberry juice. Add to pears and let sit, mixing occasionally.

At serving time, use equal portions of leaf and romaine lettuce. Break into bite size pieces. Add to pears and dressing. Toss together and serve.

PEACH SALAD
Serves: 6

1 (3 ounce) package orange
  gelatin
½ cup vinegar
½ cup sugar

1 (16 ounce) can sliced peaches
12 cloves
3 sticks of cinnamon

In a saucepan combine peaches with juice, vinegar and spices. Bring to a boil. Simmer 10 minutes. Drain, reserving juice. Take out spices. If juice is not 2 cups, add water and dissolve gelatin in it. When half congealed, add peaches and put in greased mold.

Preparation time: 20 minutes.

CITRUS SALAD
Serves: 10

2 envelopes plain gelatin
½ cup cold water
1 cup boiling water
2 large grapefruits, peeled and
  sectioned
3 large oranges, peeled and
  sectioned

1 small can crushed pineapple
Juice of 1 lemon
1 cup almonds, slivered
½ teaspoon salt
1 cup sugar

Dissolve gelatin in cold water. Add boiling water and stir. Add sugar and salt.

Drain fruit and pineapple. Measure juice, add lemon juice and enough water to make 2 cups. Add to gelatin mixture. Add fruit and almonds. Pour into molds and let congeal.

EGGNOG FRUIT SALAD

Serves: 6 to 8

1 cup eggnog, chilled

1 (2 ounce) envelope dessert topping mix

¼ teaspoon ground nutmeg

1 (13 ounce) can pineapple chunks, drained

2 medium unpared apples, cored and chopped

1 medium pear, unpared, cored and chopped

¼ cup maraschino cherries, drained and halved

⅓ cup chopped pecans

In a small mixer bowl, combine eggnog, dessert topping mix and nutmeg. Beat at high speed until soft peaks form, about 5 minutes. Combine fruits and nuts; fold in eggnog mixture. Cover and chill for several hours. Stir gently; turn salad into lettuce-lined bowl to serve.

VARIATION: Use 1 can tropical fruit in place of apples and pears.

ITALIAN TOSSED SALAD

Serves: 8 to 10

1 head lettuce, broken into bite size pieces

1 head cauliflower, broken into bite size pieces

1 large sweet purple onion, sliced into rings

¼ cup sugar, sprinkled over above

1 pound bacon, cooked, drained and crumbled

1 cup grated Parmesan cheese

1 to 2 slices Mozzarella, broken into bits

1 cup mayonnaise

Layer ingredients in airtight container, in the order listed above. Refrigerate overnight. Toss the salad when ready to serve.

ARTICHOKE SALAD

Serves: 6

1 can artichoke hearts, quartered

1 package frozen tiny green peas, cooked

1 cup diagonally cut celery

½ cup stuffed olives, sliced

Marinate the above for 24 hours

½ cup oil

¼ cup cider vinegar

1 teaspoon salt

½ teaspoon black pepper

½ teaspoon sugar

DAY AHEAD GREEN SALAD   *Serves: 8 to 10*

Iceberg lettuce in bite size pieces

Fresh spinach in bite size pieces

1 package frozen peas, uncooked

1 to 2 bunches green onion, chopped

8 pieces crisp bacon, crumbled

5 hard boiled eggs, sliced

Dressing:

1 cup sour cream

½ cup mayonnaise

1 package Good Season's Italian Salad Dressing

In a long pyrex dish, layer lettuce, spinach, peas, onions, eggs and bacon. Mix dressing ingredients and spread over top. Seal and let sit in refrigerator for 24 hours. Sprinkle with croutons before serving, if desired. If you like more salad dressing, double the amount. Do not toss.

Preparation time: 30 minutes.

ARTICHOKE-RICE SALAD   *Serves: 8*

2 cups chicken broth

1 cup uncooked rice

¼ cup green onion, chopped

¼ cup green pepper, chopped

½ cup pimento olives, drained

1 (6 ounce) jar marinated artichokes, drained and cut up

½ cup mayonnaise

½ teaspoon dill weed

½ teaspoon salt

Dash pepper

Lettuce leaves

Sliced olives as a garnish

Place broth in pan. Bring to a boil, stir in rice; reduce heat and simmer covered for 20 minutes. Cool. Stir in next 8 ingredients. Spoon salad into lettuce-lined bowl and garnish with extra olives.

CHARLESTON SALAD   *Serves: 4*

Lettuce, broken into bite size pieces

Croutons

Dressing:

1 egg	¼ teaspoon hot sauce
1 clove of garlic, minced	¼ teaspoon paprika
½ cup olive oil	½ teaspoon salt
¼ cup Parmesan cheese, grated	1 tablespoon wine vinegar

Beat the garlic, olive oil and egg with egg beater. Add the remaining ingredients. Toss with lettuce and croutons just before serving.
Preparation time: 20 minutes.

TACO SALAD
Serves: 8

Salad Bowl:

Chopped lettuce
Chopped tomatoes

Double Boiler:

1 pound Velveeta
½ can Ro-tel tomatoes

Garnish:

Corn chips

Skillet:

2 pounds ground beef
1 onion, chopped
1 green pepper, chopped
1 cup celery, chopped
1 tablespoon cumin
¼ teaspoon chili powder
Garlic salt to taste

Brown meat with onion, green pepper and celery. Add remaining skillet ingredients. Pour meat mixture over salad mixture. Pour cheese mixture over all. Crush corn chips over top.

GARIBALDI SALAD
Serves: 6

2 whole chicken breasts, cooked	1 pint olive oil
3 heads bibb lettuce	1 tablespoon red wine vinegar
Inside leaves of iceberg lettuce	2 tablespoon onion juice
Small bunch watercress	1 garlic pod
½ pound bacon, cooked and crumbled	Pinch dry mustard
	Salt and pepper to taste
2 ounces Roquefort cheese	1½ ounces Roquefort cheese

Remove chicken meat from bone and place in bowl over lettuce and watercress. Top with bacon and Roquefort cheese. Mix the last 7 ingredients in blender and whiz until smooth. Pour over salad.
Preparation time: 30 minutes.

FREEZER SLAW

Yield: 4 quarts

2 medium cabbages, chopped
6 bell peppers, chopped
8 onions, chopped
2 teaspoons celery or mustard
  seed

1 quart white vinegar
1/3 cup salt (less if desired)
4 cups sugar

Mix vegetables together. Combine remaining ingredients and boil. Pour over vegetables. Mix and package in freezer containers. The liquid should cover the chopped vegetables.
This will keep in the refrigerator 3 to 4 days after thawing.

SAUERKRAUT SALAD

1 (No. 2½) can chopped Kraut
1 large onion, chopped
1 cup celery, chopped

1 green pepper, chopped
1 (4 oz.) can pimento
1 cup sugar

Mix first 5 ingredients. Put in a container. Sprinkle sugar on top. Cover and refrigerate 24 hours. Mix well and serve.

BROCCOLI SALAD

Serves: 8 to 12

1 bunch fresh broccoli, washed
  and cut into bite size pieces
4 hard-boiled eggs, chopped
½ cup onions, finely chopped

¾ cup mayonnaise
1½ cups green olives, chopped
½ cup celery, chopped, if
  desired

Combine all ingredients. Chill and serve.,
Preparation time: 25 minutes. Can be prepared ahead and keeps well several days covered in refrigerator.

PEA-NUT SALAD
Serves: 10

1 (10 ounce) package frozen peas, cooked and chilled

6 slices bacon, cooked crisp and crumbled

½ cup celery, chopped

¼ cup onion, chopped

1 cup cashews, coarsely chopped

½ cup sour cream

Combine all ingredients and chill. Serve in hollow tomato cups, on tomatoes cut in wedges, or on tomato slices on a bed of lettuce.

Preparation time: 30 minutes. Can be prepared ahead and stored in the refrigerator.

TOMATO CONGEALED SALAD
Serves: 10

1 small can tomato sauce

1 package lemon gelatin

1 cup boiling water

Dissolve gelatin in boiling water and add sauce. Pour ½ of this mixture into shallow long container. When set, add the following which is mixed:

1 package lemon gelatin

1 carton Cottage cheese

½ cup green pepper, chopped

1 jar pimento, finely chopped

½ cup celery, chopped

Onion to taste

½ cup mayonnaise

When this second layer is congealed, add remainder of tomato mixture and let congeal. Cut into servings and place on lettuce, top with mayonnaise.

GOURMET LAYERED TOMATO ASPIC
Serves: 8

Cottage Cheese Layer:

2 cups sieved Cottage cheese

1 teaspoon salt

⅓ cup chives, minced

⅛ teaspoon paprika

1 tablespoon onion, grated

1 tablespoon unflavored gelatin

¼ cup cold water

¼ cup hot milk

Blend Cottage cheese, chives, onion and seasonings. Soak gelatin in cold water 5 minutes. Dissolve in hot milk. Add to cheese, stirring to blend. Turn mixture into 8 inch square pan, rinsed in cold water. Chill until set.
  Preparation time: 30 minutes.

Tomato Aspic Layer:

6 cloves

1 bayleaf

1 teaspoon salt

1 tablespoon lemon juice

1 small onion, sliced

1 tablespoon sugar

2 tablespoons unflavored gelatin

¼ cup cold water

2 cups tomato juice

1 stalk celery, sliced

Combine tomato juice, onion, celery, cloves, bayleaf and sugar; simmer 10 minutes. Strain; add salt and lemon juice. Soak gelatin in cold water 5 minutes. Add to hot tomato juice and stir to blend; cool. Pour cooled mixture over molded Cottage cheese layer. Chill until tomato layer is set.

GREEN DERBY HOUSE SALAD

Lettuce, bite size pieces

Parsley, chopped

Scallions, chopped

Croutons

Tomatoes, quartered

Olive oil in which pieces of garlic have been marinated

Wine vinegar

Salt to taste

Pepper to taste

Oregano, a sprinkle per salad

For each serving: Into a large salad bowl, put 2 tablespoons olive oil, 1 tablespoon wine vinegar. Add salt and pepper and oregano. Add 3 quarters of a tomato and chop into dressing. Add ⅓ head lettuce in pieces, 3 tablespoons parsley, 1 tablespoon scallions, croutons. Toss lightly and put in bowls. Sprinkle with 1 tablespoon Parmesan cheese. Salad must be served immediately.

CHEESE RING WITH
MELON BALL MELANGE
Serves: 12

Cheese Ring:

1 pound Grueyre cheese	**½ cup sour cream**
10 ounces Gouda cheese	**⅓ cup brandy**
6 ounces Bleu cheese	**2 cloves garlic, minced**

Melon Ball Melange:

2 cups watermelon	**2 cups honeydew**
2 cups cantaloupe	**½ cup brandy**

Topping:

8 ounce Cream cheese	**1 tablespoon chives, chopped**
10 ounce Bleu cheese	**1 tablespoon brandy**
1 tablespoon parsley, chopped	

For Cheese Ring: Shred Gruyere and Gouda in a large bowl. Add softened Bleu cheese with ½ cup sour cream, ⅓ cup brandy and garlic. Mix well; then pack into 6 cup ring mold. Chill 4 hours or overnight.

For Melon Balls: Combine 6 cups fruit with ½ cup brandy in a bowl and refrigerate.

For Topping: Beat Cream cheese until smooth; then add softened Bleu cheese and 1 tablespoon each parsley, chives and brandy. Beat until smooth.

To Serve: Unmold cheese mold onto serving platter. Spread topping over with slotted spoon. Lift fruit into center.

Preparation time: 45 minutes

HAM MOUSSE SALAD
Serves: 6 to 8

4 cups ground ham, finely chopped	**1 cup mayonnaise**
2 cups consomme	**½ pint whipping cream, whipped**
2 envelopes plain gelatin	**¼ cup pimentos**
1 teaspoon Worcestershire sauce	

Put plain gelatin in ½ cup cold consomme. Heat 1½ cups consomme to boiling and dissolve gelatin. Add Worcestershire sauce and let cool. Add ham and mayonnaise and fold in whipped cream.

Mold and refrigerate.

SCANDINAVIAN CUCUMBERS *Serves: 6*

½ cup sour cream

1 tablespoon sugar

2 tablespoons parsley, chopped

2 tablespoons tarragon vinegar

1 tablespoon onion, finely chopped

¼ teaspoon dried dillweed

3 small unpared cucumbers, thinly sliced (3 cups)

Place sliced cucumbers in bowl and sprinkle with salt. Toss to distribute salt evenly. Allow to stand for 30 minutes. Press out water that has accumulated. Meanwhile, mix the remaining ingredients. Fold in well drained cucumbers. Cover and chill for 2 hours. Serve on a bed of lettuce.

RUSSIAN DRESSING *Yield: 1¾ cups*

1½ cups mayonnaise

¼ cup chili sauce

4 gherkin pickles, minced

3 shallots, minced

Yolk of hard boiled egg, minced

3 tablespoons drained prepared horseradish

1 tablespoon capers, minced

1 tablespoon onion, grated

1 teaspoon Worcestershire sauce

1 teaspoon lemon juice

1 teaspoon sugar

Salt and pepper to taste

Combine all the ingredients in a bowl.

SALAD DRESSING

1 cup sugar

1 cup oil

1 cup white vinegar

¼ tablespoon paprika

¼ onion, grated

Mix and put in jar in refrigerator at least overnight. Stir before serving. Good over grapefruit and orange sections, strawberries, and avocado.

BREADS

Constitution House, Halifax

FRENCH BREAD OR FRENCH ROLLS

2 tablespoons yeast
  (2 packages)
1 tablespoon salt

2¾ cups warm water
6½ to 7½ cups flour

Mix yeast, salt, and warm water. Let proof 5 minutes. Add flour. Knead until smooth and elastic, about 10 minutes. Put in greased bowl; grease top. Let rise to double, about 1½ hours. Punch down. Form into loaf or roll size pieces. Let rise again until doubled, about 55 minutes. Slash top. Brush with:

1 beaten egg mixed with

½ cup water

1 tablespoon salt

Can sprinkle with poppy or sesame seeds. Bake at 400° 20 to 25 minutes or until done.

ITALIAN ROLLS

2½ cups warm water
2 packages yeast
1 tablespoon sugar

¾ teaspoon salt
7 to 8 cups unbleached flour
Egg white to glaze

Dissolve yeast, salt, sugar and water in large bowl. Let stand 10 minutes until foamy. Add flour gradually mixing after each cup addition, ending with a smooth but slightly sticky dough. Knead 8 minutes until smooth and elastic. Put in oiled bowl, cover and let rise 45 minutes. Punch down, let rise 45 additional minutes. Punch down, shape into lemon size rolls, put on greased baking sheet, let rise again 45 minutes. Snip across top with scissors, brush with egg white. Bake in 400° oven for 20 to 25 minutes or until slightly browned.

NAVAHO BREAD

3 cups flour
1½ teaspoons baking powder

½ teaspoon salt
1⅓ cups warm water

Mix ingredients together. Knead slightly. Divide into 12 golf ball size pieces. Roll flat; make a slit in center 1 inch to 2 inches long. Fry in hot fat ½ inch deep in frying pan, about 1 minute each side. Let drain. Can be dusted with cinnamon sugar, or served immediately with butter.

SWEET POTATO LOVE BUNS

Yield: 4 to 5 dozen buns

1 cup mashed sweet potatoes	1 tablespoon grated orange rind
½ cup scalded milk	1 teaspoon grated lemon rind
1 cup sugar	1 tablespoon orange juice
½ cup butter	1 teaspoon lemon juice
½ teaspoon salt	¼ teaspoon nutmeg
3 packages yeast softened in ½ cup warm water	5 to 6 cups flour
2 beaten eggs	

Scald milk; combine sugar, butter and salt. Into sugar mix add lukewarm milk, potatoes, yeast, eggs, rinds, juices and nutmeg. Stir in 2½ cups flour, beat until smooth. Add more flour to make a soft dough. Knead. Let rise to double; punch down; let rest 10 minutes. Shape into buns about 2 inches in diameter. Place 1 inch apart on greased baking pan. Let rise to double. Bake at 350° for 15 to 20 minutes.

Freezes well.

ANGEL BISCUITS

Serves: 40

5 cups flour	1 cup Crisco shortening
5 tablespoons sugar	2 cups buttermilk
1 tablespoon baking powder	2 packages yeast
1 teaspoon baking soda	3 tablespoons warm water
1 teaspoon salt	

Sift dry ingredients together 3 times. Cut in shortening. Dissolve yeast in water. Add yeast and buttermilk to mixture. Roll out ½ inch thick. Cut in biscuit shapes. Bake at 350° for about 10 minutes on a greased pan.

Preparation time: 1 hour. Can be frozen.

WHOLE WHEAT BISCUITS
Yield: 1½ dozen

2 cups whole wheat flour

1 heaping tablespoon shortening

1 cup buttermilk

½ teaspoon salt

1 tablespoon sugar

½ teaspoon soda

1 cake yeast

Dissolve yeast in warm buttermilk. Mix flour, soda, salt and sugar together. Add buttermilk mixture to flour mixture. Roll out in white flour and let rise until it doubles itself (about an hour at room temperature). Roll out again and cut into biscuits. Let rise about 10 minutes. Bake in hot oven at 400° 10 to 15 minutes.

SOUR CREAM CORN BREAD

1 cup self rising cornmeal

2 large eggs (or 3 small)

1 small can cream-style corn

1 cup sour cream

½ cup salad oil

Mix all together; pour into 9 inch square pan; bake at 400° for 30 to 45 minutes. Will be golden brown outside, soft inside.

This cuts in 9 squares in 9 inch square pan.

CORN LIGHT BREAD

1 teaspoon baking soda

1 teaspoon salt

¼ teaspoon baking powder

½ cup sugar

2 cups buttermilk

2 cups corn meal

½ cup plain flour

4 tablespoons shortening

Put baking soda, salt, baking powder and sugar in a bowl and add buttermilk. Stir well, then beat in flour and corn meal, alternately. Melt shortening in a 9 x 5 loaf pan and heat to 350°, swirl, stir the hot shortening into the batter. Sprinkle a little corn meal over bottom of pan. Pour batter into hot pan and bake 350° for 1 to 1¼ hours. It takes longer in glass pan. Bake for 20 minutes in muffin tins.

SWEDISH RYE BREAD

1½ cups lukewarm milk
¼ cup honey
⅓ cup brown sugar
1 tablespoon salt
2 tablespoons margarine, softened

Finely shredded rind of 1 or 2 oranges
2 packages yeast
2½ cups rye flour, sifted
2 to 2½ cups all purpose flour, sifted

Mix together all ingredients except all purpose flour. Add enough all purpose flour to make a soft dough. Turn onto lightly floured board. Let stand 10 minutes, then knead until smooth and elastic. Put in greased bowl, covered, to double — about 2 hours. Punch down; let rise 45 more minutes. Punch down; form into 2 loaves. Place on lightly greased baking sheet; let rise 1 hour. Bake at 375° for 35 minutes. Brush top with shortening or margarine after it is done. Cool on rack.

Freezes well.

CHEESE PINWHEEL BREAD

1 cup milk
¼ cup margarine
1 tablespoon honey

4 to 5 cups flour
1 package yeast

Heat milk and margarine together just until margarine melts. In food processor mix honey, 2 cups flour, yeast and half of milk-margarine mixture. Process to mix well. The texture will look like cornmeal. Add the rest of the milk-margarine mixture and 2 to 2½ cups flour. Pulse on-off a few times to gather ball. Turn out on floured board, cover and let rest 30 minutes. Roll to 10 x 20 inch oblong. Spread with cheese filling.

Cheese Filling:

2 cups Cheddar cheese, shredded
1 beaten egg
2 tablespoons Dijon mustard

1 tablespon seasoned bread crumbs
1 tablespoon sesame seeds

Toss all until well mixed.

Roll up from long side to form 20 inch roll. Cut in half. Put on greased pan. Cover with plastic wrap. Refrigerate 2 to 24 hours. Bring to room temperature for 30 minutes. Cook 425° for 10 minutes. Brush tops with egg white, sprinkle with more sesame seeds. Cook 375° for an additional 25 minutes.

Keeps in refrigerator well. Freezes well.

CAPITAL LANDMARKS
CHEESE BISCUITS

Serves: 30

½ pound sharp Cheddar
  cheese, grated
½ stick butter or margarine
2 cups Bisquick
6 drops Tabasco

¼ teaspoon pepper
½ teaspoon salt
1 teaspoon mustard powder
¼ teaspoon dill
½ cup water

   Mix cheese and butter until soft. Coat with Bisquick. Add seasonings.
Moisten to pie crust consistency with ½ cup water. Roll into small balls
(approximately 7 dozen). Bake on ungreased cookie sheet in preheated
oven for 20 minutes at 375° or until lightly brown.
   These will be slightly puffed and have a flaky texture. They freeze and
reheat well. Serve at room temperature.
   Can make ahead and freeze.

SWEET POTATO
BISCUITS

Yield: 5 dozen medium biscuits

2 cups cooked sweet potatoes
  (6 to 8 medium potatoes)
1 cup sugar
1 stick margarine, softened

4 cups self rising flour
1 cup milk
1 tablespoon Crisco

   Bake potatoes at 350-400° for 2 to 3 hours. Peel and mash. Add sugar,
margarine, milk; set aside. Sift flour; add Crisco; mix well with potatoes
(by hand). Roll, cut, let rise 20 minutes at room temperature; bake at 425°
for 12 to 15 minutes.
   Do not freeze dough. Partially cook biscuits for freezing.

PARKIE'S WHEAT GERM BISCUITS

1¾ cups Bisquick
½ pint whipping cream or
  half and half

1 to 3 tablespoons wheat germ

   Combine the above and add ¼ to ½ cup more Bisquick if dough is
sticky.
   Roll out about ¼ inch thick. Cut with biscuit cutter. Bake at 350° until
done.

HOLIDAY CARDAMOM BRAID
Yield: 1 loaf

Approximately 4⅓ cups all purpose flour, divided

⅓ cup plus 2 tablespoons sugar, divided

1 teaspoon ground cardamom

1 teaspoon salt

2 packages active dry yeast

½ cup butter

½ cup water

½ cup milk

½ cup raisins

2 tablespoons dark rum

2 slightly beaten eggs, divided

Approximately ¼ cup sliced almonds

Sprinkle rum over the raisins approximately 30 minutes before combining with other ingredients.

In a large bowl, combine 1 cup flour, ⅓ cup sugar, salt, cardamom and yeast. In a small saucepan melt butter, add water, milk and raisins with rum, and heat to 120°.

Add to flour mixture and beat with electric mixer on medium speed for 2 minutes. Remove 2 tablespoons of the beaten eggs and set aside. Add remaining eggs and 1 cup flour; beat on high speed for 2 minutes. Stir in enough of the remaining flour to make a soft dough.

Turn out on floured surface and knead 8 to 10 minutes or until smooth and elastic. Place in greased bowl; turn to grease top. Cover and let rise in warm, draft-free place 1 hour or until doubled. Punch down; turn out on lightly floured surface; using more flour if necessary, knead until smooth and elastic.

Shape using either of the following methods:

1. *Straight braid*: Cut dough into 3 equal pieces. Shape each into a rope about 22 to 24 inches in length. Pinch ends together and braid loosely, pinching other ends together and tucking pinched ends under as much as necessary to make a neat, symetrical braid. Place on greased baking sheet. Cover, and let rise in a warm, draft free place about 45 minutes or until doubled.

2. *Wreath*: Cut dough into 3 equal pieces, shape each into 30-inch long rope. Braid ropes loosely; transfer braid to greased baking sheet and shape into a wreath, neatly merging ends and pinching them firmly together. Place a 6 ounce greased custard cup, upside down in hole in center of the wreath. Cover and let rise about 45 minutes or until doubled.

For either shape: After doubled in size, brush with reserved beaten egg; sprinkle with the sliced almonds and the remaining 2 tablespoons sugar.

Bake in preheated 375° oven 25 to 30 minutes until golden and done. Watch closely as it begins to brown on top and cover with foil to prevent over-browning during last half of cooking time if necessary.

Cool on rack. Wrap airtight and store in cool place or freeze. Best eaten within one week.

SALLY LUNN BREAD

1 package yeast	¼ cup lukewarm water
¾ cup milk	½ cup butter
⅓ cup sugar	3 eggs
1 teaspoon salt	4 cups flour

Soften yeast in water. Heat milk to lukewarm. Combine with yeast. Cream butter, sugar together. Add well beaten eggs and mix. Add salt to flour and stir flour into butter alternately with milk and yeast mixture. Beat thoroughly with wooden spoon and turn into a buttered bowl. Let rise until doubled in bulk (1 to 1½ hours). Beat again and pour into a buttered ring mold or angel cake pan. Let rise again until doubled in bulk, about 40 minutes. Bake at 350° for 45 minutes. Unmold and cool on rack.

SOUR DOUGH ENGLISH MUFFINS

*½ cup sourdough starter	¾ teaspoon salt
1 cup milk	½ teaspoon soda
2¾ cups flour	Cornmeal for dusting pan
1 tablespoon sugar	

Begin the night before.

In a large bowl, mix starter, 1 cup milk, 2 cups flour; let sit 8 hours or overnight. Then add ½ cup flour, sugar, salt and soda; mix in well by hand. It will be a stiff dough. Put remaining ¼ cup flour on board and knead 2 to 3 minutes adding a little more flour if necessary. Roll dough out to ½ inch thickness. Cut with cookie cutter about 2½ inches round. Place 1 inch apart on cookie sheet that has been dusted with cornmeal, and sprinkle more cornmeal over tops. Cover and let rise again for 45 minutes. Bake on a lightly greased frying pan (or electric griddle) at about 300° - 325° medium high about 8 to 10 minutes per side, until lightly browned. Split and toast to serve.

*See sourdough starter recipe on "Sourdough Braid."

COUNTY FAIR EGG BREAD

1½ cups scalded milk

½ cup butter

2 teaspoons salt

½ cup sugar

2 cakes yeast

½ cup lukewarm water

2 beaten eggs

9 cups flour, sifted
(approximately)

Pour the scalded milk over the butter, salt and sugar. Cool. Dissolve the yeast in the lukewarm water and let stand until it bubbles, about 5 minutes. Add the yeast and the beaten eggs to the cooled milk. Gradually add the flour, add 5 cups in mixer, mix 2 minutes at medium speed, beating it in thoroughly. Do not add any more flour than is necessary to make an easily handled dough, as the bread should be light and tender. Turn out onto floured board and knead until smooth and elastic. Place in greased bowl, cover, and let rise until doubled in size, about 1½ hours. Punch down and turn out onto a lightly floured board. Shape into 3 loaves and place in greased 8 inch loaf pans. Cover and let rise until dough is just to the tops of the pans. Bake in a 425° oven for 10 minutes, then lower heat to 350° and bake 40 minutes longer, or until bread is done. Will make 2 (9 inch) loaves cooked 50 minutes at 350°.

PARMESAN CASSEROLE BREAD

1 package yeast

¼ cup lukewarm water

¼ cup scalded milk

1½ cups flour

1 tablespoon sugar

½ teaspoon salt

⅓ cup butter

1 beaten egg

½ cup shredded Parmesan
cheese

2 tablespoons parsley, chopped

Dissolve yeast in warm water. Mix all together and turn into pan. Let rise until doubled. Dot with additional butter and bake 20 to 25 minutes at 375° in round 8 inch cake pan. Cut in wedge shapes.

Freezes well.

APPLE BREAD

4 medium apples, peeled and
diced

¾ cup water

½ stick margarine

1 cup milk

6 cups flour (preferably
bread flour)

2 packages yeast

1 teaspoon salt

Cook apples in water for 5 minutes. Pour hot apples into mixing bowl and add margarine and milk. Cool to 105° and add 1 cup flour, yeast and salt. Add remaining flour and do not knead. Cover bowl and let rise until doubled. Punch down and turn onto floured board. Knead 2 or 3 times, divide into 3 greased standard size pans and let rise again. Bake for 30 minutes at 375°.

Also makes good rolls.

Freezes well.

HERBAL POPOVERS

Serves: 8

3 eggs

1 cup milk

1 cup flour (unbleached)

3 tablespoons butter, melted
with 2 cloves crushed garlic

1 teaspoon dried tarragon,
crushed

½ teaspoon celery salt

¼ cup Parmesan cheese

Preheat oven to 450°. Grease 8 (6 ounce) custard cups. Put all ingredients in blender and process at low speed until smooth. Put ⅓ cup batter in each cup. Bake 15 minutes at 450°, reduce heat to 375° and bake for 30 more minutes or until browned.

Preparation time: 5 minutes. 45 minutes cooking.

BATTER BREAD

Serves: 4 to 6

Old Recipe

Scald 1 cup of meal with a little boiling water, add 2 cups of buttermilk, 1 large tablespoon of lard melted, 1 teaspoon salt and 2 eggs, well beaten. Lastly add 1 level teaspoon of soda. Bake quickly in greased pan. Sweet milk and 1 teaspoon of baking powder can be used instead of buttermilk and soda.

Up Dated Version:

1½ tablespoons shortening
(Crisco type)

1 teaspoon salt

¾ cup white cornmeal

1 cup boiling water

1 cup sweet milk

2 eggs

2 teaspoons baking powder

Place shortening, salt and meal in mixing bowl. Pour boiling water over this and mix well. Add milk, eggs beaten lightly and mix. Add baking powder and mix well. Cook in greased 1 quart casserole 40 minutes to 1 hour at 350°.

OAT SESAME BREAD

2 cups boiling water

1 cup oatmeal

1 package yeast

½ cup water

¼ cup molasses

¼ cup honey

2 tablespoons oil

2 teaspoons salt

¼ cup sesame seeds, toasted

4½ cups whole wheat flour

Soak oatmeal in boiling water for 30 minutes. Mix yeast with ½ cup water and add to oats with molasses, honey, oil, salt and sesame seeds. Combine all with flour and knead for 10 minutes. Let rise for 1½ to 2 hours. Punch down and shape into 2 loaves. Let rise again and bake for 1 hour at 350°.

SWISS OATMEAL BREAD

1½ cups milk

¼ cup brown sugar

½ cup warm water

2 teaspoons salt

3 teaspoons butter

2 packages yeast

1 cup Swiss cheese, grated

2 cups rolled oats

4 cups unsifted flour

Scald milk, stir in sugar, salt and butter. Cool to lukewarm. Sprinkle yeast in warm water. Stir in milk mix and everything else except 2 cups of the flour. Put in enough of the remaining 2 cups flour to knead 10 minutes. Rise 1 hour; divide in half; let rise 1 hour and bake for 35 minutes at 375°.

This bread has a moist texture and is not good served hot.

Freezes well.

SOURDOUGH BRAIDS

Two days ahead, put in large bowl:

2 cups warm water

1 tablespoon sugar

1 package yeast

3 cups bread flour (or unbleached regular flour)

Cover with plastic wrap. Let stand at room temperature for 2 days. It will rise and fall many times. It is helped by stirring once or twice a day. This is more sourdough than you will need for this recipe.

About 3 hours ahead, scald ¾ cup milk and then add:

2 tablespoons margarine, cold

3 tablespoons sugar

1 teaspoon salt

When cool, add 1 package yeast dissolved in ¼ cup warm water. Put in bowl with 3 cups unbleached flour and 1½ cups starter. Stir well. Add 1 or more cups unbleached flour to make a spongy dough. Knead until smooth and elastic. Put in greased bowl; let rise to double — about 1 hour. Punch down; divide into thirds. Can make with each third: 1 dozen rolls, 1 braided loaf, and 1 long tapered loaf. Let rise again to double, 1 hour. Bake for 20 minutes or until done at 400°.

Freezes well.

DILL BREAD

2 packages yeast

1 cup lukewarm water

2 cups warm Cottage cheese

4 tablespoons sugar

2 tablespoons onion, grated

1½ teaspoon dill

2 tablespoons margarine

2 eggs

1 teaspoon soda

4 teaspoons salt

3 to 4 cups unbleached flour

2 cups whole wheat flour

Cook onion in butter until soft. Put yeast in warm water. Combine the following ingredients in large bowl: Cottage cheese, sugar, onion, dill, salt, soda, egg and yeast. Mix well. Add whole wheat flour. Mix again; add enough unbleached flour to make very soft dough. Cover bowl; let rise to double, about 1 hour. Stir down; put in two well greased loaf pans. Let rise again to double, about 40 minutes. Bake 350° for 50 to 55 minutes. Cover with foil last 15 minutes if tops get too brown.

JUDY'S EASY ITALIAN BREAD
Yield: 1 loaf

3 cups unbleached flour

1 teaspoon salt

1 tablespoon sugar

1 tablespoon margarine

1 package yeast

1 cup plus 2 tablespoons very warm water (120-130)

Put in processor with metal blade: 2 cups flour, salt, sugar, margarine and yeast. Process until thoroughly mixed. Add ½ cup water, turn on and off 4 times. Add remaining flour and water, turn on and off 4 times. Process to form ball. If still sticky, add 1 tablespoon flour at a time. Process 60 seconds past ball formation. Turn out on floured board and knead a few times. Cover and let rise 20 minutes. Roll into 10 x 15 inch rectangle. Roll up jelly roll style. Put on greased sheet dusted with corn meal. Refrigerate covered for a minimum of 2 hours and maximum of 24 hours. Leave at room temperature for 10 minutes. Bake at 425° for 20 minutes. Then brush with beaten egg and return to oven for 5 to 10 more minutes until done.

Preparation time: 10 minutes. Refrigerate: 2 to 24 hours. Cooking: 30 minutes.

COFFEE CAKE

1 cup margarine or butter

2 cups sugar

2 eggs, beaten

1 cup sour cream

¼ teaspoon salt

½ teaspoon vanilla

1¼ teaspoons baking powder

2 cups cake flour, sifted

Cream margarine, add sugar and eggs, sift dry ingredients, add to mixture alternately with sour cream. Add vanilla.

Crumb Mixture:

4 tablespoons brown sugar

2 teaspoons cinnamon

1 cup chopped pecans

Stir together. Put ½ crumb mixture on bottom of small bundt pan. Add ½ batter, follow with rest of crumb mixture and batter. Bake 350° for 60 minutes or more.

MORAVIAN LOVE FEAST BUNS

Makes 12 buns, depending on size

1 large potato

1 package yeast

⅔ cup plus 1 tablespoon sugar

½ cup water, save from cooking potato

½ teaspoon salt

2 eggs

½ cup unsalted butter, softened

4½ cups flour, approximately

GLAZE: 2 tablespoons milk plus 1 tablespoon sugar

Peel and quarter potato. Boil until tender. Reserve ½ cup potato water. Puree potato and cool (should equal ¾ cup). Mix yeast, 1 teaspoon sugar and potato water. (Cool to 110°.) Let stand 5 minutes. Mix with rest of sugar, salt, eggs, butter. Beat until smooth. Add 3½ cups flour. Put 1 cup flour on bread board and knead dough until smooth and soft but not sticky. Let rise 2 hours. Punch down. Form into 12 or 13 round buns. Place well apart on greased cookie sheet. Cover and let rise 1½ hours. Preheat oven to 350°. Bake 15 minutes. Brush on glaze. Bake another 7 to 8 minutes.

Preparation time: several hours. Freezes well.

MORAVIAN SUGAR CAKE

1 cup mashed potatoes

1 pint milk

1 cake yeast (one package)

1 tablespoon salt

2 eggs

1 cup sugar

1 cup butter or Crisco

6 cups flour

Follow directions on yeast package and add mashed potatoes. After adding half the flour, let batter rise until doubled in bulk. Stir in remainder of flour and put in refrigerator overnight.

The next day, knead about ⅓ batter adding more flour as needed. Roll out or pat out in 3 (8 x 8) inch pans to a thickness of approximately 1½ inches. Let rise about 2 hours and bake at 400°. When done and while hot, mark off indentations with knife handle or blunt object. Cover well with brown sugar and melted butter (approximately 1 pound).

Freezes well.

CREAM CHEESE BRAIDS

1 cup sour cream	½ cup butter, melted
½ cup sugar	2 packages yeast
1 teaspoon salt	½ cup warm water
4 cups flour	2 eggs, beaten

Heat sour cream over low heat. Stir in sugar, salt and butter. Cool to lukewarm. Sprinkle yeast over warm water in a large mixing bowl stirring until yeast dissolves. Add sour cream mixture, eggs and flour. Mix well. Cover tightly; refrigerate overnight.

Next day: Divide dough into 4 equal parts (easier if dough is removed from refrigerator about 30 minutes beforehand). Roll each part on well floured board into 12 x 8 inch rectangle. Spread ¼ Cream cheese filling in each rectangle; roll up jelly roll fashion, beginning with long sides. Pinch edges together, place rolled seam side down on greased baking sheet. Slit each roll at 2 inch intervals about ⅔ way through dough to resemble a braid; cover; let rise in warm place until doubled (1 hour).

Bake at 375° for 12 to 15 minutes or until lightly browned. Spread with glaze while warm.

Filling:

16 ounces Cream cheese	1 tablespoon Amaretto liqueur
¾ cup sugar	1 egg, beaten
2 teaspoons vanilla	

Mix together well.

Glaze:

2 cups powdered sugar	1 teaspoon vanilla
3 tablespoons milk	Toasted almonds
1 tablespoon Amaretto liqueur	

Mix well. Top with toasted almonds.

BANANA CORN MUFFINS
Yield: 12 muffins

¾ cup mashed extra ripe
  bananas
½ cup milk
½ cup vegetable oil
1 egg, beaten
1 cup flour

¾ cup cornmeal
¼ cup sugar
1 tablespoon baking powder
½ teaspoon salt

Put in bowl (or processor) bananas, milk, oil and egg. Process on-off. Mix in dry ingredients; process to mix well, about 10 seconds. Bake in paper lined cups ¾ full in a 425° oven 15 or 20 minutes, or until golden brown.
Freezes well.

BRAN RAISIN MUFFINS
Yield: 12 muffins

1 cup bran cereal
¾ cup milk
1 egg, well beaten
2 tablespoons salad oil
1 cup flour

3 teaspoons baking powder
¼ cup sugar
½ cup California walnuts or
  pecans
⅓ cup raisins
½ teaspoon salt

Combine bran, milk and egg; let stand 5 minutes; add salad oil. Sift dry ingredients; add bran mixture; stir just until dry ingredients are moistened but not smooth. On last 4 or 5 stirs, add nut meats and raisins. Fill greased muffin pans ⅔ full. Bake at 425° for 20 minutes.
Prepare: 10 minutes. Cooking: 20 minutes. Freezes well.

SIX WEEKS BRAN MUFFINS   *Yield: 60 muffins*

6 cups bran cereal

2 cups boiling water

1 cup shortening, melted

3 cups sugar

4 eggs, beaten

1 quart buttermilk

5 cups unsifted flour

5 teaspoons soda

2 teaspoons salt

Put 2 cups of the bran into a large bowl. Pour the boiling water over it and let stand while assembling the other ingredients. Mix in shortening. Mix the remainder of the bran with sugar, eggs and buttermilk. Sift together flour, soda and salt. Combine all ingredients. Cover and store in the refrigerator overnight. Put in paper muffin cups. Fill ⅔ full.

Bake as much as desired in a 400° oven for 20 minutes. Batter will keep up to six weeks or longer. They are better after one week. You may add raisins and nuts. This requires more than an average size box of bran.

ONION RYE BREAD

3 cups rye flour

2½ to 3½ cups white flour

¼ cup cocoa

1 tablespoon sugar

2 teaspoons salt

1 tablespoon poppy seeds

2 packages yeast

⅓ cup molasses

2 tablespoons softened
margarine

2 cups warm water

Oil to brush on tops of loaves

Mix 1 cup rye flour, 1 cup white flour, cocoa, sugar, salt, seeds, molasses and margarine. Soften yeast in 2 cups water for 5 minutes, add to previous mix. Mix with electric mixer for 5 to 8 minutes. Add remaining 2 cups rye flour and enough white flour to make medium dough. Knead on floured board. Let rise in oiled bowl to double, about 1 hour. Make into two loaves, slash tops, then oil tops. Let rise to double again, about 1 hour. Bake at 400° until done, about 30 minutes, or until sounds hollow when tapped on bottom.

OLD WORLD RYE BREAD

2 cups rye flour

¼ cup cocoa

2 packages yeast

1½ cups warm water

½ cup honey

2 teaspoons salt

2 tablespoons carraway seeds

2 tablespoons butter

2½ cups white (or whole wheat
flour)

Combine rye flour and cocoa, unsifted. Dissolve yeast in ½ cup warm water. Combine honey, 1 cup water, salt, carraway seeds in large bowl. Add rye and cocoa, yeast mixture, butter and 1 cup flour. Beat until smooth; add remaining flour, kneading. Let rise 2 hours, punch down, shape in round loaf on buttered cookie sheet dusted with cornmeal. Let rise 50 minutes. Bake 35 to 40 minutes at 375°.

DILLED CHEESE FILLED BREAD

2 teaspoons salt	4 cups flour (approximately)
3½ teaspoons sugar	½ cup butter or margarine
2 packages yeast	1 cup milk
	Sesame seeds

Put in bowl, sugar, salt, yeast and 1 cup flour. Heat in saucepan the milk and butter to 120° to 130° (no hotter). With mixer at low speed, add warm milk—butter mixture to bowl. Increase to medium speed and beat 2 minutes, scraping well. Add 1 cup flour, beat an additional 2 minutes. With spoon, add enough flour to make soft dough (about 2 cups). Turn onto floured surface and knead until smooth and elastic (about 10 minutes). Put in greased bowl, grease top, let rise to double (about 1 hour). Punch down. Roll with rolling pin on floured board to 15 inch circle. Grease 9 inch cake pan and sprinkle with 1 tablespoon sesame seeds. Place dough in pan, letting sides overlap. Place cheese filling in center and gather overhanging bread into pleats, giving the pleated circle a twist at the top to form a top knot. Brush surface with egg white and sprinkle with more sesame seeds. Cover and let rise to double (about 45 minutes). Bake at 375° for 35 to 40 minutes, or until golden. Cover with foil last few minutes, if needed, to prevent over browning. Remove from oven, tent with aluminum foil. Serve hot, warm or room temperature. Do not freeze.

Cheese Filling:

1 pound shredded Munster cheese (can be up to ½ Swiss or other cheese)	Few drops bottled hot pepper sauce
2 tablespoons breadcrumbs, Italian flavored	2 eggs
	¼ cup dried parsley
1 teaspoon ground dill	⅛ teaspoon salt
	Sesame seeds

In a large bowl, beat eggs slightly. Add remaining ingredients and mix well with spoon. Enough for 1 loaf of bread.

ITALIAN CHEESE BREAD

4 cups unbleached flour

1 tablespoon honey

1 package yeast

1 cup plus 2 tablespoons very warm water

4 to 5 tablespoons grated Parmesan (or 4 ounces crumbled Blue cheese)

2 minced shallots (or 2 large minced garlic cloves) sauteed in 2 tablespoons butter until lightly browned and slightly cooled

Cornmeal

Cooking oil

1 egg white mixed with 1 tablespoon cold water

Put 2 cups flour, honey, yeast and shallot butter in processor with steel blade. Process well. Add ½ cup water, process on-off 4 times. Add 2 cups flour, ½ cup and 2 tablespoons water and cheese and process on-off 4 times. Process to form ball on blade. May need up to 1 cup additional flour. Turn on to floured surface, knead a few minutes. Cover with bowl to rest 20 minutes. Roll dough with rolling pin to oblong, about 12 x 26 inches. Roll to form a 26 inch long roll. Cut in half, taper and seal ends. Place on oiled baking sheet that has been heavily dusted with cornmeal. Oil top of bread. Cover loosely with plastic wrap. Refrigerate at least 2 hours and up to 24 hours. When ready to bake, uncover and let rise at room temperature 15 to 30 minutes. Bake in 425° oven for 10 minutes, brush with egg-water glaze, reduce oven to 375°, and bake 25 more minutes or until sounds hollow when tapped on bottom of loaf and nicely browned. Cool on wire rack.

May be frozen after baking.

BRUNCHES

Chowan Court House, Chowan

BRIE CHEESE CREPES
Yield: 6 to 8 crepes

Crepe Batter:

3 large eggs

1 teaspoon sugar

⅛ teaspoon salt

1½ cups all purpose flour

1½ cups milk

2 tablespoons melted butter

Put eggs in blender. Add one half the flour and one half the milk. Blend until smooth. Add remainder of the flour and milk and salt. Then add butter and mix until smooth. Let sit 2 hours before using. Blend again before using.

Filling:

½ pound supreme Brie

6 tablespoons Bechamel sauce

4 heavy grinds of pepper

Let Brie come to room temperature. Mash it and mix with the Bechamel sauce and pepper. Fill crepe. Fold crepes in thirds (never roll). Place seam side down in casserole.

Topping:

Fresh grated Parmesan cheese

Major Grey chutney

Butter

Put Parmesan and 2 teaspoons chutney on top of each crepe. Melt butter and drizzle on top. Bake at 400° for 10 minutes.

HAM AND SWISS SANDWICHES

½ pound melted butter (or margarine)

½ cup prepared mustard

Swiss cheese slices

Sandwich rolls

⅓ cup chopped onion

2 tablespoons poppy seeds

Ham slices*

Mix butter, mustard, onion and poppy seeds. Spread on both sides of rolls. Add ham and cheese slices to make sandwiches. Wrap individually in aluminum foil.

Bake at 350° for 20 minutes. Serve hot. Can be made ahead and refrigerated or frozen.

*Double recipe: 1 Hostess ham thinly sliced makes about 30 sandwiches.

GOURMET CHEESE CASSEROLE

9 slices stale bread

Salt and pepper

1½ tablespoons minced onion, instant or fresh

1 pound very sharp cheese, grated

1 package frozen chopped spinach, squeezed dry

4 eggs

½ pound mushrooms, sliced and sauteed or ½ pound crabmeat or shrimp

3 cups milk

1 teaspoon dry mustard

1 teaspoon Worcestershire sauce

Black olives, sliced in half

Cut bread in 3 strips each. Fit 9 strips tightly in bottom of a greased 2 quart casserole. Sprinkle with salt, pepper, ⅓ onions and ⅓ cheese. Press down. Sprinkle spinach evenly over first layer, then layer of cheese, layer of mushrooms or seafood. Top with cheese.

Beat eggs. Add milk, mustard, and Worcestershire. Pour over bread. Put halved olives around top in a circle, top up. Let stand overnight in refrigerator. Remove 2 hours before serving. An hour before serving, bake in a preheated 325° oven for 50 to 60 minutes, or until firm in center. (Note: To double this recipe, use only 5 cups milk.)

Variation:

Omit spinach, mushrooms and seafood and add 1½ pound hot sausage, cooked and crumbled. If desired, both the sausage and the mushrooms could be used.

CHEESE VELVET
Serves: 6 to 8

8 ounces sharp cheese

10 slices white bread, crusts removed and buttered on one side

4 eggs

2 cups milk

1 teaspoon salt

½ to ¾ teaspoon dry mustard

1 teaspoon baking powder

If using processor, put cheese broken into chunks and all other ingredients in bowl. Blend until smooth.

Put in ½ of cheese, bread, eggs and milk in blender and turn on high until thoroughly mixed. Pour into bowl and blend the rest with salt and mustard. Mix two together well and pour into greased 2 quart casserole. Bake 1 hour at 350°. This is delicious and never fails. Can be made a day ahead or at last minute.

OYSTERS PARMESAN

3 English muffins, split, or
   patty shells, or toast points
½ pint oysters, drained
1 tablespoon chopped onion
1 cup milk, divided
1½ tablespoons butter
2 tablespoons flour

¼ teaspoon salt
Dash pepper
¼ teaspoon celery salt
¼ cup Parmesan cheese
1 teaspoon chopped parsley

Combine oysters, onion and ½ cup milk and cook over medium heat 15 minutes. (Do NOT overcook oysters.) Melt butter and blend in flour and seasonings and rest of milk and cook until thick, stirring constantly. Add Parmesan and parsley and stir well. Add oyster mixture and cook 5 minutes. Serve over lightly toasted and buttered muffins, toast points or patty shells.

You may also serve oysters in a chafing dish for added elegance.

SHRIMP AND ARTICHOKE DIVAN

1½ sticks butter
9 tablespoons flour
1½ cups milk
1½ cups cream or half
   and half
Salt
Freshly ground pepper
2 cans artichoke hearts or
   1 package frozen

2 pounds cooked shrimp
1 to 1½ pounds mushrooms,
   sliced
½ cup dry sherry
2 tablespoons Worcestershire
½ cup grated Parmesan cheese
Paprika
Few shakes Tabasco

Heat oven to 375°. (If using frozen hearts, cook by directions.) Melt 9 tablespoons butter and stir in flour. When blended, add milk and cream, stirring constantly with whisk. Season.

Arrange artichokes over bottom of buttered dish. Scatter shrimp over artichokes. Cook sliced mushrooms in remaining butter for 6 minutes. Spoon mushrooms over shrimp. Add sherry and Worcestershire to cream sauce and pour over casserole. Sprinkle with cheese and paprika. Bake 30 minutes.

OPEN-FACED CRAB SANDWICH

7½ ounce can white crab meat or fresh crab

¼ cup mayonnaise

1 teaspoon lemon juice

Mix above and refrigerate several hours or overnight.

Mix together the following:

3 ounces Cream cheese, softened

1 egg yolk

1 teaspoon finely chopped onion

¼ teaspoon prepared mustard

Dash salt

Split, butter and toast lightly 3 English muffins. Spread crab mixture over all 6 pieces. Top with cheese mixture. Place on cookie sheet and broil 5 to 6 inches from the heat until brown and bubbly.

NEW ORLEANS CRABMEAT
Serves: 8 individual or 4 double servings

1 pound mushrooms

½ stick butter

1 pound fresh crabmeat

2 tablespoons butter

2½ cups heavy cream sauce

Anchovy paste

1 cup fresh bread crumbs

4 English muffins, buttered and lightly toasted

Slice mushrooms and saute in butter 5 minutes. Make cream sauce. Add crab and mushrooms. Spread anchovy paste lightly on muffins. Pile crab mixture on top. Sprinkle with crumbs. Bake about 15 minutes at 350°. Can be prepared ahead of time and baked when ready to serve.

STRAWBERRY CORNUCOPIAS
Yield: 32 small sandwiches

3 cups fresh strawberries

1 (8 ounce) package whipped Cream cheese

2 tablespoons 10X sugar

¼ cup walnuts (or pecans), finely chopped

32 slices soft white bread

Wash and hull strawberries. Mash enough to measure 2 tablespoons; set remainder aside. Beat the Cream cheese and 10X sugar into the mashed strawberries until smooth; stir in walnuts. Cut a 3 inch round from the center of each slice of bread; roll each piece thin with a rolling pin. Spread a rounded teaspoon of Cream cheese mixture over each flattened bread round; roll into cornucopia shape. Place sandwiches in a single layer on a cookie sheet. Halve the remaining berries. Tuck one half strawberry into top of each cornucopia. Cover and chill.

May be made up to 1 to 3 hours ahead. Easy to prepare, colorful and delicious!

FRENCH SCRAMBLED EGGS WITH ASPARAGUS

1 garlic bud
20 eggs, beaten well and sieved
2 tablespoons unsalted butter
¾ stick unsalted butter, melted

1 pound asparagus, sliced diagonally
½ teaspoon salt
¼ teaspoon white pepper

Saute asparagus in a little butter and then add 2 tablespoons water. Cover and steam a few minutes until crunchy-tender. Set aside. Beat eggs with fork on which garlic bud has been placed.

Melt 2 tablespoons butter in top of a large double boiler (Bain Marie). Add eggs, stirring constantly with a wire whip. Fix heat so water is simmering, not boiling, and add melted butter. Keep stirring slowly. The eggs are finished when they are creamy or custard-like. Take off heat and fold in asparagus. Serve on warm platter garnished with fresh sliced tomatoes and parsley.

EGGS FILANTI

Serves: 6 to 8

2 tablespoons butter
¼ cup breadcrumbs
1 pound Mozarella cheese, grated

8 eggs
¼ cup freshly grated Parmesan cheese
Freshly ground pepper to taste

Preheat oven to 450°. Butter a deep pie or quiche pan and sprinkle with breadcrumbs. Grate the Mozarella and evenly cover bottom of the pan. Break eggs over cheese in a single layer. Completely cover the eggs with the remaining Mozarella. Sprinkle with Parmesan and pepper and bake for 15 minutes or just until egg yolks have set. Serve immediately.

COTTAGE CHEESE EGGS

10 large eggs

1 cup plus 1 tablespoon
cream-style Cottage cheese

½ teaspoon salt

Dash pepper

2 tablespoons fresh parsley,
chopped

3 tablespoons butter

3 tablespoons flour

1 cup milk

Beat eggs, Cottage cheese and seasonings in large bowl. (If you want very creamy eggs put in blender.) Melt butter in large skillet. Add flour and stir 1 minute. Stirring constantly, add the milk and cook until the mixture begins to thicken and boil. Add egg mixture. Cook eggs on low heat stirring slowly and carefully, lifting mixture occasionally from bottom and sides of pan. Cook until thickened but still very moist. Transfer to heated serving dish.

This is delicious, mild in flavor and has an unusual custard-like texture.

BAKED EGGS

4 eggs

4 to 6 pieces cooked, crumbled
bacon

Chopped chives

Sour cream

½ cup Swiss cheese (or more)

Salt and pepper

Butter 4 small individual ramekins. Sprinkle generously with Swiss cheese. Break 1 egg (or 2 depending on size of ramekin) over cheese. Spoon about 1 tablespoon sour cream on top of each egg. Season with salt and pepper. Sprinkle chives over top.

Bake 350° until whites are cooked but yolks are still a little soft. Top with crumbled bacon and serve.

MAKE AHEAD SCRAMBLED EGGS

¼ cup butter

12 eggs

1⅓ cups milk

1 teaspoon salt

⅛ teaspoon pepper

2 tablespoons flour

1 tablespoon chopped pimento

1 tablespoon chopped parsley

Scramble all ingredients together and cook to a soft scramble on top of stove in skillet. Pour into casserole and leave on warmer or in oven for at least 30 minutes at 200° to 225°.

EGGS WITH ARTICHOKE HEARTS
Serves: 6

2 packages frozen creamed spinach, cooked according to package directions

12 canned artichoke hearts, drained

12 poached eggs*

2 cups Hollandaise sauce

In a saucepan, warm the artichoke hearts in salted water until heated through. Place 2 artichoke hearts in 6 individual au gratin dishes. Fill them with the spinach and place 1 poached egg on each spinach filled artichoke heart and top with the Hollandaise Sauce. Run under a preheated broiler for a few minutes until sauce is browned.

*You may use 6 eggs if containers are too small for 2 eggs each.

Hollandaise Sauce:

8 egg yolks

Pinch salt

Juice of 2 lemons

2 cups butter, melted

Place the egg yolks, salt and lemon juice in a blender. Whip for 1 minute. Turn blender to low speed and slowly add the butter. The sauce is ready when it thickens.

EASY OVEN OMELETTE

6 eggs, separated

6 tablespoons hot milk

¾ teaspoon salt

1½ tablespoons butter

Beat egg yolks until thick. Add milk and salt. Beat egg whites until stiff and fold into yolks. Heat butter until slightly brown in 10 inch iron skillet. Pour mixture into skillet and bake in 325° oven for 20 minutes.

For variety add grated cheese, sauteed onions, bell peppers, or mushrooms.

QUICK SOUR CREAM SAUCE

1 cup mayonnaise (Hellmann's or homemade)

1 cup sour cream

¼ cup fresh lemon juice

Blend thoroughly and heat slowly. Good on cooked or raw vegetables.

119

TOMATO ZUCCHINI SAUCE

Serves: 3

2 tablespoons butter
1 tablespoon oil
1 medium onion
1 (#2 can) tomatoes

¼ teaspoon basil
¼ teaspoon oregano
Salt and pepper to taste
1 medium zucchini

Saute onion in melted butter and oil. Run tomatoes in blender a few seconds. Add to onion mixture. Add seasonings and simmer 20 to 30 minutes. Add cut up zucchini and cook until zucchini is just tender. Serve over omelet.

ZUCCHINI ROUNDS

Mix together:

⅓ cup Bisquick
¼ cup Parmesan cheese
⅛ teaspoon pepper

Add:

2 slightly beaten eggs just until moistened

Fold in:

2 cups shredded unpeeled zucchini

Fry approximatley 2 tablespoons of mix in frying pan for 2 to 3 minutes on each side. Pour melted butter over and serve.

CRUNCHY PINEAPPLE CASSEROLE

2 large (15½ ounce) cans
  pineapple chucks, drained
2 cups sharp cheese, grated
6 tablespoons flour

¾ cup sugar
½ stick butter, melted
Ritz crackers

Mix flour and sugar. Add to pineapple and cheese. Put in greased 1½ quart casserole. Crumble Ritz crackers over top. Pour ½ stick melted butter over and bake at 350° for 30 minutes.

MELON COMPOTE
Serves: 12

6 cantaloupes

1 pint raspberries or blackberries

1 pineapple, peeled and diced

1 cup fresh blueberries (optional)

Green grapes (optional)

¼ cup Kirsch or Grenadine

Halve melon and cut flesh into balls. Scallop shell. Marinate all in Kirsch overnight and serve in melon shells.

CURRIED HOT FRUIT COMPOTE

2 cups peach halves, well drained

2 cups pear halves, well drained

2 cups apricot halves, well drained

2 cups dark pitted cherries or pitted purple plums, well drained

2 cups pineapple chunks, well drained

¾ cup brown sugar

1 stick melted butter or margarine

4 teaspoons curry

Put drained fruit in 2 quart shallow casserole. Mix brown sugar into melted butter and add curry. Cook until sugar is melted and dissolved. Pour over drained fruit and cook 45 minutes in 325° to 350° oven.

BAKED APRICOTS
Yield: 1 quart casserole

2 (#2 size) cans apricots, drained

⅔ cup brown sugar

2 rolls Ritz crackers, rolled into fine crumbs

1 stick butter, melted

1 teaspoon cinnamon

Add brown sugar and cinnamon to crumbs and mix well. Layer apricots, crumbs, butter. Repeat. Bake 325° for 40 minutes.

WHITE CHOCOLATE FONDUE

1 pound white chocolate
½ cup half and half

2 teaspoons corn syrup, clear
1 tablespoon Amaretto
(optional)

Put ingredients into saucepan and put on warm until it melts (about 10 minutes). Stir well. Serve with fresh strawberries, bananas, pineapple and green grapes.

CRUSTLESS QUICHE   *Serves 4*

1 cup Swiss cheese
¾ cup Cheddar cheese
2 cups milk
½ cup Bisquick
4 eggs

½ teaspoon salt
Dash cayenne
⅓ cup minced onion
1 package broccoli, chopped
    and well drained

Preheat oven to 350°. Grease 10 inch pie pan. Sprinkle broccoli and cheese in pan. Blend eggs, milk, Bisquick and seasonings in blender. Pour over mixture. Bake 50 minutes or until set. Let stand 5 minutes before serving.

GARLIC GRITS SOUFFLE   *Serves: 6 to 8*

1 cup quick grits
1 teaspoon salt
4 cups water
Bread crumbs

1 stick butter or margarine
1 (6 ounce) roll Kraft garlic or
    Nippy cheese or 1 to 3 cups
    grated sharp Cheddar cheese
2 eggs

Cook grits in salted water. Add grated or chopped cheese and butter and melt in grits. Cool a little and add beaten eggs. (At this point you may refrigerate and bake the next day.) Top with bread crumbs and bake at 350° about 1 hour and 15 minutes until firm. If you use Cheddar, add Tabasco, cayenne pepper, garlic powder and seasoned salt to taste. You may use Pepperidge Farm Herb Crumbs.

MARINATED CHICKEN LIVERS　　　*Serves: 8*

2 pounds chicken livers, cut in
　bite size pieces
1 bottle soy sauce (3 ounces)
Flour

⅛ teaspoon pepper
½ stick butter

　Marinate livers overnight in soy sauce in refrigerator. Drain. Mix livers
with flour and pepper and saute in butter about 5 minutes until browned
but slightly pink in center. Take out and keep warm. Can make gravy with
drippings and little water.

SAUSAGE SUPPER　　　*Serves: 4*

2 acorn squash, medium to
　large
1 pound bulk pork sausage,
　mild or hot

1 cup packaged cornbread
　stuffing mix
½ cup water

　Preheat oven at 350°. Halve squash and scoop out seeds. Place squash
halves, cut side up, in shallow baking dish and cover with foil. Bake until
soft, about an hour. Meanwhile, cook sausage in skillet, crumbling while
browning, until done. Mix stuffing mix with water and 1 tablespoon
sausage drippings. Drain rest of drippings from sausage and add stuffing
mix to sausage. Pile into squash cavities and bake until browned or about
15 minutes.

APPLE SAUSAGE BAKE　　　*Serves: 12*

1 dozen apples, cooking apples
　or Golden delicious
6 tablespoons butter or
　margarine
Juice of ½ lemon
½ teaspoon nutmeg

1 tablespoon cinnamon
⅛ teaspoon salt
½ cup brown sugar
1 pound mild sausage cooked in
　patties until crisp

　Core and slice apples (leave skins on). In large frying pan, cook apples
and next 6 ingredients on medium heat, covered, until done. Cut sausage
bite size and add to apples.

CHICKEN PIE
Serves: 10

4 ounces Cheddar cheese, shredded

1 tablespoon flour

1 cup almonds, slivered and toasted

3 cups chicken, cooked and chopped

1½ cups celery slices

1 tablespoon lemon juice

1 cup mayonnaise

½ teaspoon poultry seasoning

½ teaspoon salt

⅛ teaspoon pepper

2 (9 inch) pie crust shells

Toss shredded cheese and flour. Use ¾ cup cheese and ½ cup almonds combined with remaining ingredients. Pour into 2 pie shells and top with the remaining cheese and almonds. Bake at 400° for 30 to 35 minutes.
Garnish with parsley and lemon twists.

BRUNCH CASSEROLE
Serves: 6

6 hard boiled eggs, sliced

1 pound hot bulk sausage

1½ cups sour cream

½ cup dry breadcrumbs

1½ cups Cheddar cheese, grated

Salt and pepper

Place eggs in buttered casserole. Season to taste. Cook sausage. Drain and sprinkle over eggs. Spread sour cream over sausage. Combine crumbs and cheese. Sprinkle over casserole. Brown under broiler after heating thoroughly in oven.

EGG AND SHRIMP CASSEROLE
Serves: 6 to 8

8 eggs, hard boiled and deviled

2 pounds shrimp in shell

4 cups thick cream sauce

1 cup sharp cheese, grated

1 cup buttered breadcrumbs

Cook and clean shrimp. Make cream sauce, and add 1 cup of the shrimp chopped in small pieces. Add cheese to sauce.
In a 2 quart casserole, cover bottom with deviled eggs. Sprinkle remainder of shrimp over and around eggs. Pour cream sauce over all. Top with crumbs and heat just enough to have sauce bubbling in 300° oven.

Deviled Eggs:

8 eggs, hard boiled

½ teaspoon salt

½ teaspoon dry mustard

½ teaspoon lemon juice

¼ cup mayonnaise

1½ tablespoons light cream

Dash Tabasco

HUEVOS RANCHEROS

Serves: 4

¼ cup olive oil

1 crushed clove garlic

2 medium onions, finely chopped

1 large green pepper, finely chopped

1 cup peeled, chopped tomato, fresh or canned

½ teaspoon salt

¼ teaspoon pepper

2 teaspoons chili powder

¼ teaspoon oregano

2 tablespoons catsup

6 strips bacon, cooked and crumbled

1 teaspoon Accent

1 cup Cheddar cheese, grated

4 to 8 eggs

Saute garlic in oil for 5 minutes; remove garlic, add and saute onions and peppers. Add remaining ingredients and simmer covered until thickened.

In greased baking dish put sauce, making nests for eggs. Break one egg in each nest. Bake in 450° oven until eggs are set. Sprinkle with crumbled bacon and Cheddar cheese. Heat until cheese is melted.

BRUNCH EGGS AND CHICKEN LIVERS

½ pound livers, cut in bite sizes

½ pound fresh mushrooms

1 tablespoon chopped pimento

¼ cup chopped onion

6 eggs, poached

1 package sliced ham or Canadian bacon

½ stick butter

2 tablespoons sherry

3 tablespoons flour

Salt to taste

Pepper to taste

Holland rusk or lightly toasted English muffin

Saute mushrooms, pimento and onion in butter until soft. Add livers and cook until barely pink inside (more done if desired). Remove all from butter and add flour to make roux. Add enough water to make thick gravy. Season to taste. Add livers and vegetables. Just before serving, add sherry. Poach eggs. Place slice of ham that has been heated on muffin, then egg, then the liver sauce. Top with parsley. Sauce can be made day ahead. Fruit casserole and cheese grits are good with this.

EGGS CREOLE STYLE

Serves: 4

½ stick butter

2 green peppers, finely chopped

2 medium onions, finely chopped

3 stalks celery, finely chopped

1 pound can tomatoes

1 cup medium white sauce

6 hard cooked eggs, sliced ¼ inch thick

½ teaspoon salt

Pepper to taste

Bread crumbs

Few shakes Tabasco

Sliced almonds

To make creole sauce, melt butter in skillet and fry peppers, onions and celery until tender. Add tomatoes, and cook until thick. Season. Make white sauce using 2 tablespoons flour, 2 tablespoons butter and 1 cup milk.

In baking dish, put a layer of egg slices, a layer of white sauce and then a layer of creole sauce. Top with bread crumbs and almonds. Place in pan of water in 350° oven. Heat well, but do not bake — about 45 minutes.

EGGS HUSSARDE

Serves: 4 individual or 2 doubles

4 slices Canadian bacon or thin slices ham

2 English muffins halved, buttered and toasted

4 slices tomato

4 soft poached eggs

½ cup Hollandaise sauce

½ cup Marchard de Vin sauce

Paprika

Place ham or bacon on muffins. Cover with Marchand de Vin sauce, then tomato, then poached egg. Top with Hollandaise, garnish with sprig of parsley and dust with paprika.

Marchand De Vin Sauce:

¾ cup butter

⅓ cup mushrooms, finely chopped

½ cup minced ham

2 tablespoons flour

¾ cup beef stock

½ teaspoon salt

⅓ cup chopped shallots

½ cup onion, finely chopped

2 tablespoons minced garlic

⅛ teaspoon pepper

½ cup red wine

Dash cayenne

Saute all vegetables and ham in butter until golden. Add flour and seasonings and brown well for 7 to 10 minutes. Blend in stock and wine and simmer about 45 minutes.

126

SOUR CREAM OMELETTE FOR TWO

4 eggs

¼ teaspoon cayenne pepper

3 ounces Cream cheese

½ teaspoon salt

¼ cup sour cream

2 teaspoons chopped chives, fresh or frozen

Mix together by mashing: Cream cheese, sour cream, cayenne, salt and chives. Let sit in bowl while preparing eggs.

Put a sliver of garlic on prongs of fork and mix eggs until blended. Let fork and garlic sit in bowl while heating butter in omelette pan. When butter is bubbly, remove garlic, pour in eggs — cook as for regular omelette. Just before top of omelette solidifies, spoon Cream cheese mixture onto ½ of the omelette. Turn edge over mixture. Heat 1 minute or so to warm filling. Slide out on plate.

In summer, serve with sliced fresh tomatoes sprinkled with chopped fresh basil, parsley, and vinagrette or toasted French bread rounds.

Or serve with Piperade Sauce (A French Sauce).

PIPERADE

"OMELETTE PIPERADE"   *Serves: 4 to 6*

A Provencal French Sauce:

3 tablespoons oil (try 2 tablespoons oil first)

1 cup onion, chopped

1 cup green pepper, chopped

2 garlic slivers, finely chopped

1 cup tomatoes, peeled, seeded, and chopped (no juice)

½ teaspoon salt

½ teaspoon ground pepper

½ teaspoon basil

Saute onion, garlic, pepper in oil 5 to 10 minutes until soft. Add tomatoes and simmer 5 minutes. Add spices, salt and pepper. Simmer 5 minutes.

You do not want this sauce to be too juicy, so evaporate juice if any.

Add 3 tablespoons fresh chopped parsley.

Will make enough sauce for 8 egg omelette.

ITALIAN SAUSAGE EGG BRUNCH

Serves: 8

12 slices white bread, crusts removed

2 to 3 tablespoons butter, softened

½ cup butter

½ pound fresh mushrooms, trimmed and sliced

2 cups yellow onions, thinly sliced

1 teaspoon salt

⅛ teaspoon pepper

1½ pounds mild Italian sausage

¾ to 1 pound Cheddar cheese, grated

5 eggs

2½ cups milk

3 teaspoons Dijon mustard

1 teaspoon dry mustard

¾ to 1 teaspoon ground nutmeg

2 to 3 tablespoons fresh parsley, finely chopped

Butter the bread with the softened butter and set aside. In a 10 to 12 inch skillet, melt the ½ cup butter and brown the mushrooms and onions over medium heat for 5 to 8 minutes or until tender. Season to taste with salt and pepper and set aside. Cook the sausage and cut into bite size pieces. In a greased 3 quart shallow casserole, layer ½ of the bread, mushroom mixture, sausage, and cheese. Repeat the layers, ending with the cheese. In a medium-size mixing bowl, mix the eggs, milk, both mustards, nutmeg, 1 teaspoon salt, and ⅛ teaspoon pepper. Pour over the sausage and cheese casserole. Cover the casserole and refrigerate overnight.

When ready to bake, sprinkle the parsley evenly over the top of the casserole and bake uncovered in a preheated 350° oven for 1 hour or until bubbly. Serve immediately with a fruit salad and crusty bread.

Must be prepared 24 hours in advance.

(For a milder variation, substitute 1⅓ cups chopped scallions for the yellow onions and ¾ to 1 pound sliced American cheese for the Cheddar cheese.)

SKILLET MUSHROOMS, GREEN PEPPERS AND ONIONS

Serves: 8

½ pound bacon, cooked and drained

1 pound fresh mushrooms

2 large fresh tomatoes

2 large green peppers

2 large sweet onions

¼ pound butter or margarine

Slice mushrooms into thick slices, including stem. Cut the green peppers, tomatoes and onions into 1 inch slices. Melt the butter in a large skillet, add vegetables, and saute very slowly, stirring frequently. (The vegetables may be cooked ahead and reheated.) Do not overcook. Vegetables should be crisp. Salt and pepper to taste.

Serve over sauteed liver, toast points or omelettes.

HOT CHICKEN SALAD

½ to 1 cup slivered almonds

6 cups cooked, diced chicken (approximately 8 chicken breasts)

2 tablespoons chicken stock

3 cups celery

2 to 3 teaspoons grated onion

3 to 4 tablespoons lemon juice

1 to 1½ teaspoons salt

2 cups mayonnaise

Dash of cayenne

1 cup mild Cheddar cheese, grated

1⅓ cup crushed potato chips

Combine chicken and celery. Add seasonings, then mayonnaise, almonds and stock. Put into 3 quart shallow casserole. Mix potato chips and cheese and spread on top. Bake 375° for twenty minutes. (Do not overcook.)

CRUSTLESS HAM AND ASPARAGUS QUICHE

Serves: 4

*1 pound fresh asparagus

3 tablespoons butter

½ teaspoon salt

1 cup sharp cheese, grated

¾ cup minced ham

1 green onion, chopped

4 eggs beaten

1¼ cups evaporated milk

4 tablespoons grated Parmesan cheese

Place asparagus in bottom of 9 inch greased pan. Sprinkle cheese, ham and onion over. Combine beaten eggs with milk and salt. Pour over mixture in pan. Sprinkle with Parmesan cheese. Bake at 325° for 35 to 40 minutes.

*You can substitute 1 package frozen chopped spinach, cooked, for asparagus.

CRANBERRY CASSEROLE

Serves: 8

3 cups chopped, unpeeled
    cooking apples (York,
    Stayman, or Cape Granny
    Smith)

2 cups raw cranberries

1 cup sugar

1 tablespoon cornstarch

1½ cups quick-cooking oatmeal

½ cup brown sugar

⅓ cup flour

⅓ cup chopped pecans

1 stick margarine, melted

In 7 x 11 inch casserole (or 2 quart) mix apples and cranberries. Sift sugar and cornstarch and stir to mix. Spoon over fruit. Mix remaining ingredients and spread over top of casserole. Bake at 350° for 1 hour. Serve hot or cold. This is nice to serve with your main course or to use as a dessert topped with whipped cream or ice cream.
    Can be made ahead.

SOUR CREAM MUSHROOMS

Serves: 4

¾ pound mushrooms, fresh or
    frozen

1 cup sour cream

4 hard boiled eggs, coarsely
    chopped

⅓ cup butter or margarine

⅓ cup chopped onion

2 to 3 teaspoons lemon juice

¼ cup flour

¾ cup milk

Salt

White pepper

Saute onions and mushrooms in margarine. Add lemon juice and flour. Thicken. Add sour cream and milk. Add eggs and seasonings. Serve on toast. Chicken may be added to this dish.
    Preparation time: 20 minutes.

SPINACH TORTE

Serves: 6 to 8

Crust:

2 cups lightly spooned flour

½ teaspoon salt

1 cup butter, cut in pieces

3 tablespoons water

1 egg yolk and 3 tablespoons
    water

Mix flour, butter and salt with pastry blender. Mix egg yolk with water and blend into the dry mixture. Add 3 tablespoons water to dry mixture. Chill dough at least ½ hour.

Filling:

2 packages frozen spinach or 2 pounds fresh spinach (washed)

2 large onions

3 tablespoons olive oil

3 (1 inch thick) smoked pork chops, trimmed

1 cup Ricotta cheese

1½ cups Parmesan cheese

½ teaspoon salt

Pepper to taste

4 eggs, lightly beaten

Cook spinach without adding water until just wilted. Drain well. Saute onions in olive oil until translucent. Chop spinach and add to onions. Combine and let cool. Dice pork chops. Add meat to spinach and onions. Add cheeses, salt and pepper. Add eggs and mix all together. Divide crust in half. Roll crust and brush bottom and sides with beaten egg whites. Pour in filling. Top with other half of crust. Make a large steam hole in top (use top of juice glass to press out hole). Fold edges together tightly; stretch and press down. Roll extra dough and cut out 5 to 7 leaves with diamond cookie cutter. Use egg whites to adhere leaves to crust. Brush top of crust with egg whites. Bake at 425° for 45 minutes and let stand for 15 minutes before serving.

May make a day ahead. May be frozen.

MINIATURE BREAD OMELETTES

1 cup soft bread crumbs, crusts removed

1 cup milk

2 eggs, beaten slightly

¼ teaspoon salt

1 tablespoon butter or margarine

Mix milk and bread crumbs together and allow to soften several hours or overnight. Add salt and eggs. Mix well. Melt the butter in a large skillet. Drop the mixture by tablespoons to make 3 to 4 inch circles. When bottoms are brown, fold the two sides toward the center, overlapping a little. Turn and brown on the other side. Drizzle tops with melted butter and serve plain or with warmed maple syrup.

SAVORY EGG CASSEROLE

2 cups grated cheese (1 cup Cheddar and 1 cup Harvarti)
¼ cup butter, melted
1 cup half and half
¼ teaspoon pepper

½ teaspoon salt
2 teaspoons Dijon mustard
12 eggs, slightly beaten

Sprinkle cheese in greased 13 x 9 x 2 inch baking dish. Pour butter over cheese. Combine cream with seasonings. Pour ½ of this over cheese. Pour eggs into baking dish. Add remaining cream mixture. Bake 325° about 40 minutes until set.

CHEESE PASTRY CASSEROLE

1 package Pillsbury Crescent Rolls (refrigerator)
¼ pound Monterey Jack cheese
¼ pound Swiss cheese
¼ pound Muenster cheese
¼ pound Sharp Cheddar cheese

8 ounces Cream cheese, room temperature
1 egg, beaten slightly
¼ to ½ bunch fresh parsley, chopped
½ cup chopped sesame seeds

In an 8 inch square pan pat ½ of rolls in bottom. Pat to cover completely. Grate all hard cheeses and mix well with Cream cheese. Mix egg with parsley and add to cheese. Mix well. Spread on top of roll layer. Roll out rest of roll sections to fit pan and cover cheese mixture. Brush with melted butter and sprinkle with sesame seeds. Bake 350° for 30 minutes. Cut in 6 or 9 squares. Cook until nicely browned on top.

CHEESE CROQUETTES

Serves: 4

1 cup bread crumbs
2 tablespoons butter
2 cups sharp cheese, grated
2 eggs, beaten

½ teaspoon salt
¼ teaspoon pepper
¼ teaspoon paprika
1 teaspoon Worcestershire

Mix all together and roll into balls. Deep fry until lightly browned. Drain on paper towels. Sprinkle with paprika and serve hot. Can make ahead and refrigerate. Fry when serving.

CURRIED EGGS

8 hard boiled eggs

½ cup golden raisins

Water to cover raisins

1 tablespoon Cointreau or Grand Marnier

4 tablespoons butter

2 medium onions, roughly chopped

3 tablespoons flour

1 tablespoon curry powder

1 cup milk

1 pint half and half

1 cup toasted slivered almonds

Slice eggs in half and place in oven-proof dish. Add Cointreau or Grand Marnier to raisins covered with water and simmer 10 minutes. Drain and set aside. Saute onions in butter until translucent — about 5 minutes. Add flour and curry. Cook 4 minutes, over low heat. Add milk and half and half, continuing to stir until sauce is medium thick. Add drained raisins to cream sauce; and salt to taste. Pour sauce over eggs and sprinkle top with almonds. Decorate with snipped parsley. Can hold in 250° oven one hour or on 300° hot plate for ½ hour.

CURRIED SHRIMP

Serves: 6 to 8

1 cup butter

1 large onion, chopped

1 large apple, chopped

1 cup celery, chopped

5 tablespoons flour

2 tablespoons chutney, chopped

2 tablespoons curry powder

1 cup half and half

½ teaspoon salt

Dash of white pepper

2 cups cooked shrimp

1 pound flaked crabmeat

2½ cups chicken broth

Dash of Tabasco

In a large heavy skillet, melt butter. Saute shrimp until just cooked. Remove from pan and add more butter or chicken fat if necessary. Add apple, celery, and onion and cook gently until just tender. Sprinkle curry and flour over mixture until blended well. Remove from heat and gradually add chicken broth and lemon juice. Add cream slowly and mix well. Return to burner and cook until thick. Add salt and pepper. Add shrimp, crabmeat and chutney and simmer for 15 minutes. Do not overcook. Serve with rice and condiments of your choice.

CREAMY EGGS AND SPINACH

1 (10 ounce) package frozen chopped spinach

Dash nutmeg

1 (3 ounce) package Cream cheese

¼ to ½ teaspoon salt

Dash pepper

4 soft poached eggs

Hollandaise sauce

Cook spinach in small amount of water until barely done. Drain well and mix with Cream cheese and seasonings. Soft poach the eggs. Place on 4 nests of spinach. Pour Hollandaise over all and serve.

This can also be placed in individual ramekins. If so, put raw egg on spinach and bake at 350° for 15 minutes or until eggs are soft cooked.

Quick Hollandaise Sauce:

½ stick margarine

Juice of 1 lemon

¼ teaspoon salt

1 egg, slightly beaten

¼ cup hot water

Melt butter over low heat. Remove from heat and add egg. Beat well with fork. Add juice and water and return to burner. Cook, stirring, until thick.

GARLIC GRITS   *Serves:* 4 to 6

1½ cups quick cooking grits

½ pound sharp Cheddar, grated

1 tablespoon Worcestershire sauce

½ to 1 teaspoon Tabasco sauce

½ teaspoon garlic powder

½ stick butter

1 egg, beaten

Paprika

Cook grits according to package directions. While hot, add remaining ingredients. Place in 2 quart greased baking dish. Sprinkle with paprika. Bake 300° for 40 minutes or until firm.

DIET ICED TEA

14 regular size tea bags

2 cups boiling water

2 tablespoons Sweet and Low or Equal

½ cup fresh or frozen lemon juice

Sprigs of mint (optional)

In a ceramic glass container, brew tea in 2 cups of water for 8 minutes. (Put 4 to 6 sprigs of mint in with tea if you prefer a strong mint flavor.) In a 1 gallon pitcher put the Sweet and Low and juice. Add the hot tea (bags removed) and fill with tap water to make 1 gallon.

OLD FASHION TEA

9 tea bags
2 cups water
1¾ cups sugar

Juice of 5 lemons
4 to 6 sprigs of mint

Bring water to boil and pour over tea and sugar. Steep for 5 to 6 minutes. Remove tea bags and add lemon juice and mint. Add enough water to make 1 gallon.
You can add ½ cup Tang if desired.

ICED CINNAMON COFFEE

10 cups strong coffee (coffee cups)
¼ cup sugar

½ cup water

Boil the sugar and water for 5 minutes and chill.
Mix sugar syrup with coffee. Pour over ice. Top with whipped cream with cinnamon in it. Put stick of cinnamon in glass and serve.

KENTUCKY MILK PUNCH

2½ gallons milk (1 gallon)
1 fifth bourbon

½ gallon vanilla ice cream
Few drops almond extract

Pour all together and mix until consistency of thick eggnog. Mix no more than 30 minutes before serving.

"SALTY DOG"

For individual serving use:

5 ounces fresh grapefruit juice
1½ ounces vodka

Combine and shake well. Rim a glass with piece of lime. Dip rim in salt and let dry. Pour in juice and serve.

BLOODY MARY

46 ounces Sacramento tomato juice

½ cup fresh lemon juice

⅓ cup Worcestershire sauce

3 tablespoons black pepper, fine or coarse

5 tablespoons celery salt

Combine and shake well. Add 15 ounces Vodka and refrigerate until ready to serve.

PERFECT FRUIT DAIQUIRI

In a blender, combine:

1 can frozen limeade

1 can light rum (use limeade can)

Add 1 or 2 of the following fruits:

6 to 10 strawberries

1 banana

1 banana plus 1 peach (unpeeled)

2 unpeeled peaches

Add:

½ cup vanilla ice cream

2 to 3 tablespoons powdered sugar

Add a few pieces of ice and turn the blender on. Continue adding ice until blender is nearly full and mixture is very thick.

VARIATION: Children's Daiquiri: Omit rum from above recipe and add can of orange juice, gingerale or 7-Up.

O'HENRY'S MIMOSA COCKTAIL

Use equal portions of fresh orange juice and champagne. Serve over ice in champagne or wine glasses. Garnish with a sprig of mint.

MEATS

Andrew Johnson Birthplace, Raleigh

CROWN PORK ROAST

Seasonings:

Ground oregano   **Pepper**
Salt

Use equal amounts of the above and rub into roast which is at room temperature. Cover exposed rib tips with pieces of foil and bake at 325°. Use meat thermometer as guide.

APPLE RAISIN DRESSING

1 cup raisins   **½ teaspoon salt**
4 cups soft breadcrumbs   **½ cup onions, chopped**
3½ cups chopped apples   **½ cup butter**
1 teaspoon apple pie spice

Place raisins in boiling water for 3 to 5 minutes. Then drain and add bread crumbs, apples, apple pie spice, and salt. Saute onions in butter and add to mixture. Place in center of crown pork roast for the last 45 minutes or cook in a casserole dish for 45 minutes or until golden brown.

ROAST PORK   *Serves: 6 to 8*

3 to 4 pound pork roast   **1 or 2 medium onions, sliced**
1 teaspoon rosemary   **1 carrot, sliced**
¼ teaspoon thyme   **½ cup cider, apple juice or**
Salt and pepper   **dry white wine**
                                     Sprig of parsley

Preheat oven to 325°. Trim fat from roast if very thick. Sprinkle roast with herbs, salt, pepper and pat in seasonings. Place in casserole with carrots and parsley on one side and onions on the other. Add liquid with 1 tablespoon flour stirred in to thicken if desired. Seal casserole tightly with top or foil. This recipe works well with a cooking bag, also.

Bake at 325° for 2 to 2½ hours or until meat thermometer reads 170°.

CALIFORNIA PORK CHOPS
Serves: 4

4 thick pork chops
1½ teaspoons Kitchen Bouquet
2 tablespoons fat
2 tablespoons minced onion
1 teaspoon salt

1⅛ teaspoons marjoram
1 (3 or 4 ounce) can
    mushrooms, undrained
1 unpeeled lemon, thinly sliced
1 tablespoon flour
2 tablespoons sherry or
    vermouth

Brush chops on both sides with Kitchen Bouquet. Melt fat. Add chops and brown quickly. Sprinkle chops with onion, salt and marjoram. Cook 1 minute longer. Add mushrooms and their juice and lemon slices. Cover pan, lower heat, simmer until done. Remove chops and discard lemon. Combine flour and wine. Stir wine mixture into pan and cook, stirring until sauce thickens and is clear. Pour over chops and serve.

BAKED PORK CHOPS
WITH BARBEQUE SAUCE

8 lean chops, ¾ to 1 inch thick

Sauce:

1 cup catsup
⅓ cup Worcestershire sauce
1 teaspoon chili powder

8 slices onion and lemon

2 dashes Tabasco
2 cups water

Combine ingredients for sauce and bring to boil.
Place chops in shallow baking pan with slice of onion and lemon on each chop. Secure with toothpick. Cover with sauce and bake at 350° for 1 hour or until tender. Baste with sauce during baking and serve with sauce spooned over chops.

DIJON PORK
Serves: 4

4 thick pork chops
1 teaspoon butter
2 chopped shallots
2 teaspoons flour
⅓ cup dry white wine

½ cup chicken bouillon
½ to 1 cup heavy cream
Salt and pepper to taste
2 tablespoons Dijon mustard

Brown chops in butter; remove and keep warm. Add shallots and flour, simmering until shallots are golden. Gradually stir in wine, bouillon and cream. Add salt and pepper and stir over medium heat for 5 minutes.

Replace pork in pan, cover and simmer 10 to 15 minutes. Remove chops to heated platter and stir mustard into sauce without boiling. Pour over chops and serve.

MAPLE PORK CHOPS   *Serves: 6*

6 pork chops, 1 inch thick
2 tablespoons shortening
¼ cup onion, chopped
1 tablespoon vinegar
1 tablespoon Worcestershire sauce

½ teaspoon pepper
½ teaspoon chili powder
¼ cup maple syrup
¼ cup water
1½ teaspoons salt

Brown chops in shortening. Mix remaining ingredients and pour over chops. Cover and bake at 375° for 45 minutes, basting often. Uncover and bake 15 minutes more.

ELEGANT PORK LOIN

1 pork loin (2½ to 3 pounds) if loin is small, 2 may be tied together, 3 to 4 inches in diameter
½ pound mushrooms, washed and sliced
2 onions, chopped
2 cloves garlic, minced
1 large tomato, chopped
1 teaspoon ground ginger or fresh, if available

½ cup unsalted almonds
1 small jar gherkin pickles, sliced
1 small jar pickled onions
4 tablespoons butter
2 tablespoons Maggie seasoning
1 tablespoon dark brown sugar
Tabasco to taste

Melt butter in heavy skillet. Do not burn. Rub meat with salt, pepper, and fresh or dried ginger. When butter is very hot, add a few drops of oil and brown pork on all sides. When meat is browned, add water (enough to reach ⅓ of meat) and 2 tablespoons Maggie seasoning (liquid). Slice vegetables, fruit and pickles—not pickled onions—and add to meat and liquid. Add dark brown sugar and Tabasco to taste. Stir until well mixed. Cover and simmer on top of stove for 1½ hours, basting frequently.

Serve sliced and garnished with fruit, vegetables, pickles, onions and a little liquid.

SPARE RIBS
Serves: 2 to 4

4 pounds pork or beef spare
   ribs

1 cup chicken bouillon

3 tablespoons soy sauce

3 tablespoons catsup

3 tablespoons sugar

3 tablespoons honey

Cook ribs in boiling water for 5 minutes skimming off foam. Drain. Cut ribs apart and marinate in combined above ingredients for 2 hours.

Bake ribs in marinade for 2 to 3 hours in 350° oven turning ribs over several times. Marinade will be absorbed.

Marinate: 2 hours. Cook: 2 to 3 hours.

SPARERIBS STUFFED WITH ITALIAN SAUSAGE
Serves: 4 to 6

2 racks pork spareribs
   (5 pounds, long not baby)

¼ pound Italian sausage

2 tablespoons olive oil

1 cup zucchini squash, chopped

½ cup celery, sliced

⅓ cup onions, finely chopped

1 medium clove garlic, minced

½ cup water

1 cup tomatoes, chopped

1¼ cups herb seasoned stuffing
   mix

Marinade:

1 cup catsup

4 tablespoons brown sugar

4 tablespoons cider vinegar

2 cloves garlic, minced

1 teaspoon crushed basil

1 teaspoon dry mustard

Cook spareribs in boiling salted water for 1 hour. Drain. Brown sausage in oil and break into bits. Add zucchini, celery, onion and garlic. Cook until tender, about 7 minutes. Remove from heat. Add water, tomatoes, and stuffing mix. Toss to blend. Stuff stuffing mixture between racks and tie up. Combine remaining ingredients for marinade. Cook ribs 6 inches from hot coals for 30 minutes, basting throughout the grilling period with marinade.

TYROLEAN BEEF

Serves: 8

6 pounds beef tenderloin,
  trimmed of fat and split
  lengthwise almost through
Salt and pepper
1 clove garlic, mashed
2 tablespoons butter

1 large onion, chopped
2 carrots, chopped
½ cup celery, chopped
6 ounces diced Swiss cheese
6 ounces sliced Swiss cheese

Rub beef with salt, pepper and garlic. Saute onion, carrots and celery in butter. Heap vegetables into the beef and add diced Swiss cheese. Fold to close and secure with wooden skewers. Place in a shallow pan and roast at 400° for 40 minutes. Remove the skewers. Place the Swiss cheese slices over the beef and roast 5 additional minutes.

SKEWERED STEAK AND MUSHROOMS

Serves: 4

1 pound sirloin steak, cut into
  1½ to 2 inch cubes

12 large fresh mushrooms

Soak meat in marinade 12 hours. Place on skewers with mushrooms. Cook over hot coals, gas grill or broil until desired doneness.

Marinade for Steak Cubes:

½ cup Burgundy
1 teaspoon Worcestershire
  sauce
1 clove garlic, crushed
½ cup salad oil
2 tablespoons catsup
1 teaspoon sugar

½ teaspoon salt
½ teaspoon MSG or Accent
1 tablespoon vinegar
½ teaspoon marjoram
½ teaspoon rosemary

Mix well all of the above.

BEEF KABOBS
Serves: 6

Juice of 1½ lemons
3 tablespoons salad oil
1 medium onion, grated
1 teaspoon salt
Several grinds of black pepper
½ inch slice fresh ginger root, crushed
2 teaspoons Worcestershire sauce
1 bay leaf

1 clove garlic, crushed
½ teaspoon prepared yellow mustard
3 pounds sirloin steak
Whole fresh mushrooms
Green pepper chunks
Fresh tomato quarters
Sweet onion chunks

Combine the first 10 ingredients in a shallow bowl to form a marinade. Cut steak into 1½ inch cubes, and add with whole fresh mushrooms (stems removed, lightly rinsed, and dried) to marinade. Refrigerate at least 4 hours, turning meat and mushrooms occasionally.

On metal skewers alternate meat cubes with mushroom caps, green pepper chunks, fresh unpeeled tomato quarters, and chunks of onion. Grill over glowing coals for about 20 minutes, turning frequently and brushing with marinade. Serve over yellow rice.

FILET MIGNON WITH MUSHROOM SAUCE

6 filet mignons
6 slices toasted French bread

Butter
½ cup sherry

Saute slices of French bread in butter, turning often. Set aside and keep hot.

Quickly saute filets in hot butter for 2½ minutes on each side. Pour sherry into pan juices. When hot, add mushroom sauce. Blend. Arrange filets on toasted bread on platter. Pour a little sauce over each. Serve extra sauce in sauceboat. Serve at once.

Mushroom Sauce:

½ pound fresh mushrooms
3 tablespoons butter
Salt and pepper

½ tablespoon flour
1 cup heavy cream

Slice mushrooms, saute in butter, sprinkle with salt and pepper and ½ tablespoon flour. Stir in warm cream. Keep hot and set aside.

TERIYAKI STEAKS
WITH PINEAPPLE WEDGES
Serves: 4

2 pounds top sirloin

2 teaspoons powdered ginger or
2 tablespoons fresh ginger,
chopped

1 clove garlic, minced

1 small onion, chopped

¼ cup water

¼ cup white wine

1 fresh pineapple, cut in
quarters lengthwise, leaving
together

2 tablespoons sugar

Cut meat into 4 servings. Combine other ingredients except pineapple quarters. Pour marinade over beef and let stand 6 to 8 hours at room temperature or overnight in refrigerator. Turn beef in marinade several times. Brush pineapple with marinade and place on grill with meat. Grill 3 to 5 minutes on each side or to taste.

PEPPER BEEF
Serves: 6

3 cups hot cooked rice

1 pound lean beef round steak,
½ inch thick

1 tablespoon paprika

2 tablespoons butter

2 cloves garlic, crushed

1½ cups beef broth

1 cup sliced green onions,
including tops

2 green peppers, cut in strips

¼ cup water

2 tablespoons cornstarch

¼ cup soy sauce

2 large fresh tomatoes, cut into
eighths

Pound steak to ¼ inch thickness. Cut into ¼ inch wide strips. Sprinkle meat with paprika and allow to stand while preparing other ingredients.

Using large skillet, brown meat in butter. Add garlic and broth. Cover and simmer 30 minutes. Stir in onions and green peppers. Cover and cook 5 minutes more. Blend cornstarch, water and soy sauce. Stir into meat mixture. Cook, stirring, until clear and thickened, about 2 minutes. Add tomatoes and stir gently.

Serve over beds of fluffy rice.

Hint: Meat is easier to slice if slightly frozen.

BEEF CURRY MADRAS
Serves: 3

1 pound sirloin steak, cut into
  1 inch cubes
¼ cup vegetable oil
1 large onion, chopped
1 teaspoon garlic powder
3 green chilies, chopped

1 tablespoon curry powder
2 tablespoons tomato paste
1 cup hot water
1 tablespoon lemon juice
Salt and pepper

Brown meat in oil in skillet. Remove and set aside. Add onion, chilies, curry and garlic powder to skillet. Cook over low heat for 10 minutes. Add meat, tomato paste and water. Simmer for about 20 minutes or until meat is tender. Add lemon juice and season to taste.

Serve over rice with the following condiments:

Bacon, cooked and crumbled

Chutney

Green onion tops, chopped

Sliced bananas

Peanuts

Coconut

BEEF BRETEN
Serves: 4 to 6

3 onions, chopped
1 clove garlic, chopped
3 pounds round steak, cut in
  1 inch cubes
4 tablespoons butter
4 tablespoons flour
½ cup Burgundy wine
½ cup water

1 cup strong black coffee
2 teaspoons salt
Rosemary
Oregano
Black pepper
Toast tips

Brown onion, garlic and meat in butter. Blend in flour and liquids. Season to taste. Simmer 1 to 2 hours. Serve on toast tips.

CHILI ROJO

Serves: 4 to 6

3 pounds round steak, cut into small cubes

2 tablespoons peanut oil

4 tablespoons chili powder

3 tablespoons flour

2 tablespoons cumin

1 tablespoon oregano

3 tablespoons garlic, chopped

Salt and pepper

1½ cups beef broth

Brown meat in oil. Add remaining ingredients and cook 2 to 3 hours. If you prefer more sauce, add more broth. Serve with grated cheese and chopped onion.

MARINATED EYE OF ROUND ROAST

1 eye of round roast

Marinade:

¼ cup tarragon vinegar

1 onion, thinly sliced

2 cloves garlic, crushed

1 tablespoon meat tenderizer

2 teaspoons Accent

2 teaspoons pepper

3 tablespoons plus Worcestershire sauce

Mix all of the marinade ingredients together. Marinate roast for at least 24 hours, turning occasionally. Broil on all sides to brown. Then bake at 250° uncovered until it barely reaches rare on meat thermometer. Slice very thin. May be served hot or cold.

CHEMISTRY ROAST

1 chuck roast (about 6 pounds)

Unseasoned meat tenderizer

2 tablespoons butter

1 tablespoon sesame seeds

½ cup strong coffee, cold

½ cup soy sauce

1½ tablespoons Worcestershire sauce

1 tablespoon dry vermouth

1 large onion, chopped

Sprinkle roast with tenderizer and prick with fork all over. Toast sesame seeds in butter. Add all other ingredients and pour over roast. Refrigerate overnight, turning once.

Cook on charcoal fire, turning several times, for about 45 minutes or until done to taste. Slice and serve.

MARINATED CHUCK OR
SHOULDER ROAST

Serves: 4 to 5

**4 to 5 pounds boneless chuck
or shoulder 2 inch thick roast**

Marinade:

1 cup of cooking oil

1 cup vermouth or white wine

Garlic salt

Meat tenderizer

Oregano

Place roast in pyrex dish and let stand in marinade approximately all day or over night, turning several times. Place on grill over medium flame approximately 6 to 8 minutes per side, or under broiler flame approximately same amount of time for medium rare.
(Grilled or Broiled).

SHERRY BEEF CASSEROLE

Serves: 6

1 pound ground chuck

½ cup sliced onion

1 (16 ounce can) tomatoes

**⅔ cup pimento-stuffed green
olives, sliced**

**1 (4 ounce) can mushrooms
with liquid**

1 cup raw rice

½ cup sherry

1 cup shredded Cheddar cheese

Preheat oven to 375°. Brown meat and onion in skillet. Add tomatoes, olives, mushrooms with liquid, rice and sherry. Bring to a slow boil. Pour into a 2½ quart casserole. Cover and bake for 30 minutes. Remove cover and top with cheese. Return to oven and bake uncovered for 15 minutes.

STUFFED HAMBURGER PATTIES

Serves: 6

2 pounds ground beef

1 medium onion, chopped

1 teaspoon salt

¼ teaspoon pepper

½ teaspoon sage

1 egg, slightly beaten

½ cup milk

1 cup dry bread crumbs

Onion slices

Tomato slices

**3 tablespoons grated American
cheese**

Combine the first 8 ingredients. Shape into 12 very thin patties. On each of 6 patties place an onion slice, tomato slice, and grated American cheese. Top with remaining patties and pinch edges together. Preheat broiler while making patties. Broil 3 inches from heat for 5 to 7 minutes. Turn carefully with pancake turner and broil on other side about 7 minutes.

YUMMY BALLS
Serves: 6

1 pound ground beef
½ pound ground lean pork
1 small onion, minced
½ cup uncooked rice
½ cup cracker crumbs

1 egg
½ teaspoon salt
Pepper to taste
1 can (10 or 11 ounce) tomato soup
1 soup can water

Mix ground meats, onion, rice, cracker crumbs, egg and seasonings. Shape into balls about the size of golf balls and place in a greased casserole. Dilute the soup with the water and pour over the meat balls. Bake in a 375° oven for 1 hour.

BASIL LIVER
Serves: 2 to 3

1 pound calves liver, thinly sliced
Flour
1 stick butter

⅓ cup dry sherry or dry white wine
1 tablespoon basil

Dredge liver in flour; saute in ½ stick butter for 4 minutes on each side. Remove liver; keep warm. Add wine to pan; scrape residue from pan; add basil and remainder of butter. Stir over low heat until butter melts; pour over liver.

STEAK DIANE
Serves: 2

1 pound beef tenderloin, thinly sliced
3 tablespoons butter
1 tablespoon shallots
1 tablespoon chives

1 tablespoon parsley
1 tablespoon Worcestershire sauce
1 tablespoon A-1 sauce
Salt and pepper

Saute shallots in 2 tablespoons butter until done. Add meat and cook. Turn. Add other ingredients and cook until done as you like it. Add salt and pepper.

FILET MIGNON IN FOIL

Serves: 6

2 tablespoons butter

6 filet mignons, about 8 ounces each

12 large mushroom caps, stems reserved

¼ cup green onion, chopped

2 teaspoons cornstarch

1 cup red wine

½ cup water

2 tablespoons chopped parsley

1 teaspoon salt

Pepper

Brown filets on both sides over moderate heat in butter. Place on squares of heavy aluminum foil.

Cook chopped mushroom stems and onions in fat remaining in pan until tender. Blend in cornstarch, add wine, water, parsley, salt and pepper. Cook and stir until sauce thickens.

Spoon 2 tablespoons sauce over each filet and top with 2 mushroom crowns. Bring sides of foil up and pinch corners. Refrigerate until 30 minutes before serving. Bake at 500° for 20 minutes for rare. Reheat remaining sauce and pour over filets.

CRAB STUFFED STEAK WITH MADEIRA SAUCE

Serves: 6

4 (8 ounce) filets

8 tablespoons butter

3 sliced shallots

½ pound lump crab meat

1 tablespoon chopped chives

8 large sliced mushrooms

2 cups beef bouillon

1 cup Madeira

Slice each steak almost in half horizontally, leaving left side still together. Saute shallots in 2 tablespoons butter until soft. Add crab and chives and cook until crab is coated with butter. Spoon mixture into pockets of steak and secure with toothpicks.

Saute the mushrooms in 2 tablespoons butter until just tender and set aside.

Heat remaining butter in the skillet, and, when very hot, sear steaks quickly on both sides. Transfer steaks to a 350° oven and cook to desired doneness.

Add bouillon to skillet, scraping juices with a fork. Add mushrooms and Madeira and boil down quickly to half its original volume. Season with salt and pepper and thicken with Beurre Marie.

Place filets on heated plates. Top with sauce.

Beurre Marie Sauce:

2 tablespoons butter, softened **3 tablespoons flour**

Work butter and flour together with a fork. Drop small portions into the boiling liquid and whisk until sauce thickens. The amount of paste determines thickness of sauce.

SHERRIED SIRLOIN TIPS

3 pounds sirloin steak, well trimmed and cut into cubes

1 tablespoon margarine

1 (3 ounce) can sliced mushrooms

½ cup dry sherry

½ cup beef broth

1 teaspoon soy sauce

½ teaspoon seasoned salt

Dash pepper

1 tablespoon chopped parsley

Heat margarine in a large heavy skillet. Place cubes of meat in pan without overlapping. Brown on one side, turn and brown on the other for a few minutes or to taste.

Remove to a heated platter and keep warm. Add the mushrooms and their liquid, sherry, beef broth, soy sauce, salt, pepper and parsley.

Boil about 1 minute, scraping pan, and pour over tips. Serve over rice or toast points.

STEAK PARMIGIANA
Serves: 4 to 6

1½ pounds round steak

1 egg, slightly beaten

½ cup flour

½ cup shredded Cheddar cheese

½ cup vegetable oil

1 large onion, chopped

1 (6 ounce) can tomato paste

1 clove garlic, pressed

Salt and pepper to taste

2 cups hot water

1 cup shredded Mozzarella cheese

Cut steak, which has been flattened, into 4 to 6 pieces. Dip in beaten egg until coated evenly. In a small, shallow dish, combine flour and Cheddar cheese. Dredge steak in cheese mixture.

In an electric skillet, heat oil. Brown steak for 2 to 3 minutes on each side. Place in a 13 x 9 x 2 inch greased casserole.

Saute onion in remaining oil in skillet. Stir in tomato paste, garlic, salt, pepper and water. Simmer 10 minutes. Pour over steak. Top with Mozzarella cheese. Cover and bake at 350° for 1 hour. Serve with noodles.

BEEF PATTIES PARMESAN

1 pound ground beef
½ cup Bisquick
⅓ cup tomato juice
¼ cup green pepper, finely chopped
1 egg, slightly beaten
1 small clove garlic, minced

1 teaspoon salt
½ teaspoon oregano
Dash pepper
½ teaspoon Worcestershire
Parmesan cheese
Green olives

Combine all but last 2 ingredients. Shape 4 patties and place in greased shallow baking pan. Bake at 400° for 20 minutes. Remove from oven and sprinkle each patty with 2 tablespoons Parmesan cheese and garnish with olive slices.

Can be served on buttered noodles.

TEXAS MEAT LOAF

Serves: 8

2 pounds lean ground beef
3 tablespoons parsley
3 tablespoons onion, finely chopped
3 tablespoons celery leaves, finely chopped
½ teaspoon pepper

1⅓ teaspoons salt
¼ teaspoon paprika
1 garlic clove, minced
½ cup dry breadcrumbs, moistened with ⅔ cup red wine

Sauce:

1 cup catsup
2 teaspoons chili powder
¼ teaspoon pepper
¼ cup red wine vinegar

2 garlic cloves, minced
2 tablespoons Worcestershire
1 teaspoon salt

Mix ingredients together thoroughly and form into a loaf. Place in baking dish and cover with sauce.

Bake at 325° for 1¼ hours basting frequently. (For a more subtle flavor, baste only once.)

IMPERIAL GOULASH

Serves: 15 to 20

8 pounds beef chuck cut into
  1 to 1½ inch cubes

1½ cups flour mixed with
  1 tablespoon salt, 1 teaspoon
  pepper, and ½ teaspoon
  savory

Butter or margarine for
  browning

2 pounds onions, peeled and
  sliced

2 pounds fresh mushrooms,
  sliced

2 cloves crushed garlic

1 teaspoon salt

¼ teaspoon pepper

½ teaspoon savory

¼ teaspoon oregano

2 to 3 tablespoons paprika

2 cups red Burgundy

1 cup sour cream

Dredge beef cubes in seasoned flour. Melt about 4 tablespoons butter in bottom of large heavy kettle and begin browning meat; continue until all meat is browned, adding more butter as needed. Drain beef on paper towels. Add more butter to kettle and saute onions, mushrooms and garlic until tender. Return meat to kettle, season with salt, pepper, savory, oregano. Sprinkle with paprika. Add 1 cup Burgundy, cover kettle, simmer slowly, stirring occasionally for about 3 hours (until meat is fork tender). Add more wine as needed to keep mixture from getting too thick. Just before serving, stir in sour cream.

Goulash gets better on standing.

CHINESE PEPPER STEAK

Serves: 4

1 pound round steak

4 tablespoons corn oil

2 green peppers, coarsely
  chopped

1 cup celery, chopped

2 tablespoons pimento, diced

½ cup onions, diced

1 cup beef broth or bouillon
  cube dissolved in hot water

½ teaspoon salt

½ teaspoon pepper

2 tablespoons cornstarch

¼ cup water

2 tablespoons soy sauce

Cut beef into small, thin slices. Season with the salt and pepper. Heat oil in large skillet and brown meat for 5 minutes. Add broth and simmer for 30 minutes. Add peppers, celery, pimento and onions. Cook until tender (about 15 minutes). Add cornstarch, water and soy sauce and stir until thick. Serve over rice with Chinese noodles.

LIVER BAKED WITH ONIONS

Serves: 6

2 pounds calves liver

1 large onion, sliced

Flour

Salt and pepper to taste

2 tablespoons minced parsley

1 bay leaf

1 (4 ounce) can sliced mushrooms, drained

4 tablespoons melted butter

¼ cup beef bouillon

2 tablespoons dry red wine

Place half the onion slices in bottom of lightly greased 2 quart casserole. Season liver with salt and pepper and dredge in flour. Place liver on onion slices and sprinkle with parsley. Place bay leaf on top. Cover liver with sliced mushrooms and remaining onion slices. Season with a little more salt and pepper. Pour butter over. Pour bouillon and red wine over. Cover and bake at 350° for 30 minutes. Uncover and bake for 30 minutes longer, or until liver is done.

VEAL AU CITRON

Serves: 12

2 veal scallops per person (24 veal scallops)

3 tablespoons olive oil

3 tablespoons butter

¼ cup fresh lemon juice

1¼ cups heavy cream

1 teaspoon salt

½ teaspoon white pepper

½ avocado per person

Bring oil and butter to a sizzle in a saute pan. Dust scallops with flour and lightly cook. (No more than 30 seconds per veal scallop.) Remove from pan and deglaze pan with lemon juice. To this add heavy cream, salt, pepper. Bring to boil and reduce by ¼. Add veal scallops and slices of ripe avocado. Heat over medium low temperature for 5 minutes and serve.

LEMON VEAL

Serves: 4

1 pound thin veal scallops

2 tablespoons flour

Salt and pepper to taste

1 chicken bouillon cube, crushed

1 tablespoon olive oil

1 tablespoon butter or margarine

¼ cup white wine

3 tablespoons water

2 tablespoons parsley, snipped

½ lemon, thinly sliced

154

Pound veal very thin. Pound in a mixture of flour, salt, pepper and bouillon granules. Heat oil and butter until very hot in large skillet sprayed with cooking spray. Quickly brown veal (1 to 2 minutes per side). Remove veal to a warm platter. Add wine and water to skillet and cook 1 to 2 minutes, loosening cooked bits in pan. Mix in parsley, lemon slices and veal; heat through. Serve with sauce poured over and garnish with lemon slices.

SWISS STYLE VEAL

1 pound boneless veal, from
  the leg

Salt and pepper to taste

3 tablespoons corn oil

¼ cup butter

2 tablespoons shallots, finely
chopped

¼ cup dry white wine

½ cup chicken stock

1 cup heavy cream

1 tablespoon minced parsley

Cut veal into ½ inch cubes. Sprinkle with salt and pepper. Heat oil to almost smoking in skillet and add veal. Stir rapidly, for meat will cook quickly and should not brown. Transfer meat to serving dish with a slotted spoon.

Immediately wipe skillet clean and add butter. When it is foaming, add shallots and stir. Do not brown. Add wine and reduce stock by half. Add liquid accumulated from meat, but do not add meat. Simmer for 1 minute, then add heavy cream. Simmer again for 1 minute, add meat and salt and pepper to taste. Bring to a boil and serve hot, with chopped parsley.

LOW CALORIE VEAL PARMESAN   *Serves: 4*

1 (8 ounce) can tomato sauce

1 teaspoon basil

¼ teaspoon salt

1 bay leaf

1 egg beaten

¼ cup bread crumbs

¼ cup Parmesan cheese

3 tablespoons olive oil

4 slices Mozzarella cheese

4 veal cutlets

Simmer first 4 ingredients in a saucepan while preparing veal. Dip each cutlet in beaten egg, then in bread crumbs mixed with Parmesan cheese. Brown on both sides in olive oil. Put into oven pan and pour sauce mixture over veal (removing bay leaf). Top each cutlet with a square of Mozzarella cheese. Cook 15 minutes at 350°.

GROUND VEAL PATTIES WITH
SLICED POTATOES AND HERBS

Serves: 6

1½ pounds (about 3 cups)
   ground lean veal

1 medium size onion, peeled
   and chopped

¾ teaspoon salt

Pepper to taste

½ teaspoon mixed herbs such
   as thyme, oregano and sage
   or Italian seasoning

Either 4 tablespoons soft butter
   or 2 ounces Cream cheese

2/3 cup lightly pressed
   down, fresh white bread
   crumbs moistened with
   3 tablespoons milk

1 egg

Flour

Olive oil or cooking oil

Puree the soaked bread crumbs with the egg in food processor with steel blade (or force together through coarse sieve). Add the meat, salt, pepper, herbs, and butter (or Cream cheese). Mix well until meat looks fluffy. Make 6 oval patties about ½ inch thick. Dredge patties in flour, shaking off excess. Brown them a minute or so on each side in a large pan with a 1/16 inch layer of oil heated to very hot but not smoking. Set aside until ready to assemble.

3 or 4 medium size all purpose
   potatoes, peeled, halved
   lengthwise, cut crosswise,
   into ⅜ inch thick slices

1 medium size onion, peeled
   and finely chopped

2 tablespoons butter

Salt and pepper

About 1 cup fresh tomato
   pulp (tomatoes peeled,
   seeded, juiced, chopped) or
   canned and drained sliced
   tomatoes

¼ teaspoon mixed herbs, same
   as veal

½ cup chopped black olives

¼ cup chopped fresh parsley

⅓ cup diced Swiss cheese

Into a quart of boiling water which has 1½ teaspoons of salt added, drop potato slices. Bring rapidly back to boil and boil 1 minute. Drain and shake dry. In a frying pan, melt the butter, add the potatoes and toss about. Add a sprinkling of salt and pepper, the finely chopped onion, the tomatoes, herbs and olives, and continue to toss over heat for several minutes until ingredients are mixed well. Remove from heat and toss with parsley and cheese.

Divide the potato mixture in half. Spread ½ over the bottom of a greased casserole (about 2 quart). Place the patties on top, and cover with the remaining potatoes. Cover with foil and bake in the middle level of a preheated 375° oven until foil is puffed with cooking steam.

BUTTERFLY LEG OF LAMB
ON GRILL
Serves: 6 to 8

6 to 8 pound leg of lamb boned and butterflied by butcher.

Place lamb in bottom of broiler pan and cover with marinade below. Leave in marinade all day.

Marinade:

2 cups of oil

1 cup white wine

Juice of 2 lemons

Garlic salt

2 to 3 teaspoons of oregano or Italian seasonings

Place on medium flame of charcoal grill, placing skin side down for 15 minutes. Turn to meat side for 20 to 25 minutes, depending on thickness of meat. Slice diagonally. Flavor of lamb is diminished after charcoaled.

LAZY LAMB STEW
Serves: 5 to 6

2 pounds lamb, cubed

1 can tiny peas

1 cup sliced carrots

2 medium size chopped onions

½ teaspoon salt

Dash of pepper

1 can cream of mushroom soup thinned with ½ can of water

2 large peeled potatoes, cubed

1 bay leaf

Several stalks celery, each cut in 3 pieces

Mix the above ingredients in a casserole and cover with lid. Put in 275° oven and cook for 5 hours.

RACK OF LAMB PERSILLE

2 racks of lamb

¾ cup bread crumbs

1 stick butter

¼ cup minced parsley

1 teaspoon minced garlic

½ teaspoon thyme

Mix all ingredients except lamb in skillet and heat for 3 to 4 minutes. Do not let bread crumbs brown. Reserve mixture.

Season lamb with salt and pepper and saute with 2 tablespoons butter for 5 to 6 minutes. Arrange in heavy baking pan. Pat crumb mixture firmly into browned lamb and place in 425° preheated oven for 12 to 18 minutes depending on taste. Remove from oven and let rest for 5 to 10 minutes prior to serving. Serve with Bearnaise Sauce.

LAMB SKISH KABOBS

Serves: 6

3 pounds lamb (from the leg)

Cut 3 pounds of tender lamb into 1½ inch cubes. Marinate in the refrigerator for 2 hours or more in the marinade.

Marinade:

Juice of 2 large lemons

4 tablespoons olive or vegetable oil

2 tablespoons grated onion

½ to 1 tablespoon ground chili powder

1 teaspoon ground ginger

1 teaspoon curry powder

2 teaspoons salt

1 clove garlic, crushed

On metal skewers alternate meat with similarly sized chunks of tomato, onion, green pepper and mushroom caps. Broil on charcoal grill, turning frequently and brushing with marinade.

ORANGE-GLAZED HAM

Cooked ham slices

1 (6 ounce) can frozen orange juice

3 tablespoons cognac

4 tablespoons prepared mustard

4 tablespoons brown sugar

3 heaping tablespoons orange marmalade

Place ham in pan. Mix together all other ingredients and pour over ham. Bake at 350° 30 to 45 minutes. Baste during cooking.

SAUSAGE AND
POTATO CASSEROLE

Serves: 4 to 6

5 links sweet Italian sausage

1 medium green pepper, chopped

2 medium onions, chopped

4 to 5 potatoes, cut in bite size portions

Parsley

Basil

Salt and pepper

Cover bottom of oblong baking pan with about ½ inch of water. Place over low heat and add sausage. Poke holes in sausage and simmer for 15 minutes. Add pepper, onions and potatoes. Add a little more water if needed. Simmer 5 minutes. Sprinkle with parsley, basil, salt and pepper. Cover and bake at 350° for 1 hour and 15 minutes.

ITALIAN SWEET
SAUSAGE IN BUNS

Serves: 4

2 pounds Italian sweet sausage links

2 to 3 large bell peppers

2 to 3 large onions

In a large skillet or electric fry pan, place sausage links. Slice rings of bell pepper and rings of onions on top of sausage. Place lid on and cook over moderate heat until all are done, approximately 15 minutes, or longer if necessary, pouring off some of liquid during cooking time. Warm large rolls or buns and put approximately 2 links with onion and pepper on top of each bun. Serve immediately for quick supper.

TORTILLA DOGS

Hot dogs

Sliced cheese

Thick corn tortillas, thawed

Vegetable oil

Slit the hot dogs, lengthwise, halfway through and stuff with cheese. Wrap the thawed tortillas around hot dogs and secure with a toothpick. Fry in hot oil until cheese is melted and tortilla is crisp.

HAM AND
NOODLE CASSEROLE

Serves: 10 to 12

6 cups cooked ham

2 (10 ounce) packages frozen
  peas

1 cup chopped celery

1 cup canned mushrooms,
  drained

¾ pound extra fine noodles,
  cooked and drained (about 6
  cups)

½ cup butter

½ cup flour

2 cups half and half

2 cups milk

1 cup chicken broth

¾ cup Cheddar cheese, grated

½ cup grated Parmesan

2 tablespoons lemon juice

3 tablespoons onion, grated

1 teaspoon dry mustard

2 tablespoons finely chopped
  parsley

1 to 2 teaspoons salt

¼ teaspoon crushed rosemary

½ teaspoon savory

⅛ teaspoon cayenne pepper

1 cup mayonnaise

Cut ham into 1 inch cubes. Cook peas until tender but still crisp. Drain.
Add celery and mushrooms to peas. Set aside. Prepare noodles and set
aside.

In a saucepan, melt butter and blend in flour. Slowly add the half and
half, milk and broth. Cook until thickened, stirring constantly. Add the
cheeses and lemon juice. Season with the onion, mustard, parsley, salt
rosemary, savory and pepper. Remove sauce from heat and stir in
mayonnaise. Mix sauce with ham and noodles.

Arrange layers of the ham mixture and vegetables in a 4 quart casserole
or in 2 (2 quart) casseroles; top with the ham mixture.

Bake uncovered, at 350° for 30 minutes or until bubbly.

Can make ahead.

POULTRY & GAME

Zebulon Vance Birthplace, Weaverville

ROASTING CHART

	TEMPERATURE	COOKING TIME	SERVINGS
Grouse	375	25 to 35 minutes	1 or 2
Quail	375	25 to 35 minutes	1
Squab	375	45 to 55 minutes	1
Pheasant	375	1 hour 15 minutes	2
Partridge	375	45 to 55 minutes	1 or 2
Wild Duck	325	1½ to 2 hours	1 to 2
Wild Goose	325	2½ to 3 hours	4 to 6

Preheat oven. Sprinkle inside with salt; place 1 lemon slice, 1 bay leaf and 3 celery tops in cavity. Tie legs together, then sprinkle with paprika and onion or garlic salt, if desired.

Place bird on rack in open roasting pan. Cover legs and breast with 3 to 4 bacon slices. Roast for time indicated until bird is tender and legs can be moved easily. Serve with sauce, as follows:

Sauce:

½ cup red currant jelly
½ cup port wine

½ teaspoon Worcestershire
¼ cup catsup

Combine all ingredients ten minutes before serving. Place in small saucepan over low heat. Cook until smooth, stirring constantly. Yield: 1 cup.

GRILLED DOVE BREASTS

16 dove breasts, cleaned and skinned (or duck breasts)

6 tablespoons butter

1 tablespoon red wine

Run long skewers sideways through breasts using right number to fit grill. Have coals hot. Heat butter and wine. Brush on breasts. Cook, turning and basting until cooked medium rare, about 20 minutes. Serve hot.

DOVE AND SAUSAGE GUMBO   *Serves: 8*

15 dove breasts

1 (10½ ounce) can consomme

1 beef bouillon cube

½ cup vegetable oil

½ cup flour

1½ cup finely chopped onion

2 stalks celery, finely chopped

2 tablespoons Worcestershire sauce

2 cloves garlic, minced

1 to 2 bay leaves

Hot cooked rice (brown, wild or combination)

½ teaspoon dried basil

¼ teaspoon poultry seasoning

¼ teaspoon freshly ground pepper

⅛ teaspoon ground red pepper

⅛ teaspoon ground allspice

⅛ teaspoon ground cloves

½ pound smoked sausage, cut into ¼ inch slices

¼ cup dry red wine

⅛ teaspoon hot sauce

Place dove breasts in Dutch oven and cover with water. Boil about 10 minutes. Cool and remove meat from bones. Reserve cooking liquid in Dutch oven, adding water if necessary to make 2¼ cups. Set meat aside.

Add consomme and bouillon cube to Dutch oven. Cook until bouillon cube is dissolved.

Brown dove in hot oil in large skillet; drain well. Pour off all but ¼ cup oil. Add flour to oil; cook over medium heat, stirring constantly until roux is color of a copper penny, about 10 to 15 minutes.

Gradually add about 1½ cups of consomme mixture to roux; cook over medium heat, stirring constantly, until thickened and bubbly. Stir in onion and celery and cook about 5 minutes or until vegetables are tender. Add roux mixture to remaining consomme mixture, and stir well. Stir in next 9 ingredients.

Boil sausage in ¼ inch of water and pour off liquid. Brown, and drain well. Stir sausage and dove into roux mixture; simmer 1½ hours, stirring occasionally. Add wine and hot sauce, stir well. Remove bay leaves, and serve gumbo over rice. Yield: about 1¾ quarts.

DOVE OR QUAIL CHASSEUR

8 doves

½ stick butter

Garlic slivers

2 tablespoons flour

¾ cup canned beef bouillon

¾ cup dry white wine

½ teaspoon thyme

1 tablespoon tomato paste

Salt and pepper to taste

Wild rice

Brown doves in butter. Add garlic slivers to the butter and sprinkle the doves with flour. Let cook a few more minutes and add bouillon, wine, thyme, tomato paste, salt and pepper to taste.

You can prepare it ahead to this point. Before serving, simmer about 15 to 20 minutes. Serve with wild rice.

QUAIL

6 quail (split down back)

6 tablespoons butter

1½ cups mushrooms, chopped

½ cup onion, chopped

¼ cup butter

1 cup consomme or beef bouillon

¾ cup wine

⅔ cup orange juice

Salt and pepper quail and roll in flour. Brown in butter for about 10 minutes. Remove and saute onions and mushrooms in same pan. Do not brown. Add browned quail, then consomme and wine. Cover and simmer 30 to 45 minutes or until tender. (This may be done in oven or top of stove.) Add orange juice and heat to boiling. Serve with wild rice. Spoon gravy over quail.

QUAIL WITH WHITE WINE   *Serves 8*

8 quail

½ cup margarine

2 cups sliced mushrooms

½ cup chopped onion

½ cup dry white wine

2 tablespoons lemon juice

Salt and pepper

Brown quail in margarine and remove. Saute mushrooms and onion in margarine. Place quail, mushrooms and onion in shallow pan and cover with heavy duty foil. Bake at 350° for 1 hour. The last fifteen minutes of cooking time, remove foil. Combine wine, lemon juice, salt and pepper and baste often. Serve over wild rice.

Preparation time: 1 hour, 30 minutes.

ROAST DUCK

Serves: 2

1 (5 pound) duckling
Salt and pepper
Lemon juice
Celery leaves

1 onion, sliced
1½ cups dry white wine
1 tablespoon honey

Wash duckling thoroughly inside and out with cold water, dry it and sprinkle with salt and pepper. Rub the cavity with lemon juice and insert a few celery leaves and the onion. Prick the skin. Place the duckling, breast side up, on rack in a roasting pan and cook in moderately slow heated over (325°) for ½ hour.

Drain the fat from pan, add 1½ cups wine and continue to roast, basting often, until tender. Allow 30 minutes cooking time per pound.

Brush duck with honey 15 minutes before taking from oven for crisp skin.

Excellent with brandied kumquats as follows:

12½ ounce jar preserved
kumquats

2 tablespoons brandy

Half hour before duckling is done, heat kumquats in their syrup, allowing the syrup to reduce slightly. Drain syrup from kumquats and add brandy. Pour off the fat from the pan juices. Add kumquat syrup and baste duck frequently until done.

Arrange duck on platter. Pour sauce over and garnish with kumquats.

DUCKS IN FOIL

1 medium or large wild duck
Salt
1 apple, cored and quartered
¼ cup honey
1 tablespoon butter

¼ cup orange juice
1 teaspoon orange peel
¼ teaspoon basil leaves
¼ teaspoon ginger

Prick skin of fatty ducks with fork. Salt inside and out of duck and stuff with apple. Heat rest of the ingredients in small saucepan until butter melts. Place duck on piece of foil large enough to wrap. Pour liquid in cavity and on outside of duck. Cover duck with foil and seal with double fold. Place in shallow pan, cook at 425° for 1½ hours or until tender. Open foil and roast 10 to 15 minutes until brown. Remove and discard apple Skim fat from gravy before serving.

ROAST DUCK WITH ORANGE SAUCE

Duck (½ per person if large duck such as mallard; 1 per person if small duck such as teal)

Onions

Oranges

Bacon

Red wine

Salt and pepper

Place duck breast side up in roasting pan. Stuff each duck with ½ onion and ¼ orange. Cut a strip of bacon in half and place 2 strips over breasts of each duck. Salt and pepper.

Pour red wine to cover bottom of pan well. Cook covered at 400° for 30 minutes. Uncover, baste with pan juices and cook 15 minutes or until brown.

Duck will be pink, tender and juicy.

Sauce:

1¼ cup stock or canned chicken broth

2 tablespoons butter

1 teaspoon grated onion

2 tablespoons flour

¼ teaspoon salt

⅛ teaspoon pepper

1 bay leaf

2 whole cloves

Generous dash of powdered ginger or to taste

4 tablespoons concentrated frozen orange juice

Melt butter and add onion. Stir in flour. Add broth, seasonings and orange juice. Cook until thick.

Slice meat off duck and pour orange sauce over and serve. Do not discard crisp bacon. It's delicious added to duck and sauce.

Makes enough sauce for 2 ducks.

WILD DUCK IN CREAM

2 to 3 wild ducks

Salt to taste

1 cup flour

1 stick butter

Light cream to cover ducks

Sprinkle ducks inside and out with salt, truss and dust with flour. In a heavy casserole, brown ducks on all sides in butter. Add enough boiling cream to cover ducks. Simmer, covered at 350° for 1 hour 40 minutes or until almost tender. Remove cover and simmer for 20 minutes. Good for doves and quail.

WILD DUCK STROGANOFF

**8 duck breasts, cleaned,
skinned, and sliced thinly**

1 medium onion, grated

3 tablespoons butter

In a large skillet, melt butter. Add meat and onions. Stir and cook over medium heat until just cooked. Remove to bowl.

**1 pound fresh mushrooms,
sliced**

1 onion, sliced

3 tablespoons butter

Melt butter in skillet. Add mushrooms and onions and cook over high heat, stirring constantly until moisture has evaporated. Add to duck breasts.

6 tablespoons flour

2 cups half and half

1 cup sour cream

1 teaspoon salt

**½ teaspoon freshly ground
pepper**

¼ teaspoon nutmeg

2 tablespoons white wine

Combine flour with ¼ cup cooled juice from ducks. Cook for 2 minutes over medium heat. Add half and half, salt and pepper and nutmeg. Cook and stir until thickened. Simmer for 5 minutes. Add wine and sour cream to hot mixture just before serving. Keep hot but do not boil. Serve with wild rice.

ROAST DUCKS WITH APRICOTS   *Serves: 6*

3 ducks (about 2 pounds each)

Salt

Pepper

¼ cup butter or margarine

1 can (1 pound) whole apricots

½ cup water

Heat oven to 425°. Wipe ducks dry with paper towels. Sprinkle insides with salt and pepper. Brush with butter or margarine. Place birds on a rack in large, shallow roasting pan. Roast 15 minutes. Pour off fat from pan. Roast 15 minutes more, basting frequently with juice from can of apricots. (Wild duck is usually cooked rare or medium rare, never well done which will toughen it.) Remove birds to serving platter. Arrange apricots around ducks. Discard fat from pan. Add water to pan. Bring to boiling. Season to taste. Strain into sauceboat. Garnish platter with watercress, if desired.

DUCK WITH BARBEQUE SAUCE

2 whole ducks

Sauce:

½ pound butter	**Ground pepper to taste**
½ cup catsup	**1 teaspoon salt**
1 tablespoon sugar	**1 clove pressed garlic**
1½ tablespoons lemon juice	**1 small onion, chopped**
1 tablespoon Worcestershire sauce	**½ teaspoon Tabasco**

Split 2 whole ducks in half and flatten with cleaver. Place on rack in large flat pan and bake at 375° for 1 hour. Baste every 10 minutes with barbeque sauce. Turn and cook other sides for 1 hour.

For sauce: Mix the above ingredients and simmer covered for 5 minutes. Makes enough sauce for 4 halves.

BURGUNDY GOOSE STEW

Goose, cooked and cubed	**Butter**
2 medium onions, sliced	**1½ cups Burgundy**
Flour	

Bake goose as in Wild Goose recipe; then cut into cubes as for creamed chicken. Cook 2 medium onions until soft (not brown). Add flour to onions and butter, and stir in liquid from pan until thick and smooth. Add goose and 1½ cups of Burgundy wine.

WILD GOOSE I

1. Stuff goose with 2 onions and 2 apples. Cover with bacon strips. Brown in 450° oven.

2. Take fat from pan and discard.

3. Add to pan, 1 onion, 1 carrot, 1 bay leaf, a little thyme, stalk of celery, 2 or 3 sprigs of parsley and 2 cans consomme with 2 cans water. Also, add about 1 cup of red wine.

4. Cover pan and roast at 375° for 2½ hours, basting often. Strain gravy and thicken with 1 tablespoon cornstarch mixed with 2 tablespoons cold water.

5. Choice part is the leg, so eat that yourself and give your guests the breast!

WILD GOOSE II

4 pound goose	1 can sherry
2 cans clear consomme	Salt and pepper
2 cans water	Arrowroot or flour

Place goose on rack in open roaster. Open 2 cans clear consomme; pour over goose. Pour water into roaster; pour sherry over bird. Salt and pepper goose well, then turn breast side down on rack. Bake at 350° for 2½ hours, or until goose is tender, basting every 15 minutes. If you are busy and cannot baste that often, cover with top. (Open pan method is preferred.) Should be rare.

Add arrowroot (or flour) to drippings for gravy.

ROAST PHEASANT

2 pheasants	⅓ cup all purpose flour (to dust breast)
4 shallots, cut in quarters	
4 sprigs fresh celery leaf	4 thin slices of fatback, enough to cover both pheasants
1 cup Cognac	
6 tablespoons salted butter (room temperature)	6 white peppercorns
	Salt to taste
½ cup dry sherry	

Dry pheasants inside and out with paper towels. Brush the insides with Cognac and insert some salt, sprigs of celery leaf, 1 tablespoon of salted butter, shallots and peppercorns. Truss each pheasant. Brush all over the outside with butter.

Place the pheasants on a rack in a roasting pan. Dust the tops lightly with flour. Cover the breasts with thin slices of fatback. Pour a little Cognac into the roasting pan and roast pheasants about 60 minutes in a 350° oven. Baste them after 10 minutes, first with 3 tablespoons Cognac, then with 3 tablespoons dry sherry, and an equal amount of water. Repeat a second time after 10 minutes. Then turn pheasants over on their breasts and continue roasting for 15 minutes. Then turn pheasants' breasts up again and remove the fatback. Brush breasts with melted butter and continue roasting. Baste again before the allotted time is up.

To make sure they are ready, the thermometer should read 150°. Be careful not to overcook.

To serve, remove the string ties from the pheasants. Serve whole or cut in quarters.

VENISON ROAST, TIPS ON COOKING

1. Always serve piping hot on heated plates and keep the "seconds" hot. This is important. If venison becomes slightly cooled, the fat turns hard and some of the taste of the meat is lost.
2. Venison always becomes a little dry while roasting. Some of this dryness can be avoided by adding butter in place of most of the fat, which should be trimmed off.
3. In the case of steaks and chops, never overcook. Serve them rare if possible. If you must have them well-done, stop cooking the second the juices stop flowing. Always spoon a little gravy over the meat on the serving platter or pour on the pan juices.
4. Always cook venison in something tart such as wine, lemon juice or sour cream. This doesn't make the meat sour. It enhances the flavor, preserves the juices and tenderizes the meat.

VENISON POT ROAST

3 to 4 pound roast   **1 small can mushrooms**
½ cup Cherry Kijafa   **3 tablespoons cornstarch**
Butter   **1 tablespoon poppy seeds**
1 package dry onion soup

Use a sheet of aluminum foil large enough to wrap roast completely making sure it will catch all juices. Place the roast on the foil, sprinkle the dry onion soup on top. Mix and dot with butter. Sprinkle ¼ cup Cherry Kijafa over all. Place the foil wrapped roast in a pan and cover the pan. Bake for 3 hours at 300° or 6 hours at 200°.

When the roasting time is up, the meat will be tender and falling apart and very brown. Place it on a hot platter. Pour juices from the foil into the pan. Rinse foil with ¼ cup Cherry Kijafa so that all juices from the foil are caught and pour into pan. Place foil over meat to keep warm.

Add 1½ cups of water and 1 small can of mushrooms plus their juice to the pan. Mix the cornstarch with a little cold water. Heat juices to boil and stir in cornstarch mixture. Keep stirring and boiling until gravy becomes thick and smooth. Slice roast, as venison rarely is pretty enough to serve as a whole roast. Spoon part of gravy over meat. Put remainder of gravy into a hot dish.

Serve over hot buttered noodles to which you have added 1 tablespoon poppy seeds.

VENISON STEW I

Serves 6

3 to 4 pounds venison round
    roast
4 tablespoons butter
4 tablespoons flour
1½ teaspoons salt
2 cups stock or canned bouillon
3 cups hot water

1 onion, peeled and sliced
6 peppercorns
2 cloves
1 bay leaf
Juice of ½ lemon
1 cup red wine

Trim meat of all fat. Rinse and wipe dry. Cut into serving size pieces.
Heat butter in Dutch oven, stir in flour and cook until browned.

Add salt, stock, hot water; stir well. To mixture add onions,
peppercorns, cloves, bay leaf, lemon juice. Bring to boil and cook 5
minutes. Put in meat and cover pot. Boil gently 1½ hours.

Add wine and mix with gravy in pot; cook 15 minutes. If too thin,
reduce liquid to ½ its amount by boiling. Use as gravy on venison.

Serve with potato dumplings or hot buttered noodles.

VENISON STEW II

Serves: 6

3 pounds venison (round or
    shoulder roast)
Red wine
½ cup flour
Olive oil
3 celery stalks, sliced

3 sliced onions
4 sliced carrots
1 pound canned Italian
    tomatoes, drained and
    chopped
2 tablespoons Worcestershire
    sauce

Marinate venison overnight or 24 hours in red wine. Do not discard
wine.

Cut meat into serving size pieces. Lightly coat venison with flour, salt
and pepper (fresh ground) and brown meat in olive oil. Add sliced onions
and celery, and brown.

Add tomatoes, carrots, wine marinade and Worcestershire sauce to
meat, celery and onions.

Cover and cook slowly for 1½ hours or until meat is tender.

Serve with buttered noodles and crisp green salad.

VENISON

3 pounds venison	Pinch rosemary
½ cup vinegar	1 cup water
¼ cup water	¼ cup flour
Salt and pepper to taste	¼ cup melted butter
2 cups celery, chopped	¼ cup red wine
2 cups onions, chopped	1 cup sour cream

Marinate venison all day in vinegar, salt, pepper and water. Drain and put in casserole dish with celery, onions, rosemary and water. Braise 2 hours in 350° oven. Remove venison; slice, keep warm, drain stock. Blend flour and butter and add to stock and cook, stirring until thick. Stir in wine and sour cream and pour over venison.

VENISON, MOOSE OR ELK ROAST

Serves: 6 to 8

2 tablespoons plain flour	1 bay leaf
1 cup dry red wine	8 whole cloves
3 to 4 pounds venison roast	1 medium onion, diced
Salt	1 teaspoon thyme

Preheat oven to 325°. Place flour in small (10 x 16 inch) oven cooking bag and shake until bag is well coated.

Place bag in 2 inch deep roasting pan. Pour wine into bag and stir until well-mixed with flour. Rub roast with salt. Put meat into bag. Add bay leaf, cloves, onion and thyme around meat. Close bag with twist.

Cook two hours or longer until tender. Liquid in bag is ready to use as gravy, or you may thicken with flour as you desire.

This may be cooked in the microwave on low for 1 hour. Be sure to use a tender cut.

LIGHT RANCH VENISON

Deer loin sliced ¼ to ½ inch thick

Marinate for 1 day in:

Wine vinegar	**Salt**
Fresh lime juice	**Pepper**
Paprika	

Roll in flour and fry.

DUCK OR VENISON
WILD GAME CASSEROLE

Pressure cook game: Ducks for 15 minutes or venison for 1 hour, depending on game and size. Remove meat from bone. Boil down broth. Need about 2 pounds of meat.

Cook half brown and half wild rice: 1 cup rice to 1½ cups water until absorbed.

To rice add meat, 1 cup sauteed fresh mushrooms, 1 can cream of chicken soup, broth, sour cream, salt and pepper. Combine well and add more broth if too dry.

Put in casserole with buttered bread crumbs on top. Cook at 350° for 25 minutes.

FLORIDA AVOCADO CASSEROLE   *Serves: 8*

1 (6 pound) hen	1 tablespoon salt
1 medium onion, chopped	¼ teaspoon black pepper
Several sprigs of celery	

Quarter hen and simmer until tender in a large pot with 1 quart water, onion, celery, salt and black pepper. Remove from broth and cool. Take meat from bones except wings and neck; put those back in broth and simmer slowly for ½ hour, for good strong stock. Strain stock and cool. Skim off excess fat.

4 tablespoons butter	Pinch of rosemary
6 tablespoons flour	Pinch of basil
2 cups stock	Dash of hot pepper sauce
2 cups light cream	2 ripe avocados, diced
½ cup sharp cheese, grated	½ cup toasted slivered almonds
½ teaspoon salt	

In a saucepan, melt butter. Blend in flour, stir in stock and light cream. Stir until thickened. Add cheese, salt, pinch of rosemary and basil, and a dash of hot pepper sauce.

In bottom of casserole, place chicken and ½ pound sliced mushrooms that have been sauteed in butter. Sprinkle lightly with salt and pepper. Pour sauce over and bake for 25 minutes in a 350° oven.

Remove casserole from oven, add avocados. Return to oven and cook covered for 10 to 15 minutes until avocado is warmed through. Just before serving, sprinkle top with toasted slivered almonds.

CHICKEN PRONTO   *Serves: 4*

8 boneless chicken breast halves	⅓ cup Italian-seasoned dry bread crumbs
¼ bottled Italian dressing	

Dip boneless chicken breast in Italian dressing, then in Italian-seasoned dry bread crumbs. Cover and bake at 450° for 15 minutes. Uncover and bake 10 more minutes.

CHICKEN CHILI

Serves: 6

4 tablespoons butter

1 clove garlic, minced

2 large onions, chopped

1 large green pepper, chopped

1 (3 pounds or more) fryer cooked, skinned boned, and cut into bite size pieces

6 ounces fresh mushrooms, sliced

2 (1 pound) cans pinto beans

½ cup black pitted olives, sliced

1 (6 ounce) can tomato paste

1 (28 ounce) can tomatoes coarsely chopped or 2 pints, home canned

2 bay leaves

3 tablespoons chili powder, or to taste

Herb salt & pepper to taste

1 tablespoon cumin

Melt butter in a skillet. Saute garlic, onions, mushrooms and green pepper until soft. Place sauteed vegetables and all remaining ingredients in a large, heavy pot or Dutch oven. Mix well. Partially cover and simmer over low heat for approximately 1½ hours, or until mixture is thick. Stir often while cooking. Best if made ahead and refrigerated for 24 hours. Reheat in covered casserole dish in 350° oven for 40 minutes. If chili becomes too dry, stir in a little water. Recipe can be doubled.

May be frozen.

CHICKEN AND WILD RICE CASSEROLE

Serves: 10 to 12

1 cup onion, chopped

1 cup butter

½ cup plain flour

2 (4½ ounce) cans sliced mushrooms, drained (reserve juice)

3 cups chicken broth

3 cups half and half

6 cups chicken, cooked and diced

1 (6 ounce) box long-grain and wild rice mix, cooked

1 cup slivered almonds, toasted (optional)

½ cup pimento, diced

4 tablespoons parsley, chopped

3 teaspoons salt

½ teaspoon pepper

In a large skillet, saute onion in butter until tender. Stir in flour, cooking 2 to 3 minutes. Combine mushroom juice with enough broth to make 3 cups. Slowly stir into onion mixture. Stir in cream. Cook until thickened. Add mushrooms, chicken, rice and remaining ingredients. Pour into a large casserole. Bake at 350° for 30 to 45 minutes.

PARTY CHICKEN

8 large chicken breasts (skin and bone removed)

8 slices bacon

1 package (4 ounce) chipped beef

1 can undiluted mushroom soup

½ pint sour cream

Wrap each breast with piece of bacon. Cover bottom of flat greased baking dish with chipped beef. Arrange chicken breasts on beef. Mix soup and sour cream and pour over all. Bake at 275° for 3 hours, uncovered.

CRAB STUFFED CHICKEN BREASTS

Serves: 6

6 boned chicken breasts

½ cup onion, chopped

½ cup celery, chopped

3 tablespoons butter

3 tablespoons white wine

1 can (7 ounce) crabmeat, or fresh

½ cup Pepperidge Farm stuffing

2 tablespoons flour

½ teaspoon paprika

Salt and pepper chicken breasts and pound. Cook onion and celery in butter. Remove from heat and add wine, crabmeat, and stuffing. Put inside chicken breasts and secure with toothpicks. Combine flour and paprika and coat chicken. Drizzle with butter and bake uncovered at 375° for 40 minutes. Pour sauce over when serving.

Sauce:

1 envelope Hollandaise Sauce Mix

¾ cup milk

2 tablespoons white wine

½ cup Swiss cheese

Heat ingredients and spoon over chicken.

CHICKEN WITH ASPARAGUS AND LEMON SABAYOU

Serves: 2 to 4

1½ pounds asparagus, trimmed and peeled

Salt and fresh ground pepper

1 large lemon (garnish)

2 whole large chicken breasts, halved, deboned and skinned

¼ cup butter

Lemon Sabayou:

½ cup chicken stock

½ cup whipping cream

6 egg yolks

2 tablespoons Armagmac or brandy

1½ teaspoons fresh thyme or ½ teaspoon dried

1½ to 2 tablespoons fresh lemon juice

1 tablespoon fresh chives (garnish)

Cook asparagus until tender, about 8 minutes. Cut tips of spears into 5 inch lengths (use asparagus stems in soups or salads). Sprinkle with salt. Using zester or paring knife, remove 6 equally spaced strips of peel from stem to tip of lemon. Cut lemon into thin rounds. Boil 10 minutes in reserved liquid. Drain well.

Preheat oven to 425°. Gently pound chicken breasts. Melt butter in shallow baking pan. Remove from heat and add chicken. Sprinkle with salt, pepper, and lemon juice. Cover chicken with buttered parchment paper or heavy brown paper bag. Cover pan and bake until chicken is opaque and springs to touch, about 8 minutes.

For sabayou: Combine yolks, stock, cream, Armagmac, lemon juice, thyme, salt and pepper in top of double boiler. Wisk until mixture thickens and doubles in volume, about 3 minutes.

Preheat broiler. Transfer chicken to heat proof serving platter, surround with asparagus and garnish with lemon slices. Spoon sabayou over top and sprinkle with chives. Run under broiler until sauce is brown and bubbly, about 3 minutes. Serve immediately.

CHICKEN BREASTS IN WINE
Serves: 4

2 whole chicken breasts,
   separated

⅓ cup flour

1½ teaspoons garlic salt

1½ teaspoons salt

1½ teaspoons paprika

¼ cup cooking oil

1 can pitted dark cherries
   (Bing)

1 cup sauterne

4 cups hot rice, cooked

Mix together flour, salt, garlic salt and paprika. Coat chicken with mixture. Brown in oil. Drain cherries. Measure ½ cup cherry syrup. Add cherries, cherry syrup and wine to chicken. Cover. Simmer until chicken is tender, about 1 hour. Serve over hot rice.

CHICKEN AND ARTICHOKE HEARTS IN NEWBERG SAUCE

6 tablespoons butter

6 cups cooked chicken, cut in
   2 inch pieces

3 tablespoons sherry

1½ cups half and half

4 egg yolks, well beaten

1 tablespoon and 1 teaspoon
   lemon juice

½ teaspoon salt

⅛ teaspoon white pepper

2½ cups canned artichoke
   hearts

Melt 3 tablespoons butter, add chicken and heat. Add sherry and ¾ cup of cream. Let come to a boil. Add rest of cream mixed with beaten egg yolks, stirring all the time. Add lemon juice, salt and pepper and remaining butter. Add artichoke hearts and heat until thickened at low heat. Do not boil. This sauce is not as thick as a cream sauce and will take 10 minutes to cook after eggs are added. If made ahead of time, reheat over hot water.

CHICKEN LIVERS/WILD RICE

2 medium onions, chopped

2 tablespoons soft butter

2 cups wild rice

½ cup white wine

2 dozen chicken livers, cut up

Pinch bay leaf

Pinch thyme

2 to 3 cups stock or consomme

Salt and pepper to taste

Lightly butter a casserole. Cut up chicken livers. Add remaining ingredients, using enough stock to cover contents. Add salt and pepper to taste. Bake 350° for 1 hour or until rice is tender and liquid absorbed.

CHICKEN SPAGHETTI

Serves: 8 to 12

1 (5 to 6 pound) hen
1 pint English peas
1 (16 ounce) box of spaghetti
1 pound sharp cheese, cut in small pieces
2 medium fried onions (finely cut and cooked in butter)

1 small can pimentos
1 pod hot pepper
1 teaspoon black pepper
2½ cups chicken broth

Thoroughly cook chicken and cool in broth. Cut meat into fine pieces. Put 2½ cups of chicken broth in cut up chicken. Simmer with onion and pimento. Cook spaghetti (broken up) separately. Drain and add to chicken mixture. Slowly add pieces of cheese stirring until thoroughly melted. Add pod of hot pepper or few drops of Tabasco. Let pod remain in mixture until desired taste; then remove. Add peas, stir slightly, simmer all together for a few minutes. Remove from heat and let stand a few moments before serving.

Preparation time: 4 hours.

HO PO DAI DING
(Chicken with Walnuts)

Serves: 4

4 chicken breasts, boned and chopped into bite size pieces
1 teaspoon salt
1 teaspoon sugar
½ teaspoon ginger powder
3 tablespoons soy sauce
2 cloves garlic, minced

3 tablespoons peanut oil
1 cup walnut halves or pecan halves
1 (8 ounce) can bamboo shoots, drained
1 tablespoon cornstarch
1 cup water

Combine salt, sugar, ginger, soy sauce and garlic; mix well. Mix in chicken pieces. Let stand 20 minutes. Heat peanut oil in wok at high heat. (Oil should bubble up around chopstick when end is pressed to bottom.) Stir fry walnuts or pecans for 1 minute. Remove nutmeats and set aside. Add marinated chicken mixture to hot oil. Stir fry 5 minutes, stirring constantly.* Mix in bamboo shoots. Blend cornstarch in water and add to mixture. Stir until thickened. Simmer 2 minutes longer without stirring. Mix in nutmeats. Serve immediately over cooked rice.

Preparation time: 1 hour. May not be frozen.

*If using electric skillet, let chicken cook until meat turns white, may take more than 5 minutes.

180

CHEESEY CHICKEN
Serves: 4

1 slice bacon, diced

¼ cup onion, minced

¼ cup green pepper, minced

1 cup cooked chicken, diced

1 cup Cheddar cheese, shredded

2 tablespoons pimento, chopped

1 cup cooked green beans

½ teaspoon salt

¼ cup teaspoon pepper

Garlic powder to taste

1 tablespoon chopped parsley

1 cup cooked macaroni

¼ cup buttered breadcrumbs

½ cup broth

Cook bacon. Add onion and green pepper and cook until tender. Combine all ingredients except breadcrumbs. Spoon mixture into a buttered 1 quart casserole. Sprinkle with breadcrumbs. Bake at 350° for 15 to 20 minutes.

Preparation time: 30 minutes (cook chicken ahead.) Can be prepared 24 hours ahead, but leave breadcrumbs off until baking time.

COLD LEMON CHICKEN
Serves 6

6 whole boneless, skinless chicken breasts, separated

4 tablespoons butter

½ cup white wine

⅓ cup lemon juice

Salt and pepper

1½ cups mayonnaise

¼ cup lemon juice

Saute chicken breasts in butter until brown. Remove. Add white wine to pan and cook to reduce liquid to ⅓ cup. Add ⅓ cup lemon juice, salt and pepper. Put chicken in oven proof dish and pour liquid over. Cover and bake at 350° for 30 minutes or until tender, basting several times. Remove chicken and reduce sauce by one half. Pour over chicken and refrigerate overnight.

Mix mayonnaise with ¼ cup lemon juice and put over chicken before serving at cool room temperature. Mayonnaise mixture may be omitted for lower calories.

Prepare ahead.

CHICKEN PIE WITH OYSTERS

Boiled young hen and broth

1 quart of oysters

Seasoning to taste

Pie crust for a 2 quart serving dish

Boil the chicken until tender. Drain off the liquor from the oysters, boil, skim and set aside. Line the sides of the baking dish with a rich pastry crust; put in a layer of chicken, then a layer of raw oysters and repeat until dish is filled; seasoning each layer with pepper, salt and butter, and adding the oyster liquor and a part of the chicken broth until the liquid is even with the top layer. Cover loosely with a crust having an opening in the center to allow steam to escape. If the liquid cooks away, add chicken broth or hot water. Bake 40 minutes in a moderate oven, 350°.

Gravy:

Add to chicken broth left in pot (one quart or more) two tablespoons flour, rubbed smooth with two tablespoons butter and seasoned highly with pepper; let cook until there is no raw taste of flour and salt.

CHICKEN RATATOUILLE   *Serves:* 4

¼ cup corn oil

2 whole broiler-fryer chicken breasts, skinned, boned and cut in 1 inch pieces

2 small zucchini, unpared and thinly sliced

1 small eggplant, peeled and cut into 1 inch cubes

½ pound mushrooms, sliced

1 (16 ounce) can tomato wedges

2 teaspoons garlic salt

1 onion, sliced

1 green pepper, sliced

1 teaspoon monosodium glutamate

1 teaspoon dried sweet basil, crushed

1 teaspoon dried parsley

½ teaspoon black pepper

Heat corn oil in large fry pan. Add chicken and saute about 2 minutes on each side. Then add zucchini, eggplant, onion, green pepper and mushrooms.

Cook, stirring occasionally for about 15 minutes or until tender and crisp. Add tomatoes stirring carefully. Add garlic salt, monosodium glutamate, basil, parsley and pepper. Simmer about 5 minutes or until fork can be inserted in chicken with ease. Serve on large platter with mound of rice in center.

COLD PASTA — NEW ORLEANS STYLE

Serves: 8

½ pound vermicelli, broken in half and cooked in salted water for 4 minutes
1 cup dressing (to follow)

1 (3 pound) chicken, cooked and chopped
1 cup mayonnaise
Chopped parsley

Dressing:

¼ cup wine vinegar
2 teaspoons Dijon mustard
2 teaspoons chopped garlic

Salt and pepper to taste
½ cup French olive oil

Mix vinegar, mustard, garlic, salt and pepper. Whisk in olive oil.

To assemble: Mix vermicelli with dressing in a large bowl. Cover and refrigerate overnight. Add chicken and mayonnaise and refrigerate until ready to serve (overnight, if possible). Garnish with chopped parsley.

Note: This can be put on a platter filled with lettuce and neatly arranged with pickled beets, marinated mushrooms, artichokes and cherry tomatoes.

ORANGE CHICKEN IN A CLAY POT

1 (3 to 4 pound) chicken
Salt and pepper

1 clove garlic, crushed
2 medium oranges

Rub the salt, pepper and garlic on inside of chicken. Grate orange skins and slice oranges. Stuff oranges inside chicken. Place in pot with the breast down. Sprinkle grated rind on top. Place covered pot in cold oven and bake at 480° for 90 minutes.

Make a sauce of the following and boil until thick:

½ cup orange juice
¼ cup soy sauce
1 teaspoon ginger

¼ teaspoon allspice
1 tablespoon brown sugar

Ten minutes before chicken is done, pour the liquid sauce into pan. Return pot, uncovered, to oven.

BREAST OF CHICKEN FLORENTINE

Serves: 8

Flour for dredging

4 whole chicken breasts, skinned, boned and halved

Salt and freshly ground pepper

1 egg

1 tablespoon water

½ cup dry bread crumbs

¼ cup grated Parmesan cheese

¾ cup butter

2 packages frozen spinach, chopped, cooked, and drained

1 pound mushrooms, sliced

1 tablespoon lemon juice

Chopped parsley

Mix flour, salt and pepper. Mix crumbs and cheese. Mix egg and water and beat lightly. Dredge chicken breasts in flour, dip in the egg mixture and coat with crumb mixture. Refrigerate 1 hour or more.

In a large skillet, heat ½ cup of the butter, add the chicken and brown on both sides. Lower heat and cook until tender, about 25 minutes.

Meanwhile cook spinach and season with lemon juice. Place spinach on platter, arrange chicken breasts on top and keep hot.

Add 1 tablespoon of remaining butter and mushrooms and saute until tender. Spoon over chicken.

Brown remaining butter in pan and pour through a fine sieve over the dish. Sprinkle with parsley.

CHICKEN CORDON BLEU

Serves: 8

4 whole chicken breasts

8 (3 inch square) slices boiled ham

8 (2 x 2 inch pieces, 1 ounce each) Gruyere cheese

1 stick butter

1 cup fresh breadcrumbs

1 teaspoon salt

¼ teaspoon paprika

Have the butcher halve, bone and skin the chicken breasts. Pull each half breast open in the middle to form pocket. Melt butter in pie pan. Make fresh bread crumbs in blender. Mix with salt and paprika in a second pie pan. Roll stuffed chicken breasts in melted butter and then in the crumbs. Coat well. Place in a buttered baking dish and bake at 400° for 40 minutes or until brown.

Preparation time: 20 minutes.

CHICKEN CURRY

1 box Uncle Ben's long grain
  and wild rice (discard sauce)

1 can cream of chicken soup

1 can cream of celery soup

½ package onion soup mix

1 can dry white wine

½ can water

Chicken breasts (skinned and
  boned)

Mix first 6 ingredients and allow to sit 2 to 4 hours. Layer chicken breasts on top. Bake covered 1 hour at 350°. Add fruit curry sauce.

Fruit Curry Sauce:

1 can mixed fruits for salad

½ stick butter

⅓ cup brown sugar

1½ teaspoons curry powder

Heat butter, sugar and curry. Pour over fruit. Place on top of chicken and bake uncovered at 325° for 1 hour.
  (May omit the fruit addition, if desired.)

CHICKEN DIVAN

Serves: 6 to 8

2 bunches fresh broccoli,
  cooked

3 whole chicken breasts, cooked
  and boned

½ cup soft bread crumbs

1 tablespoon butter, melted

2 cans condensed cream of
  chicken soup

1 cup mayonnaise

1 teaspoon lemon juice

½ teaspoon curry powder

½ cup shredded sharp
  processed cheese

Arrange cooked broccoli in buttered 11 x 7 inch baking dish. Place chicken on top. Combine soup, mayonnaise, lemon juice and curry powder. Pour over chicken. Sprinkle with cheese. Combine bread crumbs and butter; sprinkle over casserole. Bake 350° for 25 to 30 minutes. Trim with pimento strips.
  One (8 ounce) carton of sour cream may be added for richness.

TURKEY BROCCOLI CASSEROLE

Serves: 6

3 cups cooked diced turkey (or chicken)

2 (10 ounce) packages frozen broccoli (cook according to package directions)

1 can mushroom soup

½ cup milk

⅛ teaspoon pepper

¼ teaspoon rosemary

2 tablespoons sherry

1 teaspoon Worcestershire sauce

6 slices of cheese, sharp Cheddar

Buttered bread crumbs

Line the bottom of a 9 x 13 inch casserole with broccoli. Make sauce of the next six ingredients. Place turkey over broccoli; pour sauce over all; top with cheese and bread crumbs. Bake 400° for 30 minutes.

Preparation time: 45 minutes. May be prepared ahead and frozen.

SEAFOOD

Cape Hatteras Lighthouse, Cape Hatteras

SEAFOOD GUMBO

Yield: 1½ gallons

12 tablespoons flour

1 cup shortening

6 cloves garlic

1 cup onion, chopped

1 cup celery, chopped

3 to 4 bay leaves

1 teaspoon thyme

2 cans tomatoes

½ to ¾ teaspoon Tabasco

Freshly ground black pepper

12 ounce can tomato sauce

3 quarts water

1 pound crabmeat

3 pounds shrimp

1½ bags frozen okra

1 quart oysters and liquor

Lemon juice to taste

Salt to taste

8 slices bacon, crisply fried, with grease reserved

1½ teaspoons Lea and Perrins Worcestershire sauce

Make a roux with flour and shortening. Add garlic and cook until medium brown, being careful not to burn it. Add onions and celery and cook until transparent. Remove garlic (optional). Add tomato sauce and simmer 10 minutes. In skillet simmer okra in bacon grease until almost done. Add to tomato sauce mixture. Add water and seasonings and cook ½ to 1 hour. Just before serving, add shrimp and crabmeat and cook about 10 minutes. Then add oysters and cook until they are plump, about 3 minutes.

This dish is best if made early in the day and then reheated slowly, with seafood added just before serving. Serve in bowls over rice with crumbled bacon on top, or serve over wild rice.

DOWN EAST FISH STEW

This recipe is fun to do in a big black iron pot over an open fire, but it can be prepared in a large pot on the stove. Fry enough fat back or bacon to cover the bottom of the pot. On top of the bacon place a layer of sliced potatoes, a layer of sliced onions, and a layer of fish filets or chunks (such as rockfish or catfish). Salt and pepper to taste. Cover this first layer with water. Repeat layers, but do not add any more water. Let simmer until done (several hours). Do not stir. When the stew is nearly done, add a small bottle of catsup, a little Worcestershire sauce, and/or Texas Pete if desired. Some people add cornmeal dumplings (made of cornmeal, water, and salt) to the stew and poach until done. Others break eggs into the stew and poach until done. Serve the stew in bowls.

THANKSGIVING OYSTERS

Serves: 8 to 10

1 cup butter
¾ cup flour
1 teaspoon paprika
½ teaspoon salt
¼ teaspoon pepper
Dash of cayenne
1 clove garlic, minced

1 medium onion, chopped
½ medium green pepper,
  chopped
1 quart fresh oysters
1 tablespoon lemon juice
2 teaspoons Worcestershire
  sauce
¼ cup cracker crumbs

Preheat oven to 400°. Grease a 2 quart shallow casserole. Melt butter in a large skillet over medium heat. Remove from heat, add flour, and stir until smooth. Return to heat and cook, stirring constantly, for 5 minutes or until light brown. Add paprika, salt, pepper, cayenne, garlic, onion and green pepper. Cook at least 5 minutes, stirring constantly. Drain about half the liquor from the oysters; then add oysters, lemon juice and Worcestershire sauce. Stir well. Pour into prepared casserole. Sprinkle with cracker crumbs. Bake at 400° for 20 minutes.

Excellent dish served with turkey or country ham. May be prepared early in the day and set aside until time to bake. This dish is not good warmed over, but it so good that there is usually not any left over.

SCALLOPED OYSTERS

Serves: 4

1 pint oysters
2 cups medium coarse cracker
  crumbs
¼ cup oyster liquor

¾ cup milk
2 beaten eggs
½ cup melted butter

Alternate, 3 layers each, cracker crumbs and oysters in a buttered casserole dish. Salt and pepper each layer. Combine oyster liquor, milk and beaten eggs. Pour over layers of oysters and crumbs. Pour melted butter over all. Bake at 350°, 40 to 60 minutes, or until brown.

DEVILED OYSTERS

Serves: 6

1 cup crushed Ritz crackers
¼ pound melted butter
1 pint oysters (with liquor
  reserved)
1 medium onion, grated
¼ cup fresh parsley, minced

1 green pepper, minced
5 eggs, beaten lightly
1 tablespoon Worcestershire
  sauce
Salt and pepper
Paprika

Put crackers in blender (or food processor) with melted butter, reserving enough buttered crumbs for topping. Add oysters and liquor to processor and process for a few seconds. Mix all ingredients together and place in a shallow baking dish. Top with reserved buttered crumbs. Bake at 350° for 30 minutes.

Preparation time: 15 minutes.

POACHED FISH
WITH TOMATO SAUCE
Serves: 6

6 fish steaks, such as mackeral, wahoo or dolphin

1 cup dry white wine

Juice of 1 lemon

Herbs of choice (tarragon, thyme, parsley)

Additional fish stock or water

In a large saute pan or fish poacher combine wine, lemon juice and enough additional liquid to cover steaks. Add herbs. Poach fish 10 to 15 minutes or until done. Remove skin. Serve steaks covered with fresh tomato sauce.

Tomato Sauce With Limes:

3 tablespoons butter or olive oil

½ cup onion, chopped

1 small clove garlic, finely chopped

½ cup celery, chopped

⅔ cup sliced fresh mushrooms

Juice of ½ lime

Zest of 1 lime, or 1 lime cut in eighths

2 cups canned Italian plum tomatoes

3 tablespoons tomato paste

Salt and freshly ground black pepper to taste

Heat the butter and in it saute the onion, garlic and celery. When the onion is transparent, add the mushrooms and cook 3 minutes longer, stirring occasionally. Add the tomatoes and simmer 15 minutes. Stir in the tomato paste and lime juice and cook 10 minutes longer. Season to taste with salt, pepper and lime zest (or lime pieces). Serve over poached fish.

ELEGANT FLOUNDER
Serves: 4

3 to 3½ pounds flounder filets

2 teaspoons lemon juice

Salt and pepper

2 cups sour cream

Preheat oven to 350°. Butter a shallow baking dish just large enough to hold filets in 1 layer. Season filets with the lemon juice and sprinkle lightly

with the salt and pepper. Spread the 2 cups sour cream evenly over the filets and bake for 12 to 15 minutes, or until they flake easily when tested with a fork. Garnish with parsley if desired, and serve at once.
Preparation time: 20 minutes.

PESCADO A LA MARIA ISABEL
(Baked Fish Maria Isabel)
Serves: 6

Salt and pepper

1 (4 to 5 pound) red snapper

1 large Bermuda onion, sliced in rings

Juice of 1 lemon

1 thin lemon round, cut in half

1 small green pepper, sliced in rings

1 (#2) can whole tomatoes

1 garlic clove, minced

1 bay leaf

1 teaspoon crushed oregano

½ teaspoon thyme

1 tablespoon flour

½ cup olive oil

½ cup dry white wine

Salt and pepper the fish, inside and out, to taste. Place half of the onion slices in bottom of suitable shallow greased baking pan. Place the fish over the onion rings and squeeze the lemon juice inside and over the fish. Make 2 incisions on top of fish about 1½ inches apart and insert ½ of the lemon round in each incision.

Cover fish with the remaining onion rings and green pepper rings. Give the tomatoes a swirl in the electric blender and pour over the fish together with the minced garlic, bay leaf, crushed oregano and thyme. Sprinkle the fish with the flour. Combine the oil and wine and pour over the fish. Place in a preheated 350° oven and bake for 1 hour, or until the fish flakes easily. Baste frequently.

May be necessary to add a little water during cooking.
Preparation time: 15 minutes.

CRAB CAKES
Makes: 8

1 pound crabmeat

½ teaspoon salt

1 teaspoon dry mustard

½ cup mayonnaise

1 to 2 tablespoons bread crumbs, enough to make mixture hold together

1 egg yolk

½ teaspoon pepper

2 teaspoons Worcestershire sauce

1 teaspoon chopped parsley

1 tablespoon melted butter

Mix all ingredients well. Shape into cakes. Place in shallow baking pan and bake at 350° for 15 to 20 minutes.

TOASTED CRAB AND GRUYERE ON FRENCH ROLLS

Serves: 6

6 French sourdough rolls, split in half

3 tablespoons butter

1 pound flaked cooked crabmeat (or fish)

6 ounces Guyere or Jarlsberg cheese, shredded (1½ cups)

¼ cup mayonnaise

2 tablespoons sour cream

¼ cup pimento-stuffed olives, sliced

2 green onions, chopped

¼ cup ripe olives, sliced

Spread rolls with butter and toast lightly. Mix together crabmeat (or fish), cheese, mayonnaise, sour cream, olives and onions. Spread mixture on half of each roll. Place in a preheated 400° oven until heated through and lightly browned. Serve with other half of roll alongside.

SOFT SHELLED CRABS

This is a down East traditional home recipe usually not available in restaurants.

Select medium or small soft shelled crabs which have been cleaned. Dip lightly in flour on both sides. Shake off excess flour. Saute on both sides in bacon fat until lightly browned, but well done in the center. They may require several turnings. Crabs should not be deep fried. Serve while hot with tartar sauce or lemon juice.

Tartar Sauce:

1 cup mayonnaise

3 tablespoons sweet pickles, chopped

1 tablespoon parsley, chopped

1 tablespoon capers, chopped

1 tablespoon onion, chopped

Mix all ingredients and chill. You may vary by using chopped dill pickles instead of the sweet. This will keep in the refrigerator for weeks.

DEVILED CRAB

Serves: 6

3 tablespoons flour
3 tablespoons butter
1 cup milk
1 hard-cooked egg, chopped
1 small onion, chopped
½ teaspoon salt
1 tablespoon lemon juice

2 tablespoons Worcestershire sauce
1 teaspoon mustard
½ teaspoon Tabasco
1 pound crabmeat
Paprika

Make a thick cream sauce from flour, butter and milk. To this add the other ingredients except crabmeat. Wash and pick well the crabmeat and fold into the sauce. Correct seasonings. Place in crab shells and sprinkle with paprika. Bake at 400° until brown on top.
Preparation time: 30 minutes.

CRAB AND ARTICHOKE CASSEROLE

Serves: 10 to 12

8 tablespoons flour
4 cups milk
½ teaspoon pepper
1 tablespoon Worcestershire sauce
4 tablespoons prepared yellow mustard

Dash Tabasco
1½ pounds crabmeat
3 small cans artichoke hearts
1 cup Parmesan cheese, grated

Mix all ingredients; place in shallow casserole, and top with Parmesan cheese. Bake at 350° for 1 hour.
Preparation time: 5 minutes.

CRAB QUICHE

Serves: 4 to 6

1 (9 inch) pie shell
6 ounces crabmeat
4 ounces Monterey Jack cheese, shredded
3 eggs
1 cup half and half

½ scant teaspoon salt
¼ teaspoon pepper
Pinch of nutmeg
Dash of Tabasco
Dijon mustard (about 1 tablespoon)

Bake pie shell 5 minutes at 400°. Brush bottom with Dijon mustard. Sprinkle with crab and shredded cheese. Beat eggs and add rest of ingredients. Pour into pie shell. Bake at 425° for 15 minutes. Then lower temperature to 325° and bake 45 minutes more. Let stand 15 minutes before serving.

CRABMEAT SOUFFLE
Serves: 4 to 6

2 tablespoons minced green onions

3 tablespoons butter

3 tablespoons flour

1 cup scalded milk

½ teaspoon salt

Dash of pepper

1 tablespoon tomato paste

½ teaspoon marjoram

4 egg yolks

6 to 7 ounces of crabmeat

½ cup grated Swiss cheese

5 egg whites at room temperature

1 teaspoon cream of tartar

Preheat oven to 400°. Butter a 1½ quart souffle dish. Saute the onions in butter in a heavy pan. Add flour and cook for 2 minutes. Remove from heat and beat in scalded milk, then seasoning, and tomato paste. Bring to a boil and stir for 1 minute. Remove from heat and quickly beat in egg yolks, 1 at a time with a wire whisk. Stir in crabmeat and cheese. Beat the egg whites with the cream of tartar until stiff but not dry. Stir a large spoonful of the egg whites into the crabmeat mixture. Fold in the remaining egg whites. Pour into prepared souffle dish and place in the middle of the oven. Immediately turn heat to 375° and bake for about 30 minutes. Serve with Hollandaise Sauce.

Hollandaise Sauce:

3 egg yolks

2 tablespoons lemon juice

¼ teaspoon salt

¼ teaspoon sugar

¼ teaspoon dry mustard

½ cup butter, softened

Combine egg yolks, lemon juice, salt, sugar and dry mustard in top of double boiler or in heavy pan over low heat. Add softened butter and whisk constantly over low heat until butter melts and sauce thickens.

HAMPTON CRAB IMPERIAL

Serves: 6

1 pound backfin crabmeat

½ tablespoon pimento, chopped

½ tablespoon green pepper, chopped

1 tablespoon butter

Heavy Cream Sauce (recipe below)

1 egg yolk

¼ teaspoon dry mustard

1 rounded teaspoon capers, drained

1½ teaspoons Worcestershire sauce

Salt and white pepper to taste

1 cup mayonnaise, divided

Paprika

Heavy Cream Sauce:

4 tablespoons butter

5 tablespoons all purpose flour

1 cup milk

½ teaspoon salt

Preheat oven to 375° 10 minutes before crab is ready to go in. Pick over crabmeat and discard any bits of shell or cartilage. Refrigerate. Saute pimento and green pepper in butter. Make a heavy cream sauce by melting the butter in a heavy skillet over medium heat and stirring in the flour, milk and salt. Continue stirring until mixture is smooth and thick. Combine sauteed vegetables, cream sauce and other ingredients except crabmeat, mayonnaise and paprika. Mix in ¾ cup mayonnaise. Fold in crabmeat very gently so lumps will not break up. Spoon into shells or shallow baking dishes and spread remaining mayonnaise on top of each crab filling. Bake at 375° for 30 to 35 minutes or until golden brown. Sprinkle with paprika and serve at once.

COQUILLES ST. JACQUES

Serves: 6 as first course

Court Bouillon:

1 cup water

1 small onion, sliced

1 stalk celery, cut up

1 bay leaf

3 slices lemon

½ cup dry white wine

1 to 1½ pounds scallops

Bring water to boil. Add everything but wine and scallops. Simmer uncovered 10 minutes. Add wine and scallops and gently simmer, covered, 3 minutes or until tender. Drain. Reserve liquid.

Sauce:

¼ cup butter

¼ cup onion, finely chopped

¼ pound mushrooms, sliced

¼ cup flour

Dash of pepper

Pinch of salt

¾ cup half and half

1 cup grated Gruyere cheese (¼ pound)

2 tablespoons dry white wine

½ cup reserved court bouillon

Parsley, freshly minced (about 2 tablespoons)

In butter saute onions and mushrooms until tender (about 5 minutes). Remove from heat and stir in flour, salt and pepper, and cook until lightly browned. Slowly stir in half and half and bring to boil, stirring. Reduce heat and stir until very thick. Add Gruyere and stir until melted. Remove from heat and stir in wine, court bouillon and parsley. Add scallops and mix well. Divide into shells.

Serves 4 as main course.

CREAM OF COQUILLES ST. GEORGE WITH LEEKS

Serves: 4

2 large leeks (white part only), cut into fine 1½ inch julienne pieces

2 tablespoons butter

1 cup fish stock or 1 cup bottled clam juice

¼ cup cream sherry

1½ pounds scallops, quartered if large

1 cup whipping cream

Salt and pepper to taste

Paprika to garnish

Wash leeks well, but don't dry. Melt butter over low heat, add leeks, cover, and let sweat until tender, stirring occasionally, about 10 to 15 minutes. Remove leeks and set aside. Add stock and sherry and heat just until liquid tumbles. Add scallops and poach 2 minutes. Remove scallops with slotted spoon. Increase heat and reduce liquid to half, scraping bottom of pan. Add cream and boil until thickened. Put leeks and scallops back in pan and heat well. Serve in shells or ramekins. Sprinkle with paprika. Recipe can be halved nicely to serve 2.

Preparation time: 45 minutes.

SPINACH FETTUCCINE
WITH SCALLOPS

Serves: 4

1 pound freshly made spinach fettuccine, cooked

¼ cup firmly packed parsley

1 large clove garlic, minced

¼ cup butter

½ cup dry white wine

1 cup half and half (or whipping cream)

½ cup whipping cream

1 cup freshly grated Parmesan cheese

⅓ cup firmly packed parsley

Freshly grated nutmeg, salt and pepper to taste

¾ pound scallops

Saute ¼ cup parsley and garlic in butter, about 5 minutes. Add scallops and cook just until tender, about 1 to 2 minutes. Remove scallops from pan. Add wine to pan and reduce over medium high heat by approximately one half. Add half and half and whipping cream and cook until sauce thickens. Place cooked fettuccine in a large serving bowl. Add scallops, sauce, Parmesan cheese and spices and toss well. Serve immediately.

SCALLOP RAMEKINS

Serves: 6

2 pounds fresh spinach, trimmed

2 pounds scallops

6 tablespoons butter

Sauce Bearnaise (recipe follows)

Blanch spinach in boiling salted water until it is barely tender. Drain very well. Divide among ramekins. Saute scallops in butter just until done, about 3 minutes. Don't overcook; they will be tough. Divide over spinach. Top with bearnaise sauce and run under the broiler until golden.

Sauce Bearnaise:

½ cup wine vinegar

3 tablespoons shallots, minced

½ teaspoon tarragon

½ teaspoon chervil

½ teaspoon salt

¼ teaspoon pepper

4 egg yolks

2 sticks butter, melted

Bring wine vinegar, shallots, tarragon, chervil, salt and pepper to a boil in a saucepan. Reduce heat and cook until mixture reduces to approximately 2 tablespoons (about 5 minutes). Let cool. In a blender or food processor blend 4 egg yolks. Add reduced herb mixture and blend well. Add melted butter slowly while machine is running and process until sauce is consistency of mayonnaise.

SCALLOPS PARISIENNE

Serves: 8

1½ pounds sea or bay scallops
4 tablespoons butter
1 cup diced mushrooms
1 teaspoons salt
¼ teaspoon pepper

1 can cream of shrimp soup
2 tablespoons dry vermouth
4 tablespoons bread crumbs
3 tablespoons butter, melted

Drain scallops. Slice sea scallops; leave bay scallops whole. Melt 2 tablespoons butter in skillet and saute scallops 2 minutes. Remove. Melt remaining 2 tablespoons butter and saute mushrooms. Add to scallops and add salt and pepper. Lightly stir soup and add to mixture. Add vermouth and mix well. Divide into 8 ramekins. Sprinkle tops with crumbs and melted butter. Bake at 425° for 10 minutes until heated and brown on top.

SHRIMP HARPIN

Serves: 8

2½ pounds shrimp, deveined
1 tablespoon lemon juice
3 tablespoons salad oil
¾ cup uncooked rice
2 tablespoons butter
¼ cup green pepper, chopped
¼ cup onion, chopped
1 teaspoon salt
⅛ teaspoon pepper

⅛ teaspoon mace
Dash of cayenne pepper
1 (10 ounce) can tomato soup (undiluted)
1 cup whipping cream (or half and half)
¾ cup almonds, slivered or chopped
⅓ cup sherry (or ⅓ cup cream sherry)

Cook shrimp in boiling salted water for about 3 minutes. Drain. Save 8 cooked shrimp for garnish. Place rest of shrimp in a bowl and cover with lemon juice and salad oil. Cook rice according to directions. Saute green pepper and onions in skillet in butter for 5 minutes, and add to rice. Also add shrimp, salt, pepper, mace, cayenne, soup, cream, sherry and ½ cup almonds. Toss well. Place in a 2 quart buttered casserole and bake at 350° for about 20 minutes. Then top with reserved shrimp and ¼ cup almonds, and bake another 15 to 20 minutes until bubbly.

SCAMPI I

Serves: 5

1½ pounds medium shrimp
¼ cup butter
½ cup olive oil
8 shallots, finely chopped
  (¾ cup)
4 garlic cloves, finely chopped
1 cup stewed tomatoes

½ cup sliced mushrooms
1 teaspoon salt
Dash of pepper
⅓ cup fresh lemon juice
¼ cup parsley, minced

Shell and devein shrimp. In hot butter and oil, saute shallots and garlic, stirring for 3 minutes. Add tomatoes and mushrooms. Cook 5 minutes. Add salt, pepper, lemon juice and 2 tablespoons parsley, and shrimp. Toss to mix well. Put in shallow casserole and broil about 8 minutes or until shrimp is pink. Sprinkle with rest of parsley.

SCAMPI II

Serves: 2

1 pound large shrimp
½ cup butter
Salt
Pepper

2 tablespoons lemon juice
2 cloves garlic, pressed or minced
2 tablespoons minced fresh parsley

To vary, season with rosemary, oregano or paprika.

Preheat oven to 400°. Remove shell from raw shrimp. Slit to butterfly and remove vein. Melt butter in baking dish. Add garlic and shrimp. Bake approximately 5 minutes. Add salt, pepper, lemon juice, parsley or other seasonings, and bake another 5 minutes or until done. Serves 2 for main course or 4 for appetizer.

Recipe is easily doubled and is good served with lemon rice. (Add 2 to 3 tablespoons lemon juice to water rice is cooked in, and sprinkle with grated lemon rind when done.)

Preparation time: 25 minutes.

SHRIMP-CRAB CASSEROLE

Serves: 10

1 pound crabmeat or
   1 (12 ounce) can crabmeat
1 pound shrimp, boiled
½ green pepper, chopped
½ cup onion, chopped
2 pimentos, chopped
1 tablespoon Worcestershire
   sauce
⅛ teaspoon pepper

1 cup raw rice
1 cup celery, chopped
1 can sliced mushrooms or
   ½ pound fresh sliced
   mushrooms sauteed lightly in
   butter
1 cup mayonnaise
½ teaspoon salt
¾ cup light cream

Pick over crabmeat, removing shell. Cook rice according to package directions. Combine all ingredients. Pour into large casserole and bake at 375° for 30 minutes.

Preparation time: 1 hour.

SHRIMP WITH TEQUILLA

¾ pound raw shrimp, cleaned
¼ cup lime juice
Salt and freshly ground pepper
1 small ripe avocado
2 tablespoons butter

1 tablespoon minced shallots
¼ cup tequila
¾ cup heavy cream
1 tablespoon parsley, chopped

Place shrimp in a bowl and add the lime juice, salt and pepper. Let stand until ready to cook. Peel the avocado and cut it into ½ inch thick slices. Rinse with water. Heat the butter in a skillet; when it is hot but not smoking, add the shrimp, stirring rapidly, and cook about 2 minutes. Sprinkle with the shallots and cook, stirring, about 10 seconds. Add the tequila. Take care, for the tequila may flare up. Add the cream and cook over high heat about 1 minute. Add salt and pepper to taste. Add the avocado and just heat through. Transfer the shrimp and avocado pieces to a hot serving dish. Bring the sauce to a full rolling boil for about 30 seconds and add parsley. Spoon the sauce over the shrimp and avocado. Serve with rice.

This dish is equally good made with cubed chicken breasts or slices of veal.

SHRIMP AU GRATIN
Serves: 4

6 tablespoons butter

3 tablespoons onion, finely chopped

¼ cup flour

¼ teaspoon dry mustard

½ teaspoon salt

⅛ teaspoon white pepper

1½ cups milk

1 cup grated Swiss cheese

2 tablespoons dry white wine or vermouth

1½ pounds shrimp, peeled, deveined, and cooked

½ pound fresh mushrooms, thinly sliced

½ cup soft bread crumbs

Melt 3 tablespoons of the butter in a heavy 12 to 14 inch skillet or heavy 3 quart saucepan. Saute the onion in the butter over low heat, stirring often, for 3 to 4 minutes or until soft and tender. Stir in the flour, blending until smooth, and cook over low heat for 3 minutes. Add the mustard, salt and pepper. Cook, stirring constantly, over moderate heat until mixture is bubbling. Add the milk slowly, stirring constantly. Cook over moderate heat, stirring, for a few minutes until the mixture thickens and bubbles. Add ¾ cup of the Swiss cheese, stirring until melted and blended. Add 2 tablespoons white wine and blend. Add the shrimp to the sauce and remove from heat. In a heavy 10 to 12 inch skillet, melt 2 tablespoons butter and saute the sliced mushrooms over moderate heat for 3 to 5 minutes or until soft and tender. Remove the mushrooms with a slotted spoon and add the mushrooms to the shrimp sauce. Turn the mixture into a buttered shallow 2 quart baking dish. Combine the breadcrumbs and remaining ¼ cup Swiss cheese and sprinkle over the top of the dish. Dot with remaining 1 tablespoon butter. This recipe may be prepared up to this point early in the day and refrigerated. Bring to room temperature before baking. Bake in preheated 400° oven for 10 to 20 minutes or until the sauce is bubbly and the top is lightly browned. Serve at once.

This dish may also be cooked in individual shells or ramekins and served as a first course or luncheon dish.

SHRIMP CURRY CASSEROLE
Serves: 10

4 cups cooked rice

2 cans Campbell's shrimp soup

2 pounds cleaned boiled shrimp

1 cup celery, chopped

1 cup green pepper, chopped

3 teaspoons curry powder

1 teaspoon salt

1 tablespoon Worcestershire sauce

1 cup black pitted olives, halved

Dash cayenne

Dash Tabasco

½ cup slivered almonds

202

Combine soup, celery, green pepper, curry powder, salt, Worcestershire sauce, olives, cayenne and Tabasco. In a large casserole dish, alternate layers of rice, soup mixture and shrimp. Cover with toasted slivered almonds. Bake 45 minutes at 325°.

SHRIMP CREOLE   *Serves: 6*

2 tablespoons butter or bacon drippings
2 tablespoons flour
1 bay leaf, crushed
½ cup minced onion
½ cup diced celery
½ cup minced green pepper
1 teaspoon minced parsley
1 clove garlic, minced
Dash of cayenne pepper
Dash of hot pepper sauce

½ teaspoon salt
½ teaspoon sugar
1½ teaspoons paprika
1 (1 pound) can tomatoes and 1 (8 ounce) can tomato sauce or 6 medium size firm, ripe tomatoes or 1 (6¼ ounce) can tomato paste and 3 cups water
1½ pounds uncooked, medium size shrimp

If you are using fresh tomatoes, peel, squeeze gently to remove seeds and juice and chop coarsely. Shell the shrimp, devein them, and spread them on paper towels to drain. In a large, heavy saucepan or Dutch oven, heat the butter or bacon drippings. Add the onions and garlic and cook until onions are yellow. Blend in the flour and cook until light brown. Add green peppers and celery and, stirring frequently, cook for about 5 minutes until vegetables are soft but not brown. Stir in tomatoes and tomato sauce (or fresh tomatoes and ½ cup water or tomato paste and water), bay leaves, paprika, cayenne, parsley, pepper, salt, pepper sauce and sugar, and bring to a boil. Reduce heat to low and cook slowly, stirring occasionally, for 20 to 30 minutes. Stir in shrimp and continue to simmer for about 5 minutes until shrimp are done. If sauce is not thick enough, add 2 teaspoons cornstarch mixed with 1 tablespoon cold water and stir for 2 or 3 minutes until sauce thickens slightly. Pick out and discard bay leaf. Taste and adjust seasonigs if necessary. Serve over rice.

Preparation time: 30 minutes. Cooking time: 30 to 40 minutes.

SHRIMP CAROLYN

Serves: 6

½ cup bread crumbs

1 tablespoon butter, melted

1½ cups Gruyere cheese, shredded

1 cup mayonnaise

¼ cup dry white wine

1 tablespoon parsley, chopped

1 pound shrimp, cut up

4 tablespoons margarine

1 small jar (2½ ounce) mushrooms

½ cup onion, chopped

Toss together bread crumbs and butter. Set aside. Combine cheese, mayonnaise, wine and parsley. Set aside. Saute shrimp in 2 tablespoons margarine until pink. Drain and set aside. Saute mushrooms and onions in 2 tablespoons margarine. Drain. Combine everything except buttered crumbs. Put into shells or ramekins. Sprinkle buttered crumbs on top. Broil 6 inches from broiler for 2 to 4 minutes.

SHRIMP AND AVOCADO

Serves: 6

4 dozen medium size shrimp, peeled and deveined

2 cloves garlic, minced

1 teaspoon oregano

½ cup butter, melted

3 or 4 avocados

1 to 1½ cups bread crumbs

Saute shrimp, garlic and oregano in butter until just done. Remove from pan. Add bread crumbs to butter and cook a few minutes. Remove from heat. Arrange sliced, peeled avocados in a pinwheel fashion on ovenproof plates. Arrange shrimp over center of avocados and sprinkle with garlic-buttered bread crumbs. Broil quickly until crumbs brown and avocado is just heated. Serve immediately. Makes a good luncheon dish or use smaller portions for a first course.

CREOLE STUFFED PEPPERS

Serves: 4 to 6

1 egg beaten

2 pounds fresh shrimp (peeled and chopped) or a combination of shrimp and crabmeat

Salt and red pepper

¼ cup oil

6 bell peppers, finely chopped

½ large onion, finely chopped

½ cup celery, finely chopped

1 cup homemade bread crumbs

8 to 10 bell pepper halves

Buttered bread crumbs

Add egg to prepared seafood. Add salt and pepper and mix thoroughly. Saute in oil for a couple of minutes. Add chopped peppers, onions and celery. Cook until soft, adding a little more oil if necessary. Add bread crumbs. Blanch pepper halves and stuff with seafood mixture. Top with buttered crumbs. Cook in buttered baking dish at 350° approximately 40 minutes.

CURRIED SHRIMP IN SOUR CREAM   *Serves:* 4

3 tablespoons butter

1 green pepper, chopped

½ cup onion, chopped

1 garlic clove, crushed

1 teaspoon curry powder or to taste

½ teaspoon salt

White pepper to taste

Pinch of tumeric

1 pint (2 cups) sour cream, room temperature

1½ pounds cooked shelled shrimp, deveined

Freshly cooked rice

Melt butter in large skillet over medium-high heat. Add green pepper, onion and garlic, and saute until golden. Blend in curry powder, salt, pepper and tumeric. Just before serving, add sour cream and shrimp and stir over low heat until warmed through. DO NOT ALLOW TO BOIL. Serve over the freshly cooked hot rice.

SALMON PUFF   *Serves:* 4 to 6

1 tablespoon butter

2 tablespoons flour

¾ cup milk

1 pound can salmon, drained

1 stalk celery, chopped

1 small onion, chopped

Parsley to taste

1 tablespoon dry mustard

Dash of salt and pepper

2 eggs, separated

Preheat oven to 350°. Make a cream sauce of the butter, flour and milk, Drain salmon and flake it. Add to sauce. Combine celery, onion, parsley, mustard and seasonings. Add to sauce along with egg yolks. Mix well. Beat egg whites stiff and fold into salmon mixture. Pour into a greased 1½ quart casserole. Bake 35 minutes at 350°. Serve immediately.

CREPES AUX FRUITS DE MER

Serves: 4 to 8

3 tablespoons butter
1 medium onion, chopped
2 cups raw shrimp, cleaned
White wine
4½ tablespoons butter
4½ tablespoons flour

1 cup half and half
Shrimp cooking liquid
1 tablespoon tomato paste
Dash Worcestershire sauce
Salt and pepper to taste
½ cup grated Gruyere cheese

Melt butter in a saucepan. Add onion and saute until clear. Add shrimp and stir. Pour in enough white wine to cover shrimp. Cover and cook until shrimp are just pink. Strain, reserving liquid.

In a second saucepan, melt butter, add flour, whisk and cook for several seconds. Take pan off heat and add half and half. Return to heat and cook until thick. Add enough cooking liquid from shrimp to make a medium thick sauce, about 1 cup. Season with tomato paste, Worcestershire sauce, salt and pepper. Add ¼ cup of cheese. Reserve half of the sauce and pour other half over cooked shrimp. Blend well. Fill crepes with shrimp mixture and place in a buttered ovenproof baking dish. Top with remaining sauce and sprinkle with ¼ cup of cheese. Heat in a 350° oven for 15 minutes. Turn oven to broil and heat 5 minutes or until cheese is lightly browned. Serve immediately.

Yield: 8 crepes.

TARTE L'AVOCAT

Serves: 8 to 10

1 free standing 8 to 10 inch pie crust, baked

Filling:

2 medium avocados
7 ounces frozen artichoke hearts, coarsely chopped
¼ to ½ pound fresh cooked crabmeat
¼ pound cooked ham, coarsely chopped
½ cup mayonnaise (preferably homemade
1 tablespoon capers, rinsed and drained

2 teaspoons tomato sauce
1 teaspoon fresh lemon juice
10 medium large shrimp (cooked and peeled)
Red and Black caviar
Thin slices avocado
Tomato "rose" and parsley

Coarsely chop 1 avocado into mixing bowl. Add next 7 ingredients, salt and pepper. Mix well and spoon into pie crust. Thinly slice other avocado and arrange in spoke on top. Set shrimp upon sprinkles of caviar between slices. Arrange tomato rose, surrounded by parsley, in center. Keep refrigerated until ready to serve. Prepare as close to serving time as possible.

FRUITS DE MER
IN PHYLLO
Serves: 8 or 12 for first course

Panade:

4 tablespoons butter

4 tablespoons flour

½ teaspoon salt

Pepper to taste

1 teaspoon Dijon mustard

1½ cups milk

¼ cup light cream

Cook butter and flour together. Remove from heat and whisk in salt, pepper, mustard, milk and light cream. Set aside to chill.

8 phyllo leaves

2½ to 3 cups bread crumbs

1 cup freshly grated Parmesan cheese

1 teaspoon dry mustard

1 cup shrimp, cooked and deveined

2 cups bay scallops, sauteed in butter

1¼ pounds lobster meat, sauteed in butter

1 cup crab meat

1 cup grated Swiss cheese

4 hard boiled eggs, chopped

1½ cups sour cream

½ cup chopped parsley

¼ cup chives

½ cup shallots, chopped

2 teaspoons garlic, finely minced

Melted butter

Butter a sheet of waxed paper. Use the phyllo leaves, stacking 2 leaves at a time and brushing the top of each pair with melted butter. Mix bread crumbs, Parmesan cheese, and dry mustard together. Spread over phyllo. Using shrimp, scallops, lobster and crab meat, stack down center of phyllo. Sprinkle Swiss cheese over seafood. Add chopped eggs on top of seafood. Dot with sour cream. Sprinkle parsley, chives, shallots and garlic on top. Dot with chilled panade. Roll up like jelly roll, using waxed paper to help roll. Tuck in ends. Brush well with melted butter. Place on buttered baking sheet and bake at 375° for ½ hour or until golden. Serve with hollandaise sauce.

This dish freezes well. To freeze, wrap carefully in foil and saran wrap. To bake, remove saran wrap, and cook frozen at 375° for 1 to 1½ hours.

SEAFOOD FILLING FOR CREPES   *Serves: 4 to 6*

Seafood:

1 pound cooked seafood

1 pound fresh mushrooms, sliced

2 cloves garlic, pressed

¼ cup sherry

¼ cup parsley, chopped

2 tablespoons butter

Saute mushrooms in butter with garlic. Add cut up seafood (well drained and dried). Stir 1 minute and add sherry. Cook until sherry is evaporated. Add parsley. Put into cheese sauce, leaving excess liquid in pan.

Cheese Sauce:

2 tablespoons butter

2 tablespoons flour

1 cup half and half cream, heated

½ cup milk

½ teaspoon salt

Dash of nutmeg

Dash of Tabasco

1 egg yolk

2 cups grated Swiss cheese

2 tablespoons butter, softened

Cook butter and flour together 2 minutes. Do not brown. Add cream and milk. Stir over heat 1 minute until thickened. Add seasonings. Remove from heat. Beat in egg yolk with whisk. Stir in cheese, then butter. Stir in seafood mixture. Fill crepes.

SEAFOOD FRITTERS   *Serves: 4*

1 cup finely chopped cooked seafood

1 tablespoon parsley, chopped

1 egg

⅔ cup milk

1 cup flour

1 teaspoon baking powder

Salt and pepper to taste

Cayenne pepper, onion juice, lemon juice, dill or other flavorings as you may desire to taste

Frying oil

Make a batter with the flour, baking powder, egg and milk. Add the cut-up seafood and parsley. Add seasonings. Mix well. Drop by spoonfulls into the hot (375°) fat. Fry golden brown and drain well. Serve hot with tartar sauce or catsup.

This is an excellent way to use leftover steamed oysters.

SAUCES

Old Stone House (Braun House), near Salisbury

FIERY BARBEQUE SAUCE   *Yield: About 2 cups*

½ cup water

1 cup plus 2 tablespoons catsup

¼ cup vinegar

¼ cup Worcestershire sauce

¼ cup plus 2 tablespoons
  firmly packed brown sugar

4 tablespoons butter or
  margarine

2 tablespoons lemon juice

2 teaspoons salt

2 teaspoons dry mustard

2 teaspoons chili powder

2 teaspoons ground paprika

1 teaspoon ground red pepper

Combine all ingredients in saucepan; cook over medium heat until sugar dissolves, stirring occasionally. Use on pork chops or chicken. May be prepared ahead and stored in refrigerator.

Preparation time: 15 minutes.

EXCELLENT BARBEQUE SAUCE FOR CHICKEN OR PORK

½ cup cooking oil

1 cup cider vinegar

1 tablespoon salt

1½ teaspoons poultry
  seasoning

¼ teaspoon pepper

1 egg, beaten

Mix all ingredients well and marinate chicken or pork. This can also be cooked in the oven if you baste often. Make it in the morning and marinate until ready to cook

Will marinate 1 large chicken.

Preparation time: 10 minutes.

BEEF BARBEQUE SAUCE

½ cup Burgundy

½ cup chili sauce

¼ cup salad oil

3 tablespoons wine vinegar

1 teaspoon Worcestershire
  sauce

1 tablespoon onion, chopped

1 clove garlic, minced

1 bay leaf

Salt

Pepper

Mix. Pour over meat. Allow to marinate, turning occasionally for 3 to 24 hours. Use left over sauce for basting while grilling.

This amount will coat 3 pounds meat.

211

MRS. McCOMBS BARBEQUE SAUCE
(for lamb or pork)

Serves: 6 to 8

4 tablespoons sugar	2 egg yolks
2 tablespoons salt (scant)	6 tablespoons butter
2 tablespoons flour (heaping)	1 cup milk
2 tablespoons dry mustard	¼ cup vinegar
Cayenne pepper to taste	¼ cup water

Mix together and sift sugar, salt, flour, mustard and cayenne pepper. Add this dry mixture to slightly beaten egg yolks. Add butter which has been melted. Slowly add warmed milk. Mix vinegar and water slowly and add to above mixture. Place on stove on medium heat and cook until mixture thickens, stirring constantly. Serve hot on lamb or pork.

Preparation time: 30 minutes. May be made ahead of time and reheated in double boiler. Do not freeze.

JIM BANE SAUCE

Yield: 2 quarts

1 (14 ounce) bottle catsup	1 (10½ ounce) bottle A-1 sauce
1 (12 ounce) bottle chili sauce	2 (8 ounce) bottles chutney
1 (5 ounce) bottle Worcestershire sauce	½ cup bourbon

Place ingredients in blender and blend at low speed for a minute or two until the sauce is smooth and the chutney is well blended.

Serve with Cream cheese and crackers (as an appetizer), or with shrimp, fish, chicken, or pork (as a main dish).

Ages well, in fact, it improves when made in advance. The longer it sits the better it tastes. May be kept indefinitely if refrigerated.

GRILLED CHICKEN BARBEQUE SAUCE

4 cups vinegar	1 teaspoon A-1 sauce
1 (26 ounce) bottle catsup	1 teaspoon salt
1½ tablespoons crushed red pepper pods	1 heaping teaspoon barbeque spice
1 tablespoon soy sauce	½ teaspoon MSG
1 tablespoon dry mustard	2 tablespoons honey

Cook slowly on medium for 10 to 15 minutes. Pour over chicken about an hour before cooking, then use sauce to baste while grilling. This is enough for four chickens.

Preparation time: 20 minutes.

BARBEQUE SAUCE FOR HOTDOGS AND HAMBURGERS

1 medium onion, chopped
3 tablespoons salad oil
1 tablespoon sugar
1 teaspoon dry mustard
1 teaspoon paprika
Salt and pepper
¼ cup catsup

½ cup water
¼ cup vinegar
1 tablespoon Worcestershire sauce
1 drop Tabasco sauce

Brown onion in salad oil. Add other ingredients and simmer 15 minutes. Great over slaw with hot dogs or hamburgers.

Preparation time: 20 minutes.

BEEF MARINADE FOR ROAST

1 cup wine or wine vinegar (if you use white wine add ½ cup vinegar)
1 cup oil
½ cup Worcestershire
½ cup barbeque sauce
¼ cup Texas Pete
1 tablespoon garlic salt or powder

1 bay leaf, broken
1 tablespoon maple syrup
1 tablespoon brown sugar
½ cup soy sauce
1 tablespoon of each of the following: parsley flakes, Italian seasoning, chopped chives and basil

Marinate for 2 days. On the second day, leave the meat out for several hours before cooking. Turn several times while marinating. Cook meat over low coals 1½ hours or to desired doneness.

Preparation time: 15 minutes.

LONDON BROIL MARINADE
(to be used on flank steak)

⅔ cup dry red wine

⅓ cup olive oil

2 garlic cloves, mashed

1 teaspoon salt

½ teaspoon thyme

½ teaspoon pepper

¼ teaspoon marjoram

¼ teaspoon basil

Marinate flank steak at least 8 hours or overnight.

BEARNAISE SAUCE

½ cup red wine vinegar

3 tablespoons chopped shallots

1 tablespoon minced fresh tarragon or ½ teaspoon dried crumbled

2 teaspoons fresh chervil or ⅜ teaspoon dried

½ teaspoon salt

¼ teaspoon ground pepper

4 egg yolks

2 sticks unsalted butter, cut into pieces

¼ cup whipping cream

Combine first 6 ingredients in heavy saucepan and bring to a boil over high heat. Reduce heat and simmer until liquid is reduced to 2 tablespoons. Let cool.

Lightly whisk yolks and add to vinegar mixture. Place over low heat and whisk until thickens and becomes creamy. Whisk in butter 1 piece at a time, mixing completely before adding more butter. Whisk until consistency of light mayonnaise

Just before serving, whip cream until stiff and fold into mixture.

GRILLED FISH SAUCE

2 sticks butter, melted

¼ cup lemon juice

¼ cup barbeque sauce

Heat above ingredients, pour over fish and marinate for 30 minutes. Reserve all liquid to mop fish as they grill. Cook fish until they are fork tender. Pour remaining liquid over fish as you serve each plate.

LEMON/HORSERADISH CHICKEN BARBEQUE SAUCE

⅓ cup butter, melted

¼ cup lemon juice

2 tablespoons creamy
  horseradish

2 tablespoons catsup

2 tablespoons vinegar

2 teaspoons salt

1½ teaspoons Worcestershire
  sauce

¾ teaspoon Tabasco sauce

Combine all ingredients, and use as sauce for oven barbequed chicken, or charcoal grilled. The charcoal grilled flavor is really enhanced by this sauce. Try grilling ahead of time and pouring remaining sauce over the chicken in a casserole dish. Keep warm in low oven, or reheat later.

BLENDER BEARNAISE

1 tablespoon tarragon vineger

2 tablespoons white wine

2 teaspoons chopped tarragon

2 teaspoons shallots or onions

¼ teaspoon freshly ground
  black pepper

½ cup butter

3 egg yolks

2 tablespoons lemon juice

¼ teaspoon salt

Pinch of cayenne pepper.

Combine vinegar, wine, tarragon, shallots and pepper in a skillet. Bring to a boil and cook until almost all of the liquid disappears. In a small saucepan or in the microwave heat the butter to bubbling. Do not brown. Place the egg yolks, lemon juice, salt and cayenne in the container of an electric blender. Cover the container and start at high speed for a couple of seconds. Remove the cover, turn blender on high and gradually add the hot butter. Add the herb mixture and blend on high about four seconds.

This sauce will keep about 1 hour if placed in a preheated thermos. Preparation time: 20 minutes.

HORSERADISH CREAM SAUCE

¼ cup horseradish

1 cup heavy cream

1 teaspoon salt

Add salt to cream and whip until stiff. Fold in horseradish. Serve at once. Makes about 2 cups.

Preparation time: 10 minutes.

BLENDER HOLLANDAISE

½ cup butter

3 egg yolks

2 tablespoons lemon juice

¼ teaspoon salt

Pinch of cayenne pepper

Melt ½ cup butter but do not brown. In a blender container put the egg yolks, lemon juice, salt and cayenne. Turn the blender on low and gradually add the hot butter. Blend about 15 seconds or until sauce is smooth and thick. Makes about ¾ cup.

This sauce will keep about 1 hour if placed in a preheated thermos. Preparation time: 10 seconds.

MAYONNAISE

1 teaspoon salt

½ teaspoon dry mustard

¼ teaspoon paprika

Dash cayenne

2 tablespoons lemon juice

2 egg yolks

2 tablespoons vinegar

2 cups salad oil

Mix dry ingredients, add egg yolks and blend with beater. Add vinegar and mix well. Add salad oil a little at a time, beating all the while. At end alternate with lemon juice. Beat in 1 tablespoon hot water to cut oily appearance. Makes 2 cups.

Note: Chill oil, bowl, beaters to avoid separation.

BLENDER MAYONNAISE

In blender or food processor put 2 egg yolks or 1 whole egg, 2 tablespoons white vinegar or lemon juice, ¼ cup oil, 1½ teaspoons salt, 1 teaspoon pepper, 1 teaspoon paprika. Turn on machine. Slowly add ¾ cup oil.

MINT SAUCE FOR LAMB

Mix together about ⅔ cup mint jelly and ⅓ cup Mr. Mustard and heat slowly. Delicious over lamb chops or leg of lamb.

Preparation time: 10 minutes.

ORANGE SAUCE

¼ cup butter

¼ cup flour

1½ cups chicken stock

½ teaspoon salt

⅔ cup orange juice

Dash Tabasco

2 tablespoons sherry

Grated rind of 1 orange

Melt butter, stir in flour and cook 2 minutes. Slowly add the stock. Add salt, orange juice, Tabasco, sherry and orange rind. This is good with goose and duck.

Preparation time: 15 minutes.

WILD FOWL SAUCE

2 cups chicken broth

⅓ cup onions, diced

6 sprigs fresh parsley, chopped

½ cup celery, chopped

10 whole black peppercorns

1 bay leaf

3 tablespoons butter

4 tablespoons flour

¾ cup dry white wine

1 cup heavy cream

Salt and pepper to taste

4 tablespoons fresh parsley, chopped

3 tablespoons cognac

In saucepan, combine chicken broth, onions, parsley, celery, peppercorns and bay leaf. Bring to a boil and reduce liquid to one cup.

Melt the butter in a saucepan and add the flour. Slowly add the broth. Simmer about 5 minutes. Add wine and cook over medium heat for 5 minutes, stirring constantly. Remove from heat and add cream. Return to heat and simmer 5 more minutes. Strain sauce. Add salt and pepper to taste. Blend in chopped parsley and cognac. Use with any game bird.

Preparation time: 25 minutes.

SWEET-SOUR SAUCE

⅔ cup sugar

¼ cup catsup

⅓ cup crushed pineapple
   and juice

⅓ cup sweet pickle juice

⅝ cup vinegar

Simmer 15 minutes.

Use with cooked chicken, pork or shrimp. Serve as cold dish.

Preparation time: 15 minutes.

MUSHROOM SAUCE

Serves: 6

2 tablespoons butter

1 small onion, chopped

½ clove garlic, chopped

1 tablespoon parsley, chopped

1 tablespoon flour

1 cup chicken broth

⅛ teaspoon nutmeg

¾ pound mushrooms, thinly sliced

¼ cup dry sherry

Heat one tablespoon butter in a saucepan. Add onion, garlic, parsley, and cook over medium heat for three minutes. Stir in flour and gradually add broth while stirring constantly. Add nutmeg. In a skillet melt remaining butter. Add the mushrooms and saute 5 minutes. Add this to the saucepan and simmer for 15 minutes. Add the wine and bring to a boil. It may be served with poultry or meat.

Preparation time: 30 minutes.

POISSON CARDINALE

5 tablespoons butter

1 clove garlic, minced

¼ cup minced onions

5 tablespoons flour

1 tablespoon tomato paste

1¼ cups chicken broth

1 teaspoon salt

¼ teaspoon nutmeg

½ teaspoon Tabasco

Pinch thyme

6 sprigs chopped parsley

1 bay leaf

1 cup light cream

2 tablespoons lemon juice

2 tablespoons brandy

6 sliced mushrooms, sauteed

12 raw peeled and deveined shrimp (optional)

In a large skillet, melt butter, saute garlic and onions until tender. Do not allow to brown. Blend in flour. Add tomato paste and cook for 2 minutes. Gradually stir in chicken broth. Add mushrooms, salt, nutmeg, Tabasco, thyme, parsley and bay leaf. Mix well. Stir in cream, lemon juice and brandy to form a smooth sauce. Add shrimp if desired. Serve over broiled or baked fish. Will serve eight.

Preparation time: 20 minutes.

QUICK PEACH GLAZE

Yield: 1¼ cups

Combine 1 cup peach preserves, 2 tablespoons prepared mustard, ½ teaspoon ground cloves, 1 tablespoon soy sauce; heat. Use glaze for poultry, ham and burgers.

Preparation time: 10 minutes.

SAUCE FOR BAKED HAM
Serves: 8 to 10

1 cup brown sugar
½ cup vinegar
½ cup sherry

⅓ cup dry mustard
2½ teaspoons sifted flour
2 eggs

Beat eggs. Slowly add vinegar, sherry, dry mustard and sifted flour. Cook in double boiler until thick. Serve warm.

Preparation time: 20 minutes. May be made ahead of time and reheated in double boiler. Do not freeze.

SAUCE FOR BAKED POTATOES
Serves: 8

½ cup softened butter
½ cup mayonnaise
1 small onion, grated
2 tablespoons Worcestershire sauce

Tabasco to taste
Salt to taste
Pepper to taste

Mix all together.
Preparation time: 10 minutes.

SPICY CRANBERRY CHUTNEY

1 pound cranberries
1 cup seedless raisins
1⅓ cups sugar
1 tablespoon ground cinnamon
1½ teaspoons ground ginger
¼ teaspoon ground cloves

1 cup water
1 medium onion, chopped (½ cup)
1 medium apple, chopped (leave skins on)
½ cup celery, thinly sliced

Combine cranberries, raisins, sugar, spices and water in large saucepan. Cook 15 minutes until berries pop and mixture thickens. Stir in onions, apples and celery. Simmer 15 minutes longer or until mixture is thick. Cool. Refrigerate. Good with poultry or pork. Especially good as an appetizer spread over top and sides of a block of Cream cheese. Serve with wheat crackers. May be prepared ahead of time.

Preparation time: 30 to 45 minutes.

CRANBERRY RELISH

Serves: 12

1¾ cups sugar
½ cup water
1 teaspoon cinnamon
1 teaspoon ground cloves

4 cups fresh cranberries
1 chopped orange (skin and pulp)
½ cup brandy

Combine sugar with water and bring to boil stirring constantly for 3 minutes. Add cinnamon, cloves and cranberries. Cook about 8 minutes or until the cranberries pop. Stir occasionally. Remove from heat. Add orange and brandy. When cool refrigerate. This will keep for weeks.
Preparation time: 20 minutes.

HOT MUSTARD

1 (2 ounce) can dry mustard
Fill can with light brown sugar

1½ teaspoons salt
¾ cup vinegar

Mix dry ingredients. Boil vinegar and add gradually to dry ingredients until right consistency. May take a little more vinegar. Use immediately or store.
Preparation time: 15 minutes.

PEPPER RELISH

12 green peppers
12 red hot peppers
10 large onions
2 tablespoons salt

1 cup sugar
1 tablespoon celery seed
1 tablespoon mustard seed
1½ pints vinegar

Remove seeds from peppers. Grind peppers and onions. Add 2 tablespoons salt, cover with hot water and let stand ½ hour. Drain. Place in large pot with sugar, celery, mustard seed and vinegar. Boil slowly ¾ hour. Place in hot sterilized jars and seal.
Preparation time: 2 hours.

VEGETABLES

Hezekiah Alexander House, Charlotte

SHREDDED YAMS
Serves: 12

2 pounds raw sweet potatoes
1 gallon water
1 tablespoon salt
½ cup sugar

½ cup white corn syrup
½ cup water
1 cup pineapple juice
4 tablespoons butter

Shred yams into gallon of water with salt added. Combine sugar, syrup and ½ cup water in heavy pan. Cook until mixture forms light syrup. Drain potatoes, rinse, and pat dry. Place in 12 x 6 x 3 inch pyrex baking dish. Pour pineapple juice over potatoes. Cover with cooked syrup. Dot with butter. Bake, uncovered, at 350° about 35 minutes or until potatoes are translucent. Package and freeze part of cooked yams if desired. For a sweeter casserole, add ¼ cup sugar.

Preparation time: 30 minutes. May be prepared ahead of time or frozen.

SWEET POTATO CASSEROLE WITH TOPPING
Serves: 8

3 cups cooked sweet potatoes, mashed
1½ cups sugar
2 eggs
1 teaspoon vanilla

½ teaspoon allspice
4 teaspoons orange juice
¼ cup whole sweet milk

Combine all ingredients and beat with mixer until light. Pour into well buttered casserole (8 x 12 inch).

Topping:

⅓ cup butter
⅓ cup flour

⅔ cup brown sugar
1 cup chopped nuts

Cream butter, add sugar, flour and nuts. Sprinkle over top of potato mixture. Bake at 350° for 30 minutes.

Preparation time: 30 minutes. May be prepared ahead.

SWEET POTATO PUDDING

3 cups raw sweet potatoes,
  grated

2 cups milk

2 eggs, beaten

¾ cup brown sugar

1 teaspoon cinnamon

1 teaspoon allspice

½ teaspoon nutmeg

¼ teaspoon ginger

2 tablespoons melted butter
  or margarine

Dash of salt

Add milk, sugar, butter and seasonings to eggs. Mix with grated sweet potatoes. Pour into buttered baking dish. Bake at 325° for 1 hour. Serve warm.

May pour ½ cup bourbon over the cooked pudding.

SWEET POTATO BALLS   *Yield: 2 dozen balls*

4 to 5 large sweet potatoes

2 dozen large marshmallows

1 pound package crushed
  coconut

Boil or bake sweet potatoes. Peel and mash fine. Pat mashed sweet potato around each marshmallow and roll each in crushed coconut. Spray shallow pan with Pam and bake in 450° oven until light brown, approximately 10 minutes.

Preparation time: 30 minutes. May be made ahead and reheated.

MUSHROOMS IN SOUR CREAM   *Serves: 8*

2 pounds of mushrooms, sliced

½ cup butter or margarine

½ cup green onions, minced

1 teaspoon salt

Sprinkle of pepper

½ cup sour cream

In a 12 inch skillet over medium high heat, melt butter or margarine. Add mushrooms and minced green onions with salt and pepper. Cook, stirring frequently, about 10 minutes or until mushrooms are tender. Stir in sour cream. Heat through. Do not boil.

GERMAN MUSHROOMS
Serves: 4

1 pound mushrooms
3 tablespoons butter
1 teaspoon onion or garlic salt
1 pinch lemon-pepper
½ teaspoon salt
¾ cup sour cream

½ tablespoon flour
2 tablespoons white wine
2 tablespoons sherry
1 tablespoon fresh chopped chives or green onion tops

Saute mushrooms in butter for 4 minutes. Add seasonings. Sift in flour. Add wines and stir 1 minute. Stir in sour cream and chives. Heat and serve with toast points.

SPINACH PIE
Serves: 4 as main course

1 unbaked (9 inch) pie shell
1 cup sliced onions
1 cup sliced mushrooms (canned or fresh)

1 cup Swiss cheese, grated
1 package Stouffer's spinach souffle

Saute onions and mushrooms until onions are golden. Remove from pan and drain on paper towel. Put Swiss cheese on pie crust, place onions and mushrooms on top of cheese. Remove frozen spinach souffle from tin and put on top of mushrooms and onion mixture. Bake in 350° oven for 20 minutes; spread spinach to edge of pie pan and continue baking for another 40 minutes at 350°.
Serves: 8 as hors d'oeuvres. Preparation time: 15 minutes.

SPINACH MILANO
Serves: 8

2 packages frozen chopped spinach
¼ cup flour
⅓ cup melted butter
3 eggs, beaten

4 slices American cheese, cut into cubes
4 slices Brick cheese, cubed
1 (12 ounce) carton Cottage cheese
Salt and pepper to taste

Cook spinach. Drain. Gradually add flour to butter, blending until smooth; add to spinach with remaining ingredients, mixing well.
Spoon into lightly greased 1½ quart casserole. Bake for 1 hour at 350°.

ASPARAGUS FRIED RICE

Serves: 8

2 cups water

1 cup long-grain converted rice

2 tablespoons unsalted butter

2 large shallots, minced
(1 ounce)

1½ teaspoons salt

White pepper

2 pounds fresh asparagus
spears, stems peeled

1 cup parsley leaves, minced
(measure before mincing)

8 medium green onions
(4 ounces) thinly sliced
on diagonal

2½ tablespoons peanut oil

Combine first 5 ingredients in a small saucepan and bring to boil. Stir through once, reduce heat to low, cover and simmer until liquid is absorbed, about 15 minutes. Remove from heat and let stand, covered, 10 minutes. Fluff rice with fork, let cool and refrigerate.

Cut 1½ inches from tips of asparagus spears and set aside. Slice remaining stems thinly on the diagonal. Use slicer in food processor if desired. Blanch stems 30 seconds in 1 quart rapidly boiling water mixed with 2 teaspoons salt. Remove with slotted spoon, maintaining water at boil. Run stems under cold water until cold to touch; drain well and set aside. Blanch asparagus tips 30 seconds in same boiling water; cool and drain well. Add sliced asparagus stems, parsley, onion, salt and pepper to rice, mix lightly but thoroughly, reserving asparagus tips.

Recipe may be done ahead up to this point and refrigerated.

At serving time, heat 2 tablespoons oil in large skillet over medium high heat until sizzling. Add rice and quickly heat through, stirring gently. Heat remaining oil in small skillet over medium-high heat. Add asparagus tips and quickly heat through. Sprinkle over rice and serve immediately.

SUZANNE'S TOMATOES FLORENTINE

1 medium onion, finely
chopped

½ stick butter

2 packages frozen chopped
spinach, cooked

Salt and pepper to taste

4 medium tomatoes

Grated Romano cheese

Saute onion in butter and add cooked, seasoned spinach. Cut tomatoes in half and scoop out pulp. Sprinkle cavity with salt, then flip to drain. Fill the cavity with spinach and onion mixture. Top with grated cheese and bake 10 to 12 minutes at 300°.

ESTER'S CELERY WITH ALMONDS

4 cups sliced celery, dry
  thoroughly before chopping

4 tablespoons butter

Salt and pepper to taste

1 tablespoon finely chopped
  chives

1 cup shredded almonds,
  toasted

Parmesan cheese

1 tablespoon onions, grated

3 tablespoons flour

1 cup light cream

½ cup double strength chicken
  bouillon (2 cubes or 2
  teaspoons extract)

Cook celery in butter in covered pan until tender (10 to 15 minutes at
low heat). While this is cooking, sprinkle with chives and onions. Stir in
flour and gradually add cream and bouillon and cook. Stir until thickened.
Add almonds and seasoning to taste. Put in casserole, sprinkle with cheese
and brown under broiler.

EGGPLANT ROLLUPS
Serves: 4 to 6

1¼ to 1½ pounds eggplant

Salt and pepper to taste

½ cup flour

1 egg

1 tablespoon water

Vegetable oil

1 pound Ricotta cheese

6 tablespoons Parmesan cheese
  (or Mozzarella)

1 tablespoon dried parsley

1 tablespoon oregano

Favorite tomato sauce

Peel eggplant and cut lengthwise into ¼ inch slices. Sprinkle both sides
with salt and let drain on paper towels for 1 hour. Pat slices dry. Dredge
slices in ½ cup flour seasoned with salt and pepper, shaking off excess
flour. Dip slices in 1 lightly beaten egg with 1 tablespoon water. Saute in
oil until lightly browned on each side. Drain. Combine remaining
ingredients except tomato sauce. Put 2 to 3 tablespoons of filling on end of
each slice and roll up. Spread a thin layer of tomato sauce in shallow
baking dish. Place rollups side down (fasten with toothpicks if necessary).
Cover rolls with more sauce and sprinkle grated Parmesan or Mozarella
cheese if desired. Bake in 400° oven for 15 to 20 minutes until hot.
  Preparation time: 1½ hours.

SPINACH TIMBALES

Serves: 4 to 6

1 pound fresh spinach, washed
    well or 2 (10 ounce) packages
    frozen spinach

2 large eggs, beaten until frothy

½ cup heavy cream, heated

½ teaspoon nutmeg

½ teaspoon salt

Pepper to taste

1 lemon sliced for garnish

Cook spinach in salted water 4 to 5 minutes. Drain, cool and squeeze dry. Chop spinach finely. Place in bowl, add eggs, hot cream and seasonings. Pour in buttered timbale molds, custard or souffle cups. Place in larger pan and fill ½ full. Bake at 375° for 45 minutes. Unmold, garnish and serve.

NEW ORLEANS SPINACH

Serves: 6 to 8

2 packages frozen chopped
    spinach

1 large (8 ounce) Cream
    cheese, softened

1 lemon (juice and grated rind)

Salt to taste

½ stick butter, divided

Pepperidge Farm Herb dressing
    or bread crumbs

Cook spinach as directed and drain well. Mix softened Cream cheese, ¼ stick butter, rind of lemon and lemon juice to taste. Mix drained spinach and cheese mixture together and put in buttered casserole. Add salt to taste.

Cover top with Pepperidge Farm dressing mixed with ¼ stick melted butter. Cook at 350° for 25 minutes or until thoroughly hot. Sprinkle with parsley.

Preparation time: 20 minutes. Can be frozen.

VARIATION: Add 1 can artichoke hearts before baking.

BEAN BUNDLES

Serves: 8 to 12

2 cans vertical packed green
    beans, drained

Sauce:

3 tablespoons butter

3 tablespoons tarragon vinegar

½ teaspoon salt

½ pound bacon sliced in half

1 teaspoon paprika

1 tablespoon parsley

1 teaspon onion juice

Place 5 beans in each ½ slice of bacon, wrap and secure with a toothpick. Broil until bacon is done.

For sauce, combine all ingredients and simmer until hot and pour over beans. If you prepare ahead, reheat beans and sauce separately.

SPINACH CREPES

12 to 15 crepes
¼ cup butter
3 tablespoons flour
1 cup milk
½ teaspoon salt
Dash nutmeg
Dash pepper

1 cup Cheddar cheese, shredded
4 ounces mushrooms, drained
1 teaspoon onion, grated
1 (10 ounce) package frozen chopped spinach, cooked and squeezed dry
Butter to brush crepes
Grated Parmesan cheese

Make a cream sauce by melting ¼ cup butter, then adding 3 tablespoons flour. Slowly add 1 cup milk, ½ teaspoon salt, dash of nutmeg and pepper.

Add cheese, mushrooms, grated onion and cooked spinach to the cream sauce. Spoon 2 tablespoons filling on each crepe. Roll up and place on baking sheet that has been sprayed with Pam. Brush each crepe with 1 teaspoon butter, melted and grated Parmesan cheese.

Bake at 375° for 15 to 20 minutes.

SPINACH SUPREME

Serves: 8

2 packages frozen chopped spinach
3 tablespoons butter
3 tablespoons flour
1 teaspoon salt
½ teaspoon pepper

Juice of 1 lemon
2 eggs, beaten
1 cup Parmesan cheese
Dash nutmeg

Cook spinach and drain, reserving 1½ cups liquid (add water if necessary). Make a sauce with liquid, flour, butter, salt and pepper. When thick, remove from heat and add lemon juice and eggs. Put back on heat and stir for a minute or 2. Remove and add cheese, spinach and nutmeg to the sauce. Pour into ring mold or casserole and bake 30 minutes at 350° or until set. Takes longer for casserole. Unmold and serve with buttered carrots.

BLACK-EYED PEAS
Serves: 10

2 pounds peas

2 pounds stewed tomatoes, canned

1 pound salt pork

1 cup molasses

1 onion

Salt and pepper to taste

Soak peas ovenight in salted water. Drain. Cook salt pork in skillet until soft. Drain. Add peas, tomatoes, sliced onion, molasses and pepper. Simmer covered 2 hours or until peas are tender.

ZUCCHINI CASSEROLE
Serves: 6

4 to 6 cups zucchini

1 medium onion

2 eggs

1 cup mayonnaise

1 cup Parmesan cheese

Pepperidge Farm dressing

Chop zucchini and onions and cook in boiling, salted water until tender. Drain. Mix eggs, mayonnaise and Parmesan cheese. Mix this with the zucchini and pour in 1½ quart buttered casserole. Top with Pepperidge Farm dressing. Bake 25 to 35 minutes in 350° oven.

ZUCCHINI CASSEROLE
Serves: 12

7 small zucchini

4 ears corn (2 cans niblets)

3 medium tomatoes, diced

1 green pepper, chopped

2 medium onions, chopped

¼ cup butter

1 tablespoon flour

1 teaspoon chili powder

1½ teaspoons salt

1 teaspoon sugar

Pepper to taste

Slice zucchini, combine with remaining vegetables and put in greased 3 quart casserole with lid. Melt butter and stir in flour and then seasonings. Pour over vegetables. Cover and bake at 375° for 40 minutes covered. Uncover casserole and bake at 375° for 40 minutes.

Preparation time: 30 minutes.

BROILED ZUCCHINI STICKS
Serves: 4

4 to 5 medium zucchini
(about 1 pound)

3 to 4 tablespoons melted
butter

Salt to taste

½ cup freshly grated Parmesan
cheese

Halve zucchini crosswise and cut each half in quarters lengthwise. Dip in butter, salt lightly and coat with cheese. Broil 4 to 6 inches from heat about 5 minutes or until crisp.

To serve as hors d'oeuvre, cut smaller, as for french fries.

ZUCCHINI AND CHEESE CASSEROLE *Serves:* 6

3 medium zucchini

Salt and pepper to taste

1 cup Cheddar cheese, grated

1 cup Swiss cheese, grated

2 large basil leaves, chopped

1 clove garlic, minced

Grate zucchini, add salt and pepper and let drain in collander for 30 minutes. Combine cheeses. Combine basil, garlic and zucchini.

Place zucchini and cheeses in alternate layers in 9 inch souffle dish, ending with cheese. Bake at 325° for 25 minutes or until golden.

AUNT FANNY'S BAKED SQUASH *Serves:* 8

3 pounds yellow summer
squash

½ cup chopped onions

½ cup cracker meal or bread
crumbs

2 eggs

1 stick butter

1 tablespoon sugar

1 teaspoon salt

½ teaspoon black pepper

Wash and cut up squash. Boil until tender; drain thoroughly, then mash. Add all ingredients except ½ of butter to squash. Melt remaining butter. Pour mixture in baking dish, then spread melted butter over top and sprinkle with meal or crumbs. Bake 1 hour at 375°.

Can be frozen.

BUTTERNUT SQUASH PUDDING   *Serves: 4 to 6*

1 medium butternut squash
½ cup butter
2 eggs beaten
⅛ teaspoon maple flavoring

1 cup dark brown sugar
½ cup milk
¼ teaspoon salt

Peel, seed and slice squash. Steam until tender; drain and mash. While squash is hot, add butter and let melt. Add all other ingredients and mix well. Pour into a greased baking dish and bake about 30 minutes at 350°.

SQUASH ALFREDO   *Serves: 6*

1 medium spaghetti squash
¼ cup milk
½ stick butter

¼ pound Parmesan cheese, grated
Oregano, salt, pepper

Bake the squash at 350° for 1 hour. Cool to touch and scoop out seeds (like a pumpkin) and discard. Scoop out squash, which will separate into strings. Layer in casserole with butter and Parmesan cheese. Season to taste and stir in milk.
Bake covered at 350° for 20 minutes or until thoroughly heated.
Preparation time: 1½ hours.

VARIATION: Add tomato sauce instead of milk.

EGGPLANT PARMIGIANA   *Serves: 4 to 6*

1 medium eggplant, thickly sliced
Flour
1 egg beaten with some milk
Dried breadcrumbs, wheat germ, or cracker meal
Olive oil
½ pound Swiss cheese or Mozzarella, sliced

6 ounces tomato paste
White or red wine, as needed
Clove of garlic
Salt and pepper to taste
1 cup freshly grated Parmesan cheese
Oregano

Wash eggplant and slice, unpeeled, about ¼ inch thick. Dip slices first in flour, then egg, then breadcrumbs to coat. Saute in olive oil until browned on both sides. Arrange in baking dish; put a slice of cheese on each.

Make a thick tomato sauce by diluting the tomato paste with wine. Add oregano, salt, pepper and crushed garlic to the sauce. Spread 2 to 3 tablespoons of sauce on each slice; sprinkle grated Parmesan to top.

Bake at 400° for about 15 minutes.

Preparation time: 15 to 30 minutes.

EGGPLANT WITH CLAMS CASSEROLE

1 eggplant

¼ cup celery, chopped

¼ cup onion, chopped

¼ cup flour

½ cup milk

1 (7 ounce) can minced clams

2 eggs

¼ cup bread crumbs

Parmesan cheese

Saute onion and celery in butter. Add flour, milk and clams (with juice). Let thicken, stirring constantly. Cube eggplant and cook until tender. Place eggplant in a buttered casserole. Add the clam mixture, beat the eggs lightly and pour into casserole mixture. Top with bread crumbs, and sprinkle with Parmesan cheese.

Bake at 350° until cheese is lightly brown.

EGGPLANT CASSEROLE SIMPLE
Serves: 4

1 medium eggplant

4 tomatoes, sliced

2 medium onions, sliced

Salt and pepper to taste

½ cup grated Parmesan cheese

4 tablespoons butter or
margarine

Peel eggplant and cut into ½ inch thick slices. Cover bottom of greased 2 quart casserole with eggplant. Top with layer of tomato slices, then onion slices. Season to taste and sprinkle with part of cheese. Repeat layers until casserole is filled ending with tomatoes topped with cheese. Cover casserole and bake at 375° for around 45 minutes.

RATATOUILLE

⅔ cup fresh parsley leaves loosely packed, minced after measuring

2 large garlic cloves, minced

½ pound tomatoes (about 2 medium) peeled, seeded and coarsely chopped (or canned plum tomatoes, drained and chopped)

1 medium eggplant (about 1¼ pounds), peeled and cut into cubes

3 medium zucchini (about 1 pound), trimmed and cut into ¼ inch slices

1 tablespoon salt

¼ cup olive oil

1 teaspoon ground coriander

1 teaspoon crushed thyme

2 large onions (about ½ pound), sliced

2 small green peppers (about 6 ounces) seeded and cut into ¼ inch slices

3 tablespoons tomato paste

Pinch of sugar

1½ teaspoons dried basil

Salt and freshly ground black pepper to taste

Place the eggplant and the zucchini slices in a colander in the sink. Sprinkle them with the salt, toss, and let stand for 30 minutes to let excess moisture escape. Pat dry with paper towels.

In a 10 to 12 inch skillet with a cover, heat 2 tablespoons of the oil over high heat. Add the eggplant and zucchini and saute for 1 minute. Cover the skillet, reduce the heat to moderate and let the mixture steam for 3 minutes, shaking the pan several times. Stir in the coriander and thyme. Check the seasoning and add salt and pepper if needed. Set aside.

In a 10 to 12 inch non-aluminum skillet, saute the onions and peppers in the remaining 2 tablespoons oil over moderate heat until they are just soft. Stir in the reserved minced garlic and chopped tomatoes, the tomato sauce, tomato paste and sugar. Cover the skillet, reduce the heat to lower temperature and cook the mixture for 5 minutes. Uncover and cook until the juices evaporate. Season with the basil, salt, pepper and all but 3 tablespoons of the minced parsley. Be sure it is well seasoned.

To assemble the Ratatouille, oil a 1½ quart ovenproof casserole. Spread ⅓ of the tomato and pepper mixture over the bottom of the casserole. Cover with ½ of the eggplant and zucchini mixture. Add another layer of ½ the remaining tomato and pepper mixture, a layer of the remaining eggplant and zucchini and top with a layer of the remaining tomato and peppers.

Bake the casserole, uncovered in the middle of a preheated oven for 40 minutes or until vegetables are soft. Serve at room temperature or cold. Garnish with the remaining 3 tablespoons minced parsley if you are serving as a vegetable or stir it in if you are using it in another recipe.

RATATOUILLE A LA PROVENCALE

2 small eggplants	2 onions
4 green peppers	2 cloves garlic
6 medium tomatoes	5 tablespoons olive oil
4 medium zucchini	Salt and pepper to taste

Cut all vegetables into small pieces and place in pot. Add olive oil, salt, and pepper. Add ½ cup cold water. Cover and simmer for 1½ hours over very low heat. Vegetables should be cooked until very tender. Can be served hot or cold.

BAKED SHREDDED CARROTS *Serves: 4*

4 tablespoons butter	1 teaspoon lemon juice
¼ cup finely chopped onion	½ teaspoon ground ginger
1 bunch carrots, peeled and shredded	1 tablespoon sugar
½ cup water	¾ teaspoon salt

Saute onion in 2 tablespoons butter until tender. Mix onion and shredded carrots and pour into a 1 quart casserole. Mix water, lemon juice, ginger, sugar, salt and pour over carrots. Dot with 2 tablespoons butter. Cover and bake at 400° for 50 to 55 minutes.

CREAMED ASPARAGUS PARMESAN *Serves: 6*

2 small cans asparagus tips	⅓ cup flour
¼ cup butter	2 cups rich milk (or 1⅔ cup milk with ⅓ cup white wine)
2 to 3 tablespoons green onions, chopped	⅓ cup shredded Parmesan cheese
¼ teaspoon curry powder	
½ teaspoon salt	

Melt butter, add onion, curry and salt. Cook for several minutes. Stir in flour. Slowly add milk and cook until mix thickens. Add asparagus, turn into baking dish, sprinkle with cheese and bake 15 to 20 minutes at 400°.

PICKLED ONION SLICES

1 large Bermuda onion　　　　**Vinegar**
Salt

　　Slice onion and place in a single layer on paper towels. Using your large holed kitchen salt shaker, generously salt the top of the onion slices. Allow slices to "weep" for 3 to 4 hours. Gently pick up onion slices and place them on top of each other in a one quart freezer container (round container is best but not required). Cover onion slices with vinegar and place sealed container in refrigerator. Onions will keep 3 to 4 months.

CUCUMBERS IN SOUR CREAM　　　*Serves: 8*

8 cucumbers, thinly sliced　　　**3 tablespoons vinegar**
1 carton sour cream mixed with　**1 teaspoon salt**
**　1 carton Cottage cheese**　　　**Onion flakes**
3 tablespoons sugar

　　Mix all together and place in casserole dish. Marinate overnight. Will keep 3 or 4 days.

TOMATOES PROVENCALE　　　*Serves: 6*

6 tomatoes, seeded and sliced in　**3 shallots, finely chopped**
**　half (leaving sections**　　　　**1 clove garlic, finely chopped**
**　between pulp)**　　　　　　　　**½ teaspoon salt**
½ cup bread crumbs　　　　　　**2 tablespoons minced parsley**
¼ cup olive oil　　　　　　　　**Several grinds freshly ground**
3 tablespoons fresh basil or　　　**　black pepper**
**　1 tablespoon dried**
1½ teaspoons dried basil

　　Lightly salt inside of tomatoes and place on paper towel, cut side down, to drain until time to stuff. Mix above ingredients together. Take a large tablespoon and gently press on top of tomato. Bake at 400° in upper third of oven for 15 minutes.
　　Stuffing may be made in advance and freezes well.

236

VEGETABLE CASSEROLE   *Serves: 6 to 8*

1 large potato

2 carrots

1 onion

2 or 3 stalks celery

½ large green pepper

Few strips pimento

1 hard boiled egg,
   thinly sliced

2 cups heavy cream sauce

Grated cheese

Red pepper

Sugar

Slice or dice vegetables and cook together in small amount of water until tender. Layer in casserole vegetables, egg, pimento, cream sauce, vegetables, cheese, cream sauce. Sprinkle top with a little red pepper and sugar. Bake covered 20 to 30 minutes at 350°.

NOODLES WITH VEGETABLES   *Serves: 8*

½ pound noodles (curly)

Salt to taste

4 tablespoons butter

3 cups mushrooms, thinly
   sliced

3 cups zucchini, thinly sliced

Freshly ground pepper to taste

½ cup heavy cream

¼ teaspoon grated nutmeg

½ cup Parmesan cheese, freshly
   grated

⅓ cup toasted pine nuts or
   dry roasted peanuts

Bring water to boil for noodles. Add salt. Heat butter in a skillet and add mushrooms and zucchini. Cook, shaking the skillet and stirring, about 1 minute or until the vegetables are crisp-tender. Do not overcook.

Cook noodles and drain. Return noodles to the kettle and add salt and pepper to taste. Add the vegetables, cream, nutmeg, cheese and pine nuts. Place over low heat. Toss until ingredients are blended and serve.

May be frozen and reheated.

FETTUCINE ALFREDO   *Serves: 6*

1½ pounds fettucine noodles

6 tablespoons butter

½ cup cream (or half and half)

3 egg yolks

¾ cup Parmesan cheese

Cook noodles in boiling, salted water until tender. Drain, coat with butter. Toss. Add cream. Stir 1 minute. Add yolks and toss, so as not to scramble the eggs. Add ½ cheese and toss. Serve on plates and cover with remaining cheese.

May also use your favorite clam or meat sauce as a topping.
Preparation time: 20 minutes. Do not do ahead or freeze.

GOURMET RICE CASSEROLE   *Serves: 8*

1 cup uncooked rice

1 stick margarine, melted

1 medium onion, chopped

1 cup pecans, chopped
(optional)

1 can water

1 can mushroom soup

1 can beef consomme

Mix and bake in covered baking dish until rice is well done (about 60 minutes) at 350°.
Preparation time: 15 minutes. May prepare ahead and refrigerate.

SUZANNE'S RICE OCTAVIE

1 cup uncooked rice

2 cups water

Salt to taste

½ lemon

1 stick butter

2 to 3 large celery stalks,
chopped

½ cup green onion, chopped

¾ cup parsley, chopped

1 bunch watercress, chopped

1 bay leaf, crumbled

Pepper

Paprika

Boil rice in salted water with ½ lemon until done. Melt butter in large skillet and saute green onion. When onions are tender, but not brown, add the parsley and celery. Add rice. Cook 2 or 3 minutes longer. Add bay leaf, salt, pepper, paprika. Turn heat on low and warm. Serve immediately or may be refrigerated or frozen and reheated.

DESSERTS

Home of Thomas Wolfe, Asheville

O'HENRY'S PEARS SUPREME

8 pears, semi ripe

2 cups sugar

2 vanilla beans or ¼ cup vanilla

Brie

Apricot sauce

Peel pears and slice a thin piece off the bottom so pears will stand upright. Put pears in pot with sugar and vanilla. Add enough water to cover pears. Bring to a boil; bring to a simmer and cook until fork tender. Remove from syrup. On oven-proof plate, put pear, wedge of Brie, and 2 tablespoons apricot sauce on pear. Heat in 250° oven until cheese begins to ooze. Serve warm.

Apricot Sauce:

10 ounce bag dried apricots

⅔ cup sugar

⅓ cup apricot brandy

Place apricots and sugar in a saucepan. Add enough water to cover apricots. Bring to a boil and then turn down to a simmer and stir until ingredients are incorporated and thick, about 10 minutes. Remove from heat and add brandy.

APPLE DUMPLINGS
Yield: 1 dozen

2 to 2½ cups flour

2 teaspoons baking powder

1 teaspoon salt

1½ sticks butter

½ cup milk

4 to 6 apples, peeled, cored and cut up

sugar, cinnamon, nutmeg, butter

Sauce:

2 cups sugar

¼ teaspoon cinnamon

¼ teaspoon nutmeg

2 cups hot water

¼ cup butter, melted

Combine flour, baking powder and salt. Cut in butter and mix until like small peas. Add milk. Roll out and cut into 5 inch squares. Place 3 to 4 pieces of apple on each square and sprinkle each with 2 teaspoons sugar, a dash of cinnamon and nutmeg and bits of butter. Pull up sides and pinch in center to seal. Place dumplings 1 inch apart in a greased baking dish. Mix all the ingredients in the sauce and pour over. Bake at 375° for 35 to 45 minutes.

ORIGINAL PECAN PRALINES

Yield: 1½ to 2 dozen pralines

2 cups firmly packed brown sugar

¼ cup water

2½ cups pecans, broken into large pieces

1 tablespoon butter

Combine brown sugar and water. Bring to a boil, stirring constantly. Once it comes to a boil, add the pecans and cook without stirring until the soft ball stage (235°). Remove from heat and add the butter. Immediately drop by tablespoons onto waxed paper. Let stand until firm.

PECAN CARAMEL CREAM SQUARES

Serves: 6 to 8

16 vanilla caramels

24 large marshmallows

½ cup milk

1 cup toasted pecan pieces, chopped

1 cup heavy cream, whipped

1 cup graham cracker crumbs

4 tablespoons melted butter

In top of double boiler place caramels, marshmallows, and milk being careful not to let the bottom touch the boiling water. Cook, stirring occasionally until all is melted and smooth (about 25 minutes). Remove and cool. Stir in pecans. Carefully fold in whipped cream. Combine graham cracker crumbs and butter. Reserve ¼ cup. Press the remainder into an oiled 10 x 6 x 2 inch pan. Pour caramel mixture over. Sprinkle with remaining graham cracker crumbs. Chill overnight.

PRALINE CREME CARAMEL

Serves: 4

4 egg yolks

4 tablespoons sugar

Dash salt

1½ cups whipping cream, heated

½ teaspoon vanilla

¼ cup brown sugar

Combine yolks, sugar and salt. Whisk until thick and light. Slowly whisk in hot cream. Cook stirring constantly until mixture coats a spoon (3 to 5 minutes) and thickens slightly. (Don't overcook as mixture will separate.) Remove from heat and stir in vanilla. Pour into 4 custard dishes and chill at least 3 hours. When ready to serve top each caramel evenly with 1 tablespoon brown sugar. Place in a larger pan filled with ice and water. Boil 1 to 2 minutes or until sugar melts.

PRALINE POWDER
Makes: 2 cups

Place 2 cups slivered almonds on ungreased cookie sheet. Bake at 250° until golden brown (30 minutes to 1 hour). Let cool.

Once almonds are cool, let 1 cup sugar and 1 cup water come to a boil on high heat. Let boil until mixture gets very syrupy and a golden maple color. Pour immediately over nuts. Let set and cool. Break into pieces and process in processor with steel blade until powdered.

Praline powder will keep 2 months stored in air-tight container; do not refrigerate.

ALMOND FLORENTINE CANDY

½ cup and 2 tablespoons
   unsalted butter
½ cup sugar

2 tablespoons whipping cream
1¾ cups slivered almonds

Preheat oven to 450°. Line 15½ x 10½ x 1 inch baking sheet with heavy duty foil. Coat with vegetable oil. Melt butter. Add sugar and mix well. Add cream. Stir in almonds and bring to a boil. Reduce heat and simmer 2 minutes. Turn onto prepared baking sheet and cook until mixture is light caramel (about 8 minutes). Remove from oven. When cool enough to handle, peel off foil. Break into pieces once chilled a bit.

CHOCOLATE TRUFFLE CAKE
Serves: 8

16 ounces semi sweet chocolate
½ cup unsalted butter
1½ teaspoons sugar
1½ teaspoons flour

1 teaspoon hot water
4 eggs, separated
½ pint whipping cream,
   whipped

Preheat oven to 425°. Grease bottom of 8 inch springform pan. Melt chocolate and butter together. Add sugar, flour and hot water. Beat in yolks, one at a time, beating well with each addition. Beat whites until stiff. Carefully fold the whites into the chocolate mixture. Cook 12 minutes. (It will look very uncooked.) Let cool; then refrigerate. It can be refrigerated up to 2 weeks or frozen. When ready to serve, top with rosettes of whipped cream and garnish with grated semi-sweet chocolate.

EDWINA'S CHARLOTTE MALAKOFF
AU CHOCOLAT
Serves: 12

18 to 22 plain lady fingers

1½ cups sifted powdered sugar

2 sticks soft butter

7 squares semi-sweet chocolate

¼ cup strong coffee

¼ cup Grand Marnier

¼ teapoon almond extract

1 cup ground roasted almonds
  (use slivered almonds)

½ cup praline powder

1½ pints heavy cream, divided

Roast almonds at 250° until brown. Then grind almonds in food processor.

For praline powder: See separate recipe.

Cream butter. Add powdered sugar gradually and cream until pale and fluffy. Melt chocolate in ¼ cup coffee. To this, add Grand Marnier and almond extract. Add chocolate mixture to butter and beat until smooth. Add roasted almonds and praline powder. Beat until well blended. Beat 1 pint whipping cream until stiff. Fold ½ cream into chocolate, then fold the rest. Cut a round of waxed paper to fit bottom of 8 inch Charlotte mold. Dip lady fingers quickly into mixture of ⅔ cup cold water and ⅓ cup Grand Marnier. Place these flat side down around bottom of mold. Then overlapping a bit, line the sides of the mold. Pour chocolate mixture into ¾ of mold. Pack chocolate so there are no air holes. Put another layer of lady fingers on top of the chocolate. Press and pack down. Pour rest of chocolate onto lady fingers. Top with a round of waxed paper. Place top of mold on and weight down. Refrigerate at least 6 hours.

To remove from mold, run a dull knife around the sides. Unmold. Whip remaining ½ pint whipping cream and ice mold or pipe rosettes of cream to cover.

Freezes: 3 months. Refrigerates: 1 week.

CHOCOLATE MOUSSE
Serves: 4 *generously*

4 ounces semi-sweet chocolate

¾ cup sugar

⅓ cup water

4 egg yolks

2 tablespoons cognac or strong coffee

1 cup heavy cream, whipped

Melt chocolate. Boil sugar and water until clear and syrupy. Scrape chocolate into bowl or processor and beat in hot syrup. Add egg yolks, one at a time, beating well with each yolk. Add cognac. Cool to room temperature and fold in whipped cream. Pour into bowl or individual serving glasses.

WHITE CHOCOLATE MOUSSE
Serves: 6 to 8

6 ounces white chocolate, preferably Peter's white chocolate

⅓ cup warm milk

3 egg whites from jumbo eggs

1 cup whipping cream

¼ teaspoon lemon juice

In a double boiler, slowly melt chocolate being careful not to let the pan touch the boiling water. Remove from heat immediately after the chocolate melts. Pour the warm milk into the chocolate. It will separate but stir to get mixture smooth. Cool to room temperature. Beat whites until very stiff and very slowly and patiently fold the chocolate into the whites. Beat cream until very stiff and very slowly and carefully fold chocolate into whipped cream. Add fresh lemon juice. Chill 3 to 4 hours. If chilled longer, it will become runny.

This recipe can be doubled, but can't be made before the day of serving. This can be served in parfait glasses or tulip cups and decorated with semi-sweet chocolate curls or praline powder.

COFFEE NUT MOUSSE
Serves: 8

1 tablespoon gelatin

¼ cup cold water

3 scant tablespoons freeze-dried instant coffee

⅔ cup pecan pieces, toasted

4 large yolks

½ cup sugar

3 tablespoons dark rum

4 large whites

1½ cups whipping cream

Prepare a 1 quart souffle dish with Pam and an oiled foil collar. Combine gelatin, water and coffee in bowl and let set until water is absorbed. Dissolve this over low heat. Combine yolks and sugar in food processor and process 1 minute. Add hot gelatin through tube with machine running. Put into a pot and over medium heat, cook, whisking constantly until slightly thickened. Let cool briefly, add rum and pecans. Beat whites. Stir in ¼ of the whites, then fold in the rest. Whip cream and fold it into coffee mixture. Pour into souffle dish and chill overnight. Can decorate with more whipped cream and extra pecan halves. Nuts may be omitted.

PUMPKIN ROLL

3 eggs

1 cup sugar

⅔ cup canned pumpkin

1 teaspoon lemon juice

¾ cup flour

1 teaspoon nutmeg

½ teaspoon salt

1 teaspoon baking powder

2 teaspoons cinnamon

1 teaspoon ginger

1 cup chopped pecans

Beat eggs on high speed of mixer for 5 minutes. Gradually add 1 cup sugar. Stir in pumpkin and lemon juice. Stir together all dry ingredients and fold into pumpkin. Spread in greased and floured 15 x 10 x 1 inch pan. Top with 1 cup chopped pecans. Bake at 375° for 15 minutes. Turn out on rectangular towel sprinkled with powdered sugar. Start at short side and roll towel and cake together. Cool, then unroll.

Filling:

1 cup powdered sugar

2 (3 ounce) packages Cream cheese, softened

4 tablespoons soft butter

½ teaspoon vanilla

Combine the ingredients, spread over cake. Roll. Chill.

STRAWBERRY MERINGUE TORTE *Serves: 6 to 8*

6 egg whites, room temperature

Pinch of salt

1½ cups sugar

6 ounces semi-sweet chocolate

3 tablespoons water

2½ cups whipping cream, whipped with 1½ cups confectioners sugar

1½ pints fresh strawberries, washed, hulled and sliced lengthwise

¾ cup roasted slivered almonds

6 to 8 whole strawberries

Preheat oven to 250°. Beat whites with salt to soft peaks. Slowly add by tablespoons 1½ cups sugar. Beat until stiff. Line baking sheets with foil and trace 3 circles 8 inches in diameter. With a knife, spread meringue into 3 (8 inch) circles. Bake 1 hour. Turn off heat and open door. Let cool in oven additional 1 hour. Carefully peel off foil. (If you aren't using meringues, store in air tight containers for 3 to 4 days.) Melt chocolate with water and mix well. Spread chocolate on 2 layers of meringue. Refrigerate 20 minutes to set chocolate.

To assemble, place a piece of foil covered cardboard 8 inches in diameter on bottom of serving plate. Set one meringue on cardboard with chocolate side up. Top with whipped cream and half of the roasted almonds and sliced strawberries. Repeat with other chocolate covered layer. Top with plain meringue and top with rest of whipped cream. Garnish with whole strawberries. Refrigerate 24 hours. (Meringues will hold 24 hours and still be crunchy.)

MARRON ROLL

Serves: 10 to 12 generously

Roll:

5 eggs, separated

¼ cup sugar

¼ cup flour

1 tablespoon flavoring (brandy, rum, benedictine or vanilla)

Filling:

2 cups heavy cream

¼ cup confectioners sugar (½ cup if doing ahead)

1 tablespoon brandy

Raffeta marron pieces (chestnuts in sugar syrup)

Beat egg yolks until light and fluffy. Add sugar and continue beating until mixture is thick and lemon colored and forms ribbons when beater is lifted. Add flour and flavorings. Beat whites to a soft peak. Stir a little of the whites into the yolk mixture, then carefully fold in remaining whites. Brush an 11 x 17 inch jelly roll pan with oil. Put a piece of waxed paper in pan letting each end extend 1 to 2 inches. Oil waxed paper well. Pour in batter and bake at 400° for 12 minutes or until cake is golden brown. Unmold on lightly oiled sheets of waxed paper. With knife, release edges of cooked waxed paper and peel off. Roll the cake in the remaining waxed paper and chill 20 minutes.

To prepare filling: In a chilled bowl whip the cream with sugar and brandy until firm enough to hold shape. Drain marron pieces and reserve whole ones to decorate top of roll. Fold ½ to ⅔ of the whipped cream into the marron pieces. Unroll roll and spread with whipped cream and marron mixture. Reroll. Cover with remaining whipped cream and decorate with marron pieces giving each serving a chestnut.

WALNUT ROLL

Serves: 12

Roll:

**7 large eggs, separated, room
temperature**

¾ cup sugar

**1½ cups ground English
walnuts**

1 teaspoon baking powder

Glaze:

2 tablespoons dark rum

2 tablespoons sugar

2 tablespoons water

Filling:

1½ cups heavy cream

3 tablespoons granulated sugar

Garnish:

Walnut halves

Pan:

To prepare 10 x 15 inch jelly roll pan, brush with a pastry brush 1
tablespoon oil over entire pan. Drain excess. Line with waxed paper,
overlapping 3 inches on one side and 2 inches on other. Oil this well,
placing paper in pan evenly (no wrinkles).

For roll: Beat yolks with sugar until pale and thick. Add ground walnuts.
Sprinkle baking powder over walnuts and beat with mixer. Beat whites
until stiff but not dry. Carefully and quickly fold them in. Pour into
prepared pan and heat at 350° for 15 to 20 minutes or until golden brown.
Cool on rack in pan. Once roll has cooled, take a cold damp towel and
place over roll. Refrigerate to chill. (Can hold 1 day at this point, but keep
the towel damp.)

When ready to use, bring to a boil to glaze ingredients. Stir to dissolve
sugar. Remove from heat and let cool. Drizzle over roll in pan. Take 2 big
pieces waxed paper and sift 1¼ cups powdered sugar over it very heavily.
Turn cake onto waxed paper.

To fill: Whip cream, adding sugar until stiff. Spread ⅔ of cream on roll.
Roll cake starting with the long side. Decorate with remaining whipped
cream and walnut halves.

STRAWBERRY CREPES

Yield: 24

Basic Crepes:

3 large eggs

1 teaspoon sugar

⅛ teaspoon salt

1½ cups flour

1½ cups milk

2 tablespoons melted butter

1 tablespooon cognac

Mix eggs in blender or mixer until blended. Add sugar, salt, flour, and milk and process or mix until smooth. Add butter and cognac. Let sit at room temperature 2 hours or refrigerate overnight.

Brush a seasoned crepe pan with butter and heat on medium high until it sizzles a bit. Wipe out pan with paper towel. Remove from heat and add 2 to 3 tablespoons batter, swirl the pan around to distribute and pour out excess. Cook 1 to 3 minutes until golden turning with your fingers to brown the other side. Continue cooking the remaining batter wiping out the pan each time with a paper towel before adding the next crepe.

Crepes can be stored and frozen quite successfully by putting a piece of waxed paper between each crepe, wrapping well and freezing together.

Filling For 24 Crepes:

2 (20 ounce) packages strawberries with no sugar added

4 tablespoons Cointreau

Mash berries and mix with liqueur. Divide among crepes and roll up.

Sauce For Crepes:

In two large frying pans, combine the following in each pan and heat thoroughly.

6 tablespoons melted butter

4 tablespoons good brand strawberry preserves

2 tablespoons good brand raspberry preserves

1 to 2 drops red food coloring

1 tablespoon Grand Marnier

To serve: Place 12 crepes in each pan. Heat thoroughly. You can ignite the pans by heating 2 tablespoons Cointreau, lighting it and pouring it over the crepes. Each crepe may be topped with a dollop of whipped cream.

PRUNE SOUFFLE

Serves: 6 to 8

1 (16 ounce) box prunes
6 egg whites
½ cup sugar

¼ teaspoon salt
1 teaspoon vanilla

Topping:

½ pint whipped cream
3 tablespoons sugar

1 teaspoon vanilla

Cover prunes with water and cook until very well done. Remove seeds and use 1 cup mashed prune pulp. This can be done in advance. Beat whites until frothy. Add salt, vanilla and sugar slowly as you beat the whites to stiff. Fold in prune pulp. Butter a 2 quart souffle dish and pour prune mixture in. Make a 2 to 3 inch indentation in center of souffle. The souffle will hold several hours at this point. (The indentation is for pouring in topping). Bake at 250° for 25 minutes. Serve at once with topping.

For topping: Beat cream until soft peaks form. Add sugar and vanilla and beat until stiff.

PEPPERMINT STICK CHARLOTTE

Serves: 8 to 10

2 envelopes gelatin
¾ cup sugar, divided
¼ teaspoon salt
4 eggs, separated
2½ cups milk

Few drops red food coloring
⅔ cup crushed peppermint
2 packages lady fingers
1 cup heavy cream, whipped

Mix gelatin, ¼ cup sugar and salt. Beat yolks and milk and add gelatin to this. Place over low heat, stirring until thickens (5 minutes). Remove from heat and cool slightly. Stir in red coloring and candy. Chill, stirring some, until it mounds when dropped from a spoon. Separate lady fingers and line bottom and sides of springform pan. Beat whites with ½ cup sugar until stiff. Fold into chilled gelatin. Add whipped cream. Pour into pan and chill until set. Garnish with more piped whipped cream and crushed peppermint candy.

FROZEN CHAMPAGNE CREAM
IN CHOCOLATE SHELLS
WITH A CHOCOLATE SAUCE

Serves: 8

Champagne Cream:

¾ cup brut champagne, divided   5 egg yolks

½ cup sugar   1½ cups whipping cream

Chocolate Shells:

1½ to 2 cups semi-sweet chocolate bits (12 ounces)

Chocolate Sauce:

6 tablespoons brut champagne   1 tablespoon sugar

½ cup (3 ounces) semi-sweet   2 tablespoons unsalted butter,
   chocolate bits   softened

For Champagne Cream: Combine ½ cup champagne with the sugar. Bring to a boil over medium high heat stirring occasionally. Continue without stirring until it reaches 236° on the candy thermometer. Meanwhile in a large bowl, beat egg yolks until light and lemon colored. Add the sugar syrup slowly to yolks. Beat until thick and creamy (10 minutes). Gradually blend in the remaining ¼ cup champagne. Chill until thick but not stiff. Whip cream and fold into champagne mixture. Freeze until firm.

For Chocolate Shells: Melt the semi-sweet chocolate in a double boiler. Meanwhile tear off 8 pieces of waxed paper 6 to 9 inches wide. Put 3 to 4 tablespoons melted chocolate on a piece of waxed paper, and with the back of tablespoon spread out into a square. Quickly place a scoop of champagne cream in the middle of the chocolate. Molding with the waxed paper, pull the chocolate up on the sides of the ice cream to form a shell. The chocolate will harden as it hits the ice cream. Freeze.

For Chocolate Sauce: Combine the champagne, chocolate bits and sugar. Heat until chocolate melts. Whisk in the butter. Keep warm until ready to use.

To serve, let frozen champagne cream thaw a bit to soften and spoon sauce over.

Can be served without shells.

Can be assembled ahead except for chocolate sauce.

AMARETTO SOUFFLE
Serves: 6

4 large egg yolks
¼ cup sugar
1 tablespoon flour
¾ cup scalded milk

3 tablespoons Amaretto
6 large egg whites
Pinch salt
½ cup roasted slivered almonds

Butter a 1½ quart souffle dish and dust generously with sugar. Butter and sugar a foil band 4 inches high and put on souffle dish. In deep saucepan, beat 4 yolks with ¼ cup sugar until the mixture is light and lemony. Beat in 1 tablespoon flour. Add scalded milk in slow steady stream. Over moderate heat, bring the mixture just to the boiling point, stirring constantly. Remove from heat and transfer custard to a metal bowl and let cool. (To speed up process, place bowl in ice.) Stir in 3 tablespoons Amaretto. In large bowl, beat 6 whites with pinch of salt until stiff. Stir in about ¼ of whites into custard. Then fold in the rest of the whites along with the almonds. Pour into prepared dish and cook at 400° for 20 minutes or until golden and puffed. Serve immediately with Amaretto English Custard Sauce.

AMARETTO ENGLISH CUSTARD SAUCE
Yield: 1¼ cups

5 large egg yolks
¼ cup sugar

¾ cup scalded milk
2 tablespoons Amaretto

Beat the yolks and sugar in deep saucepan until light and lemony. Add scalded milk in a stream. Cook over low heat until custard thickens, stirring constantly. Don't let custard boil or it will separate. Remove from heat and let cool. Stir in Amaretto and pour into a serving pitcher.

KAHLUA SOUFFLE
Serves: 6 to 8

½ cup sugar, divided
1 package (1 tablespoon) unflavored gelatin
Dash salt
1 cup cold water
½ cup Kahlua or other coffee flavored liqueur as Tia Maria

3 eggs, separated
1 cup whipping cream, whipped
½ to 1 cup toasted chopped pecans
Garnish with piped rosettes of more whipped cream and chocolate curls or coffee granules

Combine ¼ cup sugar, gelatin, salt, cold water, and Kahlua in saucepan. Cook over low heat until gelatin dissolves, stirring occasionally. Stir small amount of gelatin mixture into slightly beaten yolks; gradually add yolk mixture back to gelatin mixture. Cook over low heat stirring until mixture coats a metal spoon (3 minutes). Chill until slightly thickened. Fold in whipped cream and nuts. Beat whites with a pinch of cream of tartar until soft peaks form. Slowly add ¼ cup sugar. Beat until stiff but not dry. Fold into the gelatin, Kahlua, and whipped cream mixture. Pour into 1 quart souffle dish and chill.

HOT CHOCOLATE SOUFFLE   *Serves:* 8

1 tablespoon butter

1 heaping tablespoon sugar

6 ounces semi-sweet chocolate

6 eggs

½ cup sugar

Dash salt

¼ teaspoon cream of tartar

Grand Marnier and whipped cream as garnish

Grease a 1 quart baking dish with 1 tablespoon butter. Sprinkle with a heaping tablespoon of sugar. Let all sugar absorb. Melt chocolate in top of double boiler; set aside. Separate eggs. Beat yolks in small bowl until light and lemon colored. Slowly add sugar and salt. Beat until thick and ribbony and pale in color. Cut off beater; add chocolate; then mix on low. Beat whites until foamy. Add cream of tartar and continue beating until stiff but not dry. Take ¼ of egg whites and stir into chocolate. Carefully fold remaining whites. Bake at 375° for 25 to 30 minutes. Serve immediately.

To serve, pour Grand Marnier over and garnish with whipped cream.

CHOCOLATE SOUFFLE   *Serves:* 12

2 envelopes unflavored gelatin

2 cups milk

1 cup sugar, divided

4 eggs, separated

12 ounces semi-sweet chocolate bits

2 cups heavy cream, whipped

¼ teaspoon salt

1 teaspoon vanilla

In medium saucepan mix gelatin, milk, ½ cup sugar, salt, egg yolks, and chocolate bits. Stir over low heat until chocolate is melted (about 6 minutes). Add vanilla. Chill until mixture firms slightly. Beat egg whites until stiff, but not dry, slowly adding ½ cup sugar. Fold into chocolate mixture. Beat cream and fold in. Put in a 2 quart souffle dish with a 2 inch collar. Chill until firm.

CHOCOLATE CORONET

Serves: 20

18 unfilled ladyfingers, split

¾ cup Grand Marnier liqueur

¾ cup sugar

½ cup water

3 large egg yolks

1 pound Cream cheese, room temperature

8 squares (8 ounces) unsweetened chocolate, melted and cooled

5 squares (5 ounces) semi-sweet chocolate, melted and cooled

2 cups heavy cream

1 (6 ounce) package semi-sweet chocolate pieces or broken white chocolate, optional

Lightly grease a 9 inch springform pan. Sprinkle ladyfingers with ¼ cup of the orange-flavored liqueur and use to line bottom and sides of prepared pan. In a small saucepan bring sugar and water to a boil over moderate heat, stirring until sugar dissolves. Continue cooking without stirring until syrup registers 240° F. on a candy thermometer, or until a small amount of the mixture holds its shape when dropped into very cold water. (When removed from water with fingers it will be soft and will flatten out.) While syrup cooks, in a large bowl beat egg yolks with an electric mixer at high speed until yolks are pale and thick. While beating yolks continuously, pour in hot syrup in a thin stream. Continue beating yolk mixture 2 to 3 minutes. Reduce speed to medium and beat in Cream cheese, about one sixth at a time. Then beat in remaining ½ cup liqueur and the melted chocolate. In another bowl, whip cream with an electric mixer or rotary beater until stiff. Stir about ¼ of the whipped cream into the chocolate mixture, then fold in the remainder, adding the chocolate pieces as you go (if chocolate pieces are being used). Spoon mixture into prepared pan. Smooth surface and cover with plastic wrap; refrigerate at least 4 hours or up to 6 days before serving.

Recipe may be halved. Use 7 or 8 inch springform pan.

BAVARIAN FRUIT TORTE

Serves: 8 to 10

1 stick butter, softened

⅓ cup sugar

¼ teaspoon vanilla

1 cup flour

1 (8 ounce) package Cream cheese, softened

¼ cup sugar

1 egg

½ teaspoon vanilla

⅓ cup sugar

½ teaspoon cinnamon

4 cups fruit as peaches, apples, blueberries

¼ cup slivered almonds, lightly toasted

Cream butter and ⅓ cup sugar. Stir in vanilla. Blend in flour. Press dough in the bottom and up the sides 1½ inches in a greased 9 inch spring-form pan.

Combine Cream cheese and ¼ cup sugar. Beat in egg and ½ teaspoon vanilla. Beat well. Spread over pastry. Combine ⅓ cup sugar, cinnamon and fruit tossing lightly. Spoon over Cream cheese. Sprinkle fruit with nuts. Bake at 450° for 10 minutes. Reduce heat to 400° and bake 25 minutes longer. Cool 5 minutes and loosen rim. Allow torte to cool completely before removing rim.

CREAM CARAMEL   *Serves: 4 to 6*

¾ cup sugar	½ cup sugar
3 large eggs, room temperature	2 cups half and half
Dash salt	1 teaspoon vanilla

Two days ahead preheat a heavy frying pan on medium heat. Add ¾ cup sugar and reduce heat to medium low. Continue cooking shaking the pan until sugar turns to syrup. Let syrup continue cooking until it turns to a maple color. Pour out into a 1 quart dish and coat bottom and up sides a bit. Let cool and syrup harden before adding custard.

To prepare custard: With a wire whisk, mix eggs, salt and ½ cup sugar. Meanwhile scald half and half. Slowly pour half and half into egg mixture. Add vanilla. Blend well. Pour into prepared dish. Place dish in larger pan and put warm water in larger pan until it covers ¾ of the caramel. Bake at 350° for 45 minutes or until knife comes out clean. Don't overcook. Let cool to room temperature and refrigerate.

To turn out, go around custard with a knife to loosen. Shake bowl and turn out. Syrup will be runny.

FROZEN GLACE CREAM   *Serves: 6*

1 quart vanilla ice cream, softened
1 cup bottled Nesselrode sauce

Mix and freeze.

COLD STRAWBERRY SOUFFLE $\qquad$ *Serves: 6 to 8*

**1½ tablespoons unflavored
gelatin**

**2 cups strawberries, washed
and dried**

¾ cup sugar or to taste

1½ cups heavy cream

2 egg whites

**2 tablespoons Grand Marnier,
optional**

Soften gelatin in ¼ cup cold water for 5 minutes. Dissolve over low heat and let cool. Puree strawberries with the sugar. Beat cream with whites until stiff. Fold in strawberries and Grand Marnier. Pour into mold and refrigerate until ready to serve. Garnish as desired.

This should be made 1 day ahead and served from a 3 cup souffle dish, sherbet dishes, or tulip cups. Garnish with more piped whipped cream and whole strawberries.

NOTE: Raspberries may be substituted for the strawberries.

Tulip Cups:

½ stick unsalted butter

¼ cup light corn syrup

¼ cup sugar

**4 ounces almonds, processed
medium fine**

¼ cup flour

Position rack on third level. Preheat oven to 350°. Lightly grease cookie sheet. Combine butter, corn syrup and sugar and place over medium low heat stirring often to warm the mixture. Add the almonds and flour. Mix by hand thoroughly. Place 1 heaping tablespoon on sheet making cookie. Put 2 cookies only to a sheet as they will spread. Bake until golden brown, about 10 minutes. Remove and let cool 30 seconds or until cookie can be lifted with a spatula. Immediately place over a coffee mug to form cup shape. It will cool immediately and be formed. If tulip cup can't be shaped, reheat it to remold. For saucers, leave cookies flat.

Can leave ½ the cookies flat serving as a saucer for the cups. Recipe makes 12 cups or 6 cups and 6 saucers. Cups need to be used the day they are made. Place in a cool area until ready to use.

RASPBERRY AND
STRAWBERRIES ROMANOFF $\qquad$ *Serves: 4*

**½ cup seedless raspberry
preserves**

2 tablespoons kirsch

**12 to 15 strawberries,
depending on the size**

1 quart soft vanilla ice cream

Piped dollop of whipped cream

To make the sauce, combine the raspberry preserves with the kirsch.

When ready to serve, spoon ice cream into sherbet or parfait dishes. Top with sauce. Repeat once more so it will be layered. Top with whipped cream and strawberries and serve immediately.

GRAND MARNIER SAUCE

2 cups milk	**2 tablespoons cornstarch**
½ stick butter	**1 teaspoon vanilla**
⅓ cup sugar	**⅓ cup Grand Marnier**
3 egg yolks, room temperature	**⅓ cup whipping cream**
⅓ cup sugar	

Combine milk, butter and ⅓ cup sugar. Place in saucepan and bring to a boil stirring occasionally. Beat yolks with other ⅓ cup sugar until thickened. Add cornstarch and beat until light and lemony colored. Gradually beat in enough hot milk to warm eggs. Add this back to rest of milk and bring to a boil. Remove from heat and add vanilla. Let stand until cool. Refrigerate until ready to use. Just before serving, cook over low heat, stirring in Grand Marnier and whipping cream.

GRAND MARNIER SOUFFLE   *Serves: 4 to 6*

2 cups milk	**5 egg yolks**
¾ cup sugar	**2 ounces Grand Marnier**
4 tablespoons butter	**7 egg whites**
⅓ cup flour	

Butter and dust with 3 tablespoons sugar a 2 quart souffle dish. Set aside. Combine milk and sugar in saucepan and heat to a boil. Meanwhile in another pan melt butter. Add flour and cook 1 to 2 minutes, as for a roux. Slowly add hot milk and stir over medium heat until thick and creamy. Beat yolks until thick and lemony color. Add Grand Marnier. Remove milk from heat and add yolks and Grand Marnier mixture. Mix well. Beat whites until stiff but not dry. Carefully fold this into egg-milk custard. Pour into prepared dish. Bake at 400° for 20 to 25 minutes. Dust with powdered sugar and serve immediately.

May be served with Grand Marnier Sauce.

LEMON SPONGE PUDDING
Serves: 4

3 eggs, separated
½ stick butter, softened
¾ cup sugar
⅓ cup fresh lemon juice

1 tablespoon grated lemon rind
⅓ cup flour
1½ cups milk

Beat whites until stiff but not dry. Set aside. Cream butter and sugar. Add yolks one at a time letting yolks disappear each time. Add lemon juice, rind and flour. Slowly add milk. Stir in ¼ cup beaten egg whites. Then carefully fold in remaining beaten whites. Pour into greased 1½ quart souffle dish. Set souffle dish in larger pan and pour boiling water to half the height of souffle dish. Bake at 350° for 30 to 40 minutes or until puffed and brown. To serve, garnish with powdered sugar. This pudding will separate. Serve warm or chilled.

LEMON CUSTARD IN MERINGUE TARTS
Serves: 6

Meringue Shells:

3 egg whites
¼ teaspoon vanilla

Dash salt
1 cup sugar

Beat whites until frothy. Add salt and add sugar, 1 tablespoon at a time. Continue beating until meringue is stiff. Add vanilla. Prepare baking sheet with brown paper and place 6 globs of meringue on paper. With the back of a spoon, shape the shells 4 inches wide and 1½ inches high. Bake at 225° for 1 to 1¼ hours. Cool. Fill with chilled custard.

Lemon Custard:

1 cup sugar
5 tablespoons cornstarch
Dash salt
1½ cups boiling water

3 yolks
¼ cup fresh lemon juice
2 tablespoons grated lemon rind

Combine sugar, cornstarch and salt. Stir in water. Cook over low heat stirring constantly until mixture thickens. Combine yolks with lemon juice and rind. Stir some of the hot mixture into the yolks, then add it all back. Cook, stirring constantly until mixture thickens and is smooth (about 10 minutes). Chill.

ORANGE CUSTARD
Serves: 12 or more

1 quart whole milk

3 tablespoons flour

11 eggs, reserve 5 egg whites

3 cups sugar

1 teaspoon vanilla

¼ stick butter

5 tablespoons sugar

1 teaspoon vanilla

7 oranges, sectioned, retaining juices

Combine flour with milk in a double boiler using a whisk to stir. (Water must not touch bottom of pan.) Beat eggs adding sugar slowly. Add to milk mixture and stir constantly over low heat until custard thickens (25 to 30 minutes). Remove pan from heat and add vanilla, butter, oranges and their juices. Pour into large pyrex dish. Beat reserved 5 egg whites until frothy. Add sugar and vanilla and beat until stiff. Dot meringue on top of custard and broil to brown the meringue. Let cool a bit before serving.

LEMON TRIFLE WITH STRAWBERRY MELBA SAUCE
Serves: 4 to 6

1 cup whipping cream

⅓ cup sugar

Juice of 2 lemons

Zest of 1 lemon (no white)

1 tablespoon Eagle Brand milk

30 to 35 vanilla wafers broken but not crumbled

Strawberry Melba Sauce:

Mix together and heat until bubbly the following:

6 tablespoons butter, melted

4 tablespoons good brand strawberry preserves

2 tablespoons good brand raspberry preserves

1 to 2 drops red food coloring

1 tablespoon Grand Marnier

Whip cream adding sugar slowly once soft peaks appear. Fold in the lemon juice, zest, and Eagle Brand milk. Mix in vanilla wafers and freeze in 8 inch dish. When ready to serve, let thaw at room temperature for 15 to 20 minutes. Spoon into sherbet or parfait dishes and drizzle heavily with very warm Melba Sauce.

Can be prepared ahead.

FROZEN COGNAC CREAM

Serves: 8

½ cup sugar, divided

3 tablespoons water

3 tablespoons cognac

4 egg yolks

1 whole egg

1½ cups heavy cream, whipped

Combine ¼ cup sugar and water and heat on low until sugar is melted and mixture is bubbly (about 5 minutes). Remove from heat and cool to tepid. Stir in cognac. Beat yolks and egg until frothy. Gradually beat in ¼ cup sugar. Continue beating until triple in volume (about 4 minutes). Slowly beat in cognac syrup. Carefully fold whipped cream into egg-cognac mixture. Freeze.

FROZEN GRAND MARNIER SOUFFLE IN "ORANGE CUPS"

Serves: 8

6 egg yolks

¾ cup sugar

2 cups heavy cream

3 ounces Grand Marnier

8 orange shells, with tops sliced off and pulp removed

¾ cup heavy cream

Powdered cocoa or twisted orange slice

Combine yolks and sugar. Beat until stiff. Whip 2 cups heavy cream and carefully fold into yolk mixture. Fold in Grand Marnier. Fill orange shells and freeze at least 2 hours. Whip remaining ¾ cup heavy cream to garnish orange shells. Dust with cocoa or twisted orange slice.

FROZEN LEMON CHIFFON

Serves: 4 to 6

3 egg yolks

4 tablespoons fresh lemon juice

Dash salt

Grated rind of 1 lemon

½ cup plus 1 tablespoon sugar

1 cup heavy cream, whipped

3 egg whites, stiffly beaten

Combine egg yolks, lemon juice, salt, lemon rind and sugar in top of double boiler. Cook until it thickens. Place in refrigerator to cool. Fold in whipped cream and beat egg whites. Keep the mixture light and fluffy. Pour into an icy tray filled with a vanilla wafer crust. Garnish top of chiffon with additional crushed vanilla wafers. Let soften slightly to serve.

PECAN ICE CREAM LOG
WITH WARM BOURBON SAUCE

Serves: 12

7 ounces pecans, toasted and
   finely ground

3 tablespoons unsweetened
   cocoa

8 eggs, separated

1½ cups sugar, divided

1 teaspoon vanilla

½ cup powdered sugar

2 scant tablespoons
   unsweetened cocoa

1½ quarts coffee or vanilla
   ice cream

Warm Bourbon Sauce:

1½ cups dark corn syrup

¾ cup sugar

¾ cup brown sugar

⅔ cup evaporated milk

3 tablespoons corn oil

Dash salt

¼ to ⅓ cup bourbon

Preheat oven to 350°. Prepare a jelly roll pan with waxed paper letting it overlap 3 to 4 inches. Grease it or use Pam, being sure to have paper evenly into the edges of the pan. Mix the finely ground pecans and 3 tablespoons cocoa and set aside. Beat the 8 egg whites until frothy. Continue beating whites until stiff but not dry, slowly adding ½ cup sugar. Combine yolks with remaining 1 cup sugar and vanilla. Beat until thick and pale. Beat in 1 cup whites. Then fold slowly the nut mixture and remaining beaten whites into the yolk mixture. Don't overfold. Pour into prepared pan and bake 15 to 20 mintues. (The edges will shrink slightly.) Remove from oven and cool in pan. Combine the powdered sugar and 2 scant tablespoons cocoa and sift over top of the roll. Cover the top with waxed paper and with another jelly roll pan on top remove the cake.

To assemble, spread the softened ice cream to within 1 inch of the edges of the cake. Drizzle with some of the bourbon sauce. Roll only to close. Freeze. When log is frozen, brush with more bourbon sauce and roll in toasted, chopped pecans. Freeze again. Serve with warm bourbon sauce.

For the sauce, combine all ingredients except the bourbon in a saucepan. Stir over moderate heat until it comes to a boil. Let boil 5 minutes, stirring occasionally. Remove from heat and let cool 5 minutes. Blend or process. Add bourbon and reheat before serving. Sauce will keep 1 month refrigerated.

MINT CHOCOLATE CHIP ICE CREAM
WITH CHOCOLATE SAUCE
Serves: 6 to 8

Ice Cream:

4 eggs whites, room
  temperature

Dash salt

¼ cup sugar

2 cups whipping cream

¼ cup Creme de Menthe

½ teaspoon peppermint extract

2 teaspoons sugar

1 cup semi-sweet chocolate
  morsels, melted and cooled

½ cup roasted almonds

Chocolate Sauce:

9 ounces milk chocolate,
  melted (semi-sweet or sweet)

4 to 8 tablespoons whipping
  cream

Beat whites with dash of salt until foamy. Slowly add sugar and beat until stiff but not dry. Set aside. Beat whipping cream adding creme de menthe, peppermint extract and sugar once the soft peak stage has been reached. Beat until stiff. Fold this into the beaten egg white mixture. Freeze in an elongated dish until ice crystals form. Then fold in chocolate morsels and roasted almonds. Freeze. (Chocolate pieces will form.)

Melt chocolate in heavy saucepan over low heat. Add whipping cream and heat until thoroughly warm.

To serve: Let ice cream soften at room temperature. Spoon into serving dish and top with chocolate sauce.

Makes: 1 quart.

COFFEE FILBERT ICE CREAM
Serves: 6 to 8

1½ cups milk

1 cup ground hazelnuts

5 egg yolks

¾ cup sugar

2 cups whipping cream

1 tablespoon instant coffee,
  freeze-dried

1 teaspoon vanilla

1 cup toasted almonds, coarsely
  chopped

Combine milk and hazelnuts in saucepan. Bring to a boil over medium heat. Meanwhile beat the yolks slowly adding the sugar. Slowly add the hot milk to the yolks and mix well. Bring just to a boil. Add coffee, vanilla and whipping cream. Chill to cool. Freeze and fold in almonds.

Makes: 1 quart.

PEACH ICE CREAM

5 pounds peaches (more if very
  bruised)

2½ cups sugar (when added to
  peaches will fill a 1½ quart
  bowl)

Dash of almond extract

3 pints half and half

Chop peaches with sugar and let set for 30 minutes or until very juicy.
This step will not take very long if peaches are quite ripe. Puree in blender
about ⅓ at a time. Pour into 4 quart ice cream container, add half and half
and almond extract. Will make 3 quarts liquid.
  Follow directions for your churn to process.

FRESH PEACH SHERBERT   *Serves: 4*

5 fresh medium size peaches,
  unpeeled

¼ teaspoon almond extract

¾ cup sugar

1 teaspoon fresh lemon juice

1 cup sour cream

2 to 4 tablespoons Amaretto
  or to taste

Slice and pit 4 of the peaches. Place in blender. Add remaining
ingredients and blend until smooth. Freeze according to manufacturer's
directions. Garnish with slices of the last peach.

SHERRY WALNUT ICE CREAM

1 cup sugar

2 tablespoons cornstarch

¼ teaspoon salt

2 cups milk

3 egg yolks, beaten

¾ cup cream sherry

2 cups whipping cream

1 cup chopped, toasted walnuts

Combine sugar, cornstarch, salt, milk and yolks. Cook over medium
heat stirring until it comes to a boil. Stir in cream sherry. Cool completely.
Refrigerate 1 hour. Add whipping cream and freeze. When partially frozen,
add nuts.

SPUMONI ICE CREAM

Serves: 8 to 10

2 cups milk

5 egg yolks, slightly beaten

Dash salt

1 cup sugar, divided

1 teaspoon vanilla

1 cup heavy cream

8 maraschino cherries, cut up

8 slivered almonds

4 teaspoons bourbon

2 teaspoons dry sherry

In top of double boiler, mix milk, yolks, salt and ¾ cup sugar. Cook stirring constantly until mixture is thickened and coats a metal spoon. Cool and add vanilla. Pour into a tray and freeze until almost firm. Line a 2 quart mold with this mixture. Whip cream until stiff, adding ¼ cup sugar. Then mix into the whipped cream the cherries, almonds, bourbon and dry sherry. Fill the center of the mold, cover and freeze. To unmold, put a hot cloth on bottom of mold. Slice and serve.

RASPBERRY ICE CREAM

Yield: 1 quart

2 (10 ounce) packages frozen raspberries, packed in light syrup and thawed

1 to 2 tablespoons lemon juice

3 cups half and half

½ cup sugar

4 large egg yolks

1 teaspoon vanilla

Puree raspberries, add lemon juice and refrigerate 2 hours. Combine half and half and sugar. Scald the mixture over moderate heat, stirring. Beat 4 yolks until light and thick; pour in scalded half and half, whisking. Return to pan and cook over moderate heat until mixture coats the spoon. Remove from heat and add 1 teaspoon vanilla and let custard cool. Chill in refrigerator for 2 hours. Stir in raspberry puree and freeze according to manufacturer's directions.

ICE CREAM GRASSHOPPERS

Serves: 8

12 large scoops softened vanilla ice cream

4 tablespoons green Creme de Menthe

4 tablespoons Creme de Cocoa

In a blender or food processor, combine above and process until thick. Serve in frappe glasses.

CREAM DE MENTHE ICE CREAM SQUARES

Squares:

2 cups chocolate wafer crumbs

⅓ cup soft butter

3 pints softened vanilla ice cream

5 tablespoons green Creme de Menthe

Chocolate Sauce:

3 ounces unsweetened chocolate

½ cup water

¾ cup sugar

¼ teaspoon salt

1½ teaspoons butter

¾ teaspoon vanilla

Combine chocolate crumbs and butter and press into greased 9 inch square pan. Swirl Creme de Menthe into ice cream. Place on crumbs and freeze. Drizzle with chocolate sauce. When serving, pass extra sauce.

For chocolate sauce: Combine chocolate and water. Cook on low heat until chocolate melts. Add sugar and salt and cook stirring until sugar dissolves. Remove from heat and add butter and vanilla. Cool well.

TRIPLE CAFE

Place a large scoop coffee ice cream in sherbert dish or parfait glass. Pour over 1 to 2 tablespoons Kahlua. Top with a dollop of whipped cream and sprinkle with coarse grains of freeze-dried coffee.

PEPPERMINT STICK ICE CREAM   *Makes: 1 quart*

¾ pound peppermint stick candy, crushed

2 cups milk

1 cup evaporated milk

1 cup whipping cream

Half and half

Peppermint extract, optional

Soak ½ pound candy in 2 cups milk overnight. Add the evaporated milk and whipping cream. Finish filling quart container with half and half and extra peppermint extract, if desired. Freeze. Fold in remaining ¼ pound of candy.

WALNUT CREPES WITH COFFEE BUTTERCREAM AND CHOCOLATE SAUCE

Serves: 8

Crepes:

1 cup walnuts, finely chopped	**2 eggs**
1 cup flour	**2 tablespoons sugar**
¾ cup milk	**1 tablespoon Grand Marnier**
¾ cup water	

Coffee Filling:

1 tablespoon instant coffee	**8 tablespoons unsalted butter, softened**
1 tablespoon boiling water	
1 tablespoon Grand Mariner	**12 tablespoons powdered sugar**
	1 egg yolk

Bittersweet Chocolate Sauce:

6 ounces semi-sweet chocolate	**½ to ¾ cup whipping cream**
1 ounce unsweetened chocolate	

For crepes: Using only ¾ cup ground walnuts, saving the rest for garnish, combine the rest of the crepe ingredients and beat well or process in food processor 30 seconds, scraping once. Refrigerate 1 hour or more.

For filling: Combine coffee, water and Grand Marnier and set aside. Beat butter; add sugar and yolk. Mix in coffee liquid.

For bittersweet chocolate sauce: Melt the two chocolates. Thin with whipping cream. Keep warm.

To assemble: Cook crepes according to manufacturer's directions. Top with one heaping teaspoon of butter and coffee filing. Roll up and chill 30 minutes. Top with warm chocolate sauce and remaining ¼ cup chopped walnuts. Serve immediately.

Yield: 16 crepes

CAKES, COOKIES, & PIES

Waterside Theater, Roanoke Island

CHOCOLATE ANGEL CAKE
WITH RUM TOPPING
Serves: 16 to 20

1½ cups egg whites (whites of 10 large eggs)

1½ teaspoons salt

¾ teaspoon cream of tartar

1½ teaspoons vanilla extract

1½ teaspoons almond extract

2 cups sugar

2 to 3 tablespoons cocoa (according to taste)

Flour, enough added to cocoa to measure 1½ cups

Measure sugar. Add 1 cup to cocoa/flour mixture and sift 4 times. Sift other cup of sugar 4 times and set aside. Add salt to egg whites. Beat until foamy. Add cream of tartar. Continue beating until stiff. Add the sifted cup of sugar to the whites, 2 tablespoons at a time. Use low speed on mixer.

Add flavorings. With wire whisk, fold flour mixture into egg whites, 2 tablespoons at a time. Fold in carefully. Pour into ungreased 10 inch tube pan and cut through batter with knife to remove bubbles.

Bake at 375° for 30 to 35 minutes. Invert pan on rack to cool. Remove carefully. You may eat plain, with whipped cream, frosting or Rum Topping.

Rum Topping:

1 package of instant vanilla pudding mix

1 cup milk, skim or whole

½ (8 ounce) Cool Whip container or some such topping

1 to 2 tablespoons rum, according to taste

Place milk and pudding mix in bowl. Beat with mixer. Fold in Cool Whip and add flavoring to taste.

You may "ice" cake and refrigerate or simply cut slices and put dab of topping on it.

Preparation time: 20 minutes.

FRENCH CHOCOLATE SILK CAKE

Chocolate Crumb Crust:

3 cups "Famous Chocolate Wafers", crushed

½ cup (1 stick) unsalted butter, melted

Method:

Crush cookies, enough to make 3 cups. Melt butter. Combine the two and press on bottom and completely up the sides of a 10 inch springform pan. Refrigerate or freeze.

Prepare chocolate silk and pour into chilled crust.

Prepare whipped cream topping.

Remove the chocolate silk in cookie crust from the springform pan.

Pile topping on after situating cake on doily and plate and garnish with chocolate leaves on top and sides and other choices.

Chocolate Silk Filling:

6 ounces unsweetened chocolate

3 sticks butter

2 teaspoons pure vanilla extract

2 cups light brown sugar

8 eggs

Melt chocolate in top of a double boiler on moderate heat, covered. Remove from hot water and cool.

Cream the butter in a bowl until soft. Add vanilla and brown sugar and beat well. Add melted chocolate and heat. Add eggs one at a time beating 3 minutes each. Pour the chocolate silk into the chocolate crumb crust.

With a thin knife, go around edges of springform pan. Release spring and carefully lift sides of pan. Refrigerate.

Whipped Cream Topping:

2 teaspoons unflavored gelatin

¼ cup cold water

4 cups heavy cream

1 cup confectioners sugar, sifted

3½ teaspoons vanilla extract

Sprinkle gelatin over cold water in tiny heat-proof cup and after few minutes put cup in a pan of shallow hot water on low heat. Dissolve.

Reserve ⅓ cup of the heavy cream and put rest in a medium chilled bowl. Add the sugar and vanilla and beat until the cream barely holds shape. Stir the remaining ⅓ cup cream into dissolved gelatin quickly and while beating, pour all at once into whipped cream. Continue to beat only until the cream holds a shape and is just firm enough for a topping — don't overbeat.

Spread topping over the chocolate silk mixture thickly, saving a pastry bag full. Fit bag with a fancy nozzle and flute around the edges of the cake. Put a star nozzle in and pile stars high in the middle. Decorate with chocolate leaves in a spiral fashion and if desired large chocolate leaves around the sides of crumb crust and garnish with violets and violet leaves. Keep refrigerated!

Chocolate Leaves:

8 ounces semi-sweet chocolate or Peter's bittersweet chocolate

A scant tablespoon Crisco

Camellia, Sasanqua or other waxy leaves

Melt chocolate and Crisco in top of double boiler and stir.

Spoon chocolate onto the underneath side of the leaves. Place on wax paper and put wax paper on a cookie sheet. Freeze a short while. Separate the chocolate leaves from the real leaves, starting at the stem and refreeze in zip lock bags or a box until ready to use.

CHRISTMAS PLUM PUDDING
Serves: 10 to 12

½ cup Crisco
½ cup milk
¾ cup raisins
¾ cup mixed candied fruits and peels
½ cup molasses
¼ cup brown sugar

1½ cups flour
1½ teaspoons baking powder
¼ teaspoon salt
1½ teaspoons cinnamon
1½ teaspoons nutmeg
¾ teaspoon cloves

Sift dry ingredients and mix in all other items.

Pour into greased tube pan and place over steaming water for 2 hours. Remove from pan.

After pudding is done and cooled, pour apple brandy or wine over it, wrap in cheese cloth and keep for several weeks. Moisten cloth with brandy.

When ready to serve, heat thoroughly and serve with whipped cream or hard sauce.

CHEESE CAKE I

Crust:

1 cup sifted enriched flour

¼ cup sugar

1 teaspoon grated lemon peel

½ cup butter or margarine

1 slightly beaten egg yolk

¼ teaspoon vanilla

Combine flour, sugar, and lemon peel. Cut in butter until mixture is crumbly. Add egg yolk and vanilla. Blend thoroughly. Pat one third of dough on bottom of 9 inch springform pan (sides removed). Bake in hot oven (400°) about 6 minutes or until golden; cool. Butter sides of pan and attach to bottom. Pat remaining dough evenly on sides to a height of 2 inches.

Cheese Filling:

5 (8 ounce) packages Cream cheese

¼ teaspoon vanilla

¾ teaspoon grated lemon peel

1¾ cups sugar

3 tablespoons enriched flour

¼ teaspoon salt

5 eggs

2 egg yolks

¼ cup heavy cream

Stir Cream cheese to soften; beat until fluffy. Add vanilla and peel. Mix sugar, flour and salt; gradually blend into cheese. Add eggs and yolks, one at a time, beating well after each. Gently stir in cream. Turn into crust-lined pan. Bake in very hot oven (500⁰) 5 to 8 minutes, or until top edge of crust is golden. Reduce oven heat to 200°; bake one hour longer. Remove from oven; cool in pan about 3 hours. Remove sides of pan. Top with strawberry or pineapple glaze.

Strawberry Glaze:

2 to 3 cups fresh strawberries

1 cup water

1½ tablespoons cornstarch

½ to ¾ cup sugar

Crush 1 cup of the strawberries; add the water and cook 2 minutes; sieve. Mix cornstarch with sugar (amount of sugar depends on sweetness of berries). Stir into hot berry mixture. Bring to boiling, stirring constantly. Cook and stir until thick and clear. (Add a few drops of red food coloring, if needed.) Cool to room temperature. Place remaining strawberries on top of cooled cheesecake; circle with halved pineapple rings. Pour glaze over strawberries; chill about 2 hours.

Pineapple Glaze:

3 tablespoons sugar

1 tablespoon cornstarch

1 cup unsweetened pineapple juice

¼ teaspoon grated lemon peel

Mix sugar and cornstarch; stir in pineapple juice and lemon peel. Heat, stirring until mixture comes to boiling. Cook and stir until mixture thickens. Cool to room temperature. Trim with canned pineapple; spoon over glaze. Chill 2 hours.

CHEESE CAKE II

10 graham crackers

¼ cup melted butter

¼ cup sugar (for crust)

3 (8 ounce) packages Cream cheese

4 eggs

¼ cup sugar (for filling)

1 pint sour cream

¼ cup sugar (for topping)

½ teaspoon vanilla

¼ teaspoon almond extract

Crush crackers into crumbs, combine with butter and sugar, press over bottom and sides of 9 inch pie plate (deep dish).

Beat cheese in large bowl with electric mixer until soft. Add eggs and sugar. Beat until smooth. Pour into crumb shell.

Bake at 350° for 20 minutes. Cool on wire rack for 15 minutes.

Combine sour cream, sugar, and vanilla in small bowl. Spread over cheese cake.

Bake at 475° for 5 minutes. Cool on rack and refrigerate.

PARALINE CHEESE CAKE   *Serves: 10 to 12*

Crust:

1 cup graham cracker crumbs

3 tablespoons sugar

3 tablespoons margarine, melted

Filling:

3 (8 ounce) packages Cream cheese

1¼ cups dark brown sugar, packed

2 tablespoons flour

3 eggs

1½ teaspoons vanilla

½ cup pecans, finely chopped

Topping:

Maple syrup

Pecan halves

Combine crumbs, sugar, margarine; press in bottom of 9 inch spring-form pan. Bake in preheated 350° oven for 10 minutes.

Combine softened Cream cheese, sugar and flour. Mix at medium speed until well blended. Add eggs, one at a time, mixing well after each addition. Blend in vanilla and nuts. Pour mixture over crumbs. Bake at 350° for 50 to 55 minutes. Loosen cake from rim of pan; cool before removing rim. Chill. Brush with maple syrup and garnish with pecan halves.

CHERRY "UPSIDE-DOWN" CAKE   *Serves: 12*

½ cup firmly packed brown
   sugar

1 (No. 2) can sour pie cherries,
   drained; reserve juice

1¾ cups sifted flour

2 teaspoons baking powder

½ teaspoon salt

1 cup sugar

⅓ cup shortening (liquid)

¾ cup milk

1 teaspoon vanilla

1 egg

All must be at room temperature.

Grease a 12 x 8 x 2 inch pan with butter. Sprinkle brown sugar over bottom of pan. Add drained cherries. Sift together flour, baking powder, salt and sugar. Add to shortening and milk and vanilla. Beat for 1½ minutes until batter is well blended. Add egg, unbeaten and beat for another 1½ minutes. Pour over cherries in pan.

Bake in moderate oven (350°) for 35 to 45 minutes.

Preparation time: 20 minutes.

Cherry Sauce:

½ cup sugar

2 tablespoons cornstarch

1½ cups juice (juice reserved
   from cherries plus water)

⅛ teaspoon almond extract

Combine sugar, cornstarch and juice. Cook until thickened, stirring constantly. Remove from heat and add almond extract. Serve warm over warm cake. A fluff of whipped cream for decoration may be added.

FRUIT COCKTAIL CAKE

1¾ cups sugar

2 cups flour

2 teaspoons baking soda

⅛ teaspoon salt

2 eggs

1 (15 ounce) can fruit cocktail
   (drained but reserve juice)

Mix sugar, flour, soda and salt well together. Add eggs, fruit cocktail, and ¼ cup of the juice. Bake 325° for 35 to 40 minutes in a greased and floured 9 x 13 inch pan.

Icing:

1 cup milk	**¾ cup coconut**
1 cup sugar	**¼ cup pecans**
1 stick of margarine or butter	**1 teaspoon vanilla**

Boil milk, sugar and butter for 10 minutes. Remove from the heat and add coconut, pecans and vanilla. Spread on cake while still warm. Serve warm.

TOASTED POUND CAKE WITH CREAM CHEESE TOPPING AND BURGUNDY CHERRY SAUCE

Pound Cake:

Use homemade, bought or pound cake mix. It may be slightly stale. Cut cake into slices and toast. Top each slice with a spoonful of Cream Cheese Topping and Burgundy Cherry Sauce.

Cream Cheese Topping:

1 (3 ounce) package Cream cheese, softened	**1 tablespoon cream**
¼ cup confectioners sugar	

In a small mixer bowl, blend together softened cheese, sugar and cream until light and fluffy.

Burgundy Cherry Sauce:

1 (1 pound) can pitted dark sweet cherries	**2 tablespoons cornstarch**
¼ cup sugar	**¼ cup Burgundy**

Drain cherries; reserve syrup. In a small saucepan, combine sugar and cornstarch. Gradually stir in cherry syrup until smooth. Cook over medium heat, stirring constantly, until mixture thickens and boils. Remove from heat; stir in Burgundy and cherries.

COCONUT POUND CAKE

Serves: 20 to 25

1 pound butter or margarine	**6 eggs**
2 cups sugar	**7 ounces angel flake coconut**
2 cups flour	**1 teaspoon vanilla**

Cream butter and sugar. Add 1 cup of flour and mix well. Add eggs, one at a time, mixing well. Mix remaining cup of flour with coconut and add to cake mixture. Mix in vanilla. Place in 9 inch tube pan. Bake at 350° for 1 hour and 15 minutes or until cake begins to pull away from sides of pan. Turn from pan and glaze while hot.
May be frozen.

Glaze:

1 cup sugar	**1 teaspoon coconut flavoring**
½ cup water	**or almond flavoring**

While cake is baking, combine glaze ingredients and simmer for 10 minutes. Brush onto warm cake. Let cake cool. Best served 24 hours after baking.

SHORTBREAD FROM SCOTLAND

4 tablespoons sugar	**½ pound butter**
2 cups flour	**Pinch of salt**
4 tablespoons cornstarch	

Cream butter and sugar until consistancy of mayonnaise. Sift flour, cornstarch and salt. Add to butter and sugar, working in gradually until well mixed.
Roll or pat ½ inch thick in ungreased cookie pan. Bake at 325° for ½ hour. When done and still warm cut into pieces. Return to oven after you have turned the oven off and is still warm.
This can be rolled out ¼ inch thick and cut with a cookie cutter. Makes 36 or more cookies.

Alternate Instructions:
Put all in food processor and mix well. Roll ½ inch thick in ungreased cookie pan. Bake at 325° for ½ hour.

CREAM CHEESE POUND CAKE

3 sticks butter
1 (8 ounce) package Cream cheese
3 cups sugar
6 eggs

3 cups flour
¼ teaspoon salt
1 tablespoon vanilla

Cream butter, cheese and sugar. Beat until fluffy. Add eggs one at a time. Gradually add flour and salt, beating well after each addition. Add vanilla and mix well. Pour into 10 inch tube pan which has been greased and floured. Place in a cold oven. Turn oven to 300° and bake for 1 hour and 45 minutes (or until done when tested and golden brown).

May be prepared ahead of time and/or frozen.

ORANGE DATE NUT CAKE

1 (6 ounce) package dates
1 cup chopped pecans
4 cups sifted flour
1 teaspoon baking powder
1 teaspoon soda

2 cups margarine
2 cups sugar
4 eggs
1½ cups buttermilk
2 tablespoons grated orange rind

Chop dates and nuts. Add 1 cup of the flour to the dates and nuts and blend. Sift remaining flour with baking powder, soda and salt. Cream margarine and add 2 cups sugar and cream until light and fluffy. Add eggs one at a time. Add sifted dry ingredients alternately with buttermilk, blending well. Add floured dates, nuts and orange rind. Pour into a tube or bundt pan which has been greased and floured. Bake in a 300° oven 1½ hours.

Sauce:

1 cup orange juice

1½ cup sugar

Meanwhile add orange juice to 1½ cups sugar in a saucepan and bring to a boil. Pour hot sauce over hot cake. Allow to cool in pan and turn out. It must cool. Sprinkle powdered or confectioners sugar on top.

HERMIT CAKE

Serves 25 to 30

1 pound butter

5 cups flour

3 cups brown sugar

6 eggs, beaten separately

4 packages of dates, cut each date twice

Juice of one lemon

1⅓ pounds pecans

2 teaspoons baking powder

2 teaspoons cinnamon

4 teaspoons vanilla

2 teaspoons nutmeg

Cream butter and sugar, add yolks of eggs. Sift dry ingredients and add to butter and sugar. Add nuts and flavorings. Lastly fold in egg whites, stiffly beaten. Bake in oven at 275° for 2 hours and 30 minutes. Test with straw. Don't overcook. (Test cake first 2 hours of cooking.)

Cake may be topped with whipped cream, egg nog ice cream or just plain ice cream.

BLUEBERRY CAKE WITH BROWN SUGAR SAUCE

2 eggs

2 cups sugar

¾ cup butter at room temperature

½ cup milk

2½ cups twice-sifted cake flour

1 pint blueberries

Cream butter and sugar together at room temperature until fluffy. Beat eggs separately and add to butter and sugar. Take 1 teaspoon of the cake flour and coat blueberries with it by tossing them together to prevent berries from sinking to bottom of pan. Add the remaining 2¼ cups flour to mixture along with milk. Add berries. Bake the cake in a greased and floured tube or bundt pan at 375° for 45 minutes or until firm.

Preparation time: 45 minutes.

Sauce:

2 egg whites, stiffly beaten

1 cup brown sugar added to egg whites

½ pint cream, whipped and add to egg whites and sugar

1 teaspoon vanilla

Pour this in a pitcher to spoon over cake as you serve. Cake is good served hot.

TEXAS SHEET CAKE

2 cups flour	½ cup sour cream
2 cups sugar	1 teaspoon soda
½ teaspoon salt	2 eggs

Mix the above ingredients.

In a saucepan, heat:

2 sticks margarine	4 tablespoons cocoa
1 cup water	

Bring to a boil. Add to flour mixture while hot. Beat until smooth. Pour into greased and floured sheet cake pan, or 2 (9 x 13 inch) pans. Bake at 350° for 20 minutes.

Icing:

Mix in a small bowl:

1 box powdered sugar	1 teaspoon vanilla

In a small pan, bring the following to a boil:

1 stick margarine	4 tablespoons cocoa
6 tablespoons milk	

Mix together, stir until smooth and spread on cake while warm. Sprinkle with nuts.

OATMEAL CAKE

1½ cups boiling water	1 cup white sugar
1 cup oatmeal	2 eggs
¼ stick margarine	1 teaspoon cinnamon
1½ cups self rising flour	1 teaspoon soda
1 cup dark brown sugar	

Pour boiling water over oatmeal and let sit 15 minutes. Mix other ingredients together and add to oatmeal. Cook 30 minutes at 350° in 2 greased and floured pans. Frost with Cream Cheese Frosting, adding 1 cup pecans. (Refer to recipe for Cream Cheese Frosting.)

APPLE CAKE

Yield: 2 loaves

Combine:

3 cups flour	**2 teaspoons cinnamon**
2 cups sugar	**1 teaspoon salt**
1 teaspoon soda	**1 teaspoon baking powder**

Stir into the above mixture:

3 eggs, well-beaten	**1 cup Wesson oil**
4 cups diced apples, unpeeled	**1 cup nuts**

Pour in greased loaf or tube pan. Bake 325° oven for 1 hour and 20 minutes.

Icing:

Boil for 2 to 3 minutes:

¾ cup brown sugar	**½ cup Pet milk**
1 stick margarine	

Add:

½ cup nuts	**1 teaspoon vanilla or walnut flavoring**

Cover top of cake and let it run down sides.

WHITE RAISIN POUND CAKE

1 pound butter	**1 teaspoon baking powder**
2 cups sugar	**1 pound white raisins**
6 eggs	**2 cups pecans, chopped**
3½ cups flour	**2 ounces lemon extract**

Cream butter and sugar. Add eggs, flour and baking powder, then raisins and chopped nuts. Mix well, add extract. Bake in greased tube or bundt pan at 250° for about 3 hours 20 minutes or until it tests done.

CARROT-PINEAPPLE CAKE

1½ cups oil
1¾ cups sugar
4 eggs
2¼ cups flour
2 teaspoons soda
1 teaspoon salt

4 teaspoons cinnamon
2 teaspoons vanilla
3 cups grated carrots
1 small can crushed pineapple, drained
½ cup raisins

Combine oil, sugar and eggs. Add flour, soda, salt and cinnamon. Then add vanilla and grated carrots. Stir in crushed pineapple and raisins.

Place in well greased tube pan or 9 x 13 inch pan. Bake 45 minutes at 325°. When cool, ice with Cream Cheese Frosting. (Refer to recipe for Cream Cheese Frosting.)

YOGURT APPLE COFFEE CAKE

1 stick butter or margarine
1 cup sugar
2 eggs
2 cups flour
2 teaspoons baking powder

1 teaspoon baking soda
¼ teaspoon salt
1 teaspoon vanilla
1 cup yogurt or sour cream
4 large apples, peeled and sliced
Cinnamon

Cream together butter, sugar, eggs. Stir in dry ingredients and yogurt. Place ½ batter in well greased tube pan. Layer apples on top and sprinkle with cinnamon and sugar. Pour remaining batter on top. Bake 1 hour at 350° (until knife comes out clean.)

Frosting:

1 tablespoon milk, warm
1 tablespoon butter, warm

1 cup powdered sugar
¼ teaspoon vanilla

Combine and drizzle over warm cake.

YOGURT CAKE
WITH ORANGE SYRUP

Serves: 12 to 16

1 cup butter

1 cup sugar

4 eggs

1 tablespoon grated orange peel

1 teaspoon vanilla

2½ cups all purpose flour

1 teaspoon baking powder

1 teaspoon baking soda

¼ teaspoon salt

1 cup blanched almonds, finely chopped

1 cup plain yogurt

Cream butter and sugar. Add eggs, orange peel and vanilla. Beat well. Sift together flour, baking powder, baking soda and salt. Add flour mixture and almonds and the creamed mixture alternately with yogurt. Pour into 9 inch bundt pan and bake at 350° about 1 hour.

Orange Syrup Topping:

½ cup orange juice

½ cup sugar

Stir together the juice and sugar. Pour over warm cake. Let cool in pan.

HUMMINGBIRD CAKE

Serves 16 to 20

3 cups flour

2 cups sugar

1 teaspoon salt

1 teaspoon baking powder

1 teaspoon cinnamon

1½ cups oil

3 eggs

1½ teaspoons vanilla

1 (8 ounce) can crushed pineapple, undrained

2 cups chopped banana

1 to 2 cups chopped pecans

Sift dry ingredients into bowl. Add all other ingredients and stir until mixed. Do not beat. Pour into a greased and floured 10 inch tube pan. Bake at 350° for 1 hour and 10 minutes. Cool in pan. Frost with Cream Cheese Frosting. (Refer to recipe for Cream Cheese Frosting.)

Preparation time: 20 minutes. 1 hour 10 minutes to bake; 20 minutes to frost. May be prepared 1 or 2 days ahead and kept in refrigerator.

ICE BOX CAKE
Serves: 6

3 eggs

¾ cup sugar

4 teaspoons flour

1 cup milk

1 tablespoon butter

¼ cup lemon juice

Grated rind of 1 lemon

1 (7 ounce) box Nabisco vanilla wafers

½ pint whipping cream

2 tablespoons sugar

½ teaspoon vanilla

Few drops almond

Beat yolks of eggs until light, add sugar, flour and beat until smooth. Add milk and butter, cook over hot water, stirring constantly, until thickened. Add lemon juice and rind. Cool and add well beaten whites of eggs. Line serving bowl with vanilla wafers, pour half of custard over wafers, cover with a layer of wafers and repeat. Refrigerate for 12 to 24 hours. Whip cream and add seasonings. Serve with the cake.

FUDGE ICING

¾ stick butter

1 cup sugar

⅓ cup evaporated milk

½ cup semi-sweet chocolate bits

Mix butter, sugar, milk and bring to boil on medium heat. Cook about 10 minutes; remove from heat and add semi-sweet chocolate bits. Mix well and ice cake.

CREAM CHEESE FROSTING

8 ounces Cream cheese, softened

1 stick butter or margarine, softened

1 teaspoon vanilla

1 pound confectioners sugar

Soften butter and Cream cheese at room temperature and cream together well. Mix all ingredients until smooth. Spread over cooled cake. Refrigerate to keep well.

PIE CRUST

Yield: 2 (9 inch) pie crusts

2 cups all purpose flour, sifted
1 teaspoon salt

⅔ cup Crisco
7 tablespoons ice water

Combine flour and salt, cut in shortening. Sprinkle in water, mixing lightly with fork.
Form into 2 balls and roll out on floured surface for crust.

LEMON CHESS TARTS

½ stick butter
1½ cups sugar
1 tablespoon flour
3 eggs, slightly beaten

1 teaspoon vanilla
⅛ teaspoon salt
1 lemon, grated rind and juice
2 tablespoons half and half

Cream butter and sugar. Add flour, eggs and other ingredients. Pour into 16 unbaked tart shells (approximately 3 inches in diameter). Bake in slow oven at 325° for approximately 30 minutes or until golden.

EASY LEMON CHESS

Yield: 2 pies

2 lemons
4 eggs
2 cups sugar
4 level tablespoons flour

1 cup water
1 stick margarine
Pinch salt

Cut lemons into 4 or 6 pieces (lengthwise). Remove seeds and tough center part. Mix flour and sugar. Put lemon pieces in blender first, then add remaining ingredients. Blend one minute. More interesting if small pieces of lemon are present. Pour into two unbaked pie shells. Cook in preheated 400° oven for 10 minutes. Reduce oven to 350° and bake for 30 minutes.

Preparation time: 15 minutes plus baking time. May be frozen.

MARY'S LEMON PIE

Use your favorite all-purpose pastry recipe, and line a pie pan. Smear 2 tablespoons tart jelly (red currant or crabapple) on the pastry before pouring in the following filling:

4 eggs, beaten

2 cups sugar

1 stick butter, melted

6 tablespoons cornmeal

Juice of 2 lemons

Grated rind of 1 lemon

Bake for 55 minutes at 350°. Allow to cool and set before slicing (at least 30 minutes). This makes a large pie.

OLD FASHION LEMON PIE

1½ cups sugar

⅓ cup cornstarch

¼ teaspoon salt

1½ cups boiling water

4 egg yolks, beaten

2 tablespoons butter

Juice of 1½ small lemons

Mix dry ingredients (sugar, cornstarch, and salt). Add boiling water. Cook until clear. Add beaten egg yolks, butter and lemon juice. Cook until thickness desired. Pour into previously baked pie crust, top with meringue.

Meringue:

6 egg whites

½ teaspoon cream of tartar

¾ cup sugar

Beat egg whites until frothy. Add cream of tartar. Add sugar slowly while continuing beating. Cover pie to edge of filling. Bake slowly until meringue browns.

CRUNCH TOP PEAR PIE
Yield: 1 (9 inch) pie

Unbaked 9 inch pie shell

6 sliced, peeled, and cored large winter pears

½ cup sugar

1 orange (grate peel and extract juices)

½ cup brown sugar, firmly packed

½ cup flour

½ teaspoon cinnamon

¼ teaspoon ginger

¼ teaspoon nutmeg

⅓ cup butter

Mix pears with sugar, 2 teaspoons grated orange peel and 3 tablespoons orange juice. Arrange in pie shell.

Combine brown sugar, flour and spices. Cut in butter until mixture is crumbly. Sprinkle over pears.

Bake at 400° until pears are tender (about 45 minutes).

Cool slightly. Serve with cream.

Preparation time: 1¼ hours.

PEAR MINCE MEAT
Yield: 5 pies or 40 tarts

7 pounds pears

1 cup vinegar

3 pounds brown sugar (light or dark)

1 tablespoon cinnamon

1 tablespoon cloves

1 tablespoon nutmeg

1 tablespoon salt

1 tablespoon allspice

1 pound seedless raisins

Wash and core pears, run through meat grinder or fine slicer machine — do not peel pears. Mix other ingredients into pears and cook 45 minutes — longer if necessary for pears to become tender. Seal in pint or quart jars — 1 pint is enough for one pie. Serve with whipped cream. May also be used as a relish by eliminating the whipped cream.

Preparation time: 1 hour. Will keep indefinitely in sealed jars.

YUMMY BUTTERSCOTCH PIE

2 egg yolks, beaten
Pinch of soda
1½ cups brown sugar

4 tablespoons flour
2 cups milk

Mix flour and soda with brown sugar and add to egg yolks. Stir in milk. Cook in a double boiler until thick. Mix in:

2 tablespoons butter

1 teaspoon vanilla

Pour into baked pie shell, top with meringue and brown in 325° oven.

AUNT BETTY'S CHOCOLATE PIE
(the very best chocolate pie you ever ate)

Melt 3 squares of unsweetened chocolate in top of double boiler. Add one can of Eagle Brand sweetened condensed milk. Stir together over heat until thoroughly mixed and starting to thicken. Pour into baked pie crust. Allow to cool. Top with ½ pint of cream whipped with a dash of vanilla and two tablespoons sugar.

OUR FAVORITE CHOCOLATE PIE

2 squares unsweetened
   chocolate, melted
4 eggs (leave out 3 whites)
1 cup sugar
1 cup Carnation milk

2 tablespoons cornstarch
1 teaspoon vanilla
1 tablespoon butter

Melt chocolate in a double boiler and add other ingredients. Mix together until thickened. Pour into baked pie shell. Cool. Top with meringue. Bake at 350° until meringue is brown.

Meringue:

3 egg whites
Dash of salt

¾ teaspoon vanilla (optional)
3 tablespoons sugar

Beat egg whites and salt until whites are stiff. Fold in sugar and vanilla.

FRENCH SILK PIE

Serves: 8 to 12

4 squares semi-sweet chocolate   **½ stick butter (or margarine)**

Melt together and cool the above.

**½ pound (8 ounces) Cream
cheese**

1½ sticks butter (or margarine)

**2 cups sifted confectioners
sugar**

4 eggs

**2 or 3 teaspoons Grand
Marnier or other flavored
liqueur**

Cream together Cream cheese and butter until very fluffy. Add eggs one at a time, beating well. Add sugar and beat well. Add chocolate mixture. Add liqueur. Refrigerate in any baked pie crust at least six hours. (No cooking.) Refrigerates for 2 to 3 days.

PIE CRUSTS: A nutty flavor will be given pie crust if ⅓ of the flour is whole wheat.

CHOCOLATE EGGNOG LAYER PIE

1 envelope unflavored gelatin

½ cup water

⅓ cup sugar

2 tablespoons cornstarch

¼ teaspoon salt

2 cups commercial eggnog

**1½ squares unsweetened
chocolate, melted**

1 teaspoon vanilla extract

1 (9 inch) baked pastry shell

1 teaspoon rum extract

2 cups whipping cream, divided

¼ cup powdered sugar

Chocolate curls (optional)

Soften gelatin in water; set aside. Combine sugar, cornstarch, and salt in a 1 quart saucepan; gradually stir in eggnog. Cook over medium heat, stirring constantly, until thickened; cook 2 minutes. Remove from heat and add gelatin mixture; stir until dissolved.

Divide filling in half; set one half aside to cool. Add melted chocolate and vanilla to other half of filling; stir well and pour into pastry shell. Chill until filling is set.

Add rum extract to remaining filling. Whip 1 cup whipping cream, and fold into cooled mixture. Spoon over chocolate layer and chill.

Whip remaining whipping cream; add powdered sugar. Spread over pie; garnish with chocolate curls, if desired.

SWISS CHOCOLATE ALMOND PIE   *Serves: 8*

Crust:

2 cups all purpose flour

¾ cup (1½ sticks) unsalted butter, cut into small pieces

¾ cup sliced almonds, coarsely chopped

¼ cup firmly packed brown sugar

1 ounce (1 square) semi-sweet chocolate (preferably Swiss), grated

¼ teaspoon salt

1½ teaspoons Creme de Cacao

1½ teaspoons Amaretto

½ teaspoon almond extract

Water (as needed)

Filling:

½ cup (1 stick) butter, room temperature

⅔ cup sugar

2 ounces (2 squares) unsweetened chocolate, melted and cooled

2 eggs

1½ teaspoons Creme de Cacao

1½ teaspoons Amaretto

½ teaspoon almond extract

Topping:

2 cups whipping cream

¼ cup powdered sugar

1 tablespoon Creme de Cacao

1 tablespoon Amaretto

For crust: Preheat oven to 375°. Generously grease 9 inch pie plate. Combine flour and butter in medium bowl and mix with fingertips until consistency of coarse meal. Gently blend in almonds, sugar, chocolate and salt. Sprinkle liqueurs and almond extract over mixture and toss together, adding water as needed, until dough can be formed into ball.

Press into bottom and sides of prepared pie plate. Bake until crust is set and almonds are browned, about 15 minutes. Let cool.

For Filling: Cream butter. Gradually add sugar and beat until mixture is light and fluffy. Stir in chocolate. Add eggs one at a time, beating well after each addition. Stir in liqueurs and almond extract. Turn into prepared crust, spreading evenly. Chill.

Shortly before ready to serve, beat remaining ingredients until stiff. Spoon into pastry bag fitted with large star tip and pipe over filling. Garnish with chocolate shavings.

This recipe is from Bob Passarelli, Chef, Executive Mansion.

HOT FUDGE PIE

4 tablespoons cocoa

4 tablespoons flour

1 cup sugar

2 large or extra large eggs,
  beaten

¾ teaspoon vanilla

¼ teaspoon almond extract

1 stick butter

Mix first 6 ingredients together. Add melted butter. Pour into unbaked pie shell. Bake 20 to 25 minutes at 375°.

Serve warm with scoop of vanilla ice cream or whipped cream.

CHESS PIE
Yield: 9 inch pie

3 eggs

1½ cups sugar

½ cup margarine

1 tablespoon cornmeal

1 tablespoon vinegar

1 teaspoon vanilla

Beat eggs and add sugar slowly. Add melted butter, cornmeal, vanilla and vinegar. Pour into unbaked pie shell. Bake at 325° to 350° for 20 to 30 minutes or until set. (This is a very old recipe.)

Preparation time: 20 to 30 minutes. Freezes well. Can be made the day before and just kept.

BROWN SUGAR PIE

3 eggs, beaten slightly

2 tablespoons cream

1 tablespoon melted butter

1 teaspoon vinegar and vanilla
  (combined to make
  1 teaspoon)

2 cups brown sugar

2 tablespoons sifted corn meal

Dash of salt

Mix brown sugar, meal and salt. Beat eggs into mixture. Add vanilla, vinegar, cream and melted butter. Bake in pie shell or individual tart shells at 325° for 30 minutes.

CARAMEL PECAN PIE   *Serves: 8*

4 eggs, slightly beaten   **1 teaspoon vanilla**
1 cup sugar   **3 tablespoons melted butter**
Pinch of salt   **1 cup pecan halves**
1 cup dark Karo syrup   **1 (10 inch) unbaked pie shell**

Beat eggs slightly. Add sugar, salt, syrup, vanilla and melted butter. Place pecans in bottom of pie shell and pour filling over. Bake at 425° for 15 minutes. Reduce heat to 350° and bake about 35 minutes longer.
Preparation time: 20 minutes.

CHERRY AMBROSIA PIE

1 #2 can sour cherries, drained   **1 (3 ounce) package cherry or**
1 #2 can crushed unsweetened   **   orange gelatin**
**   pineapple, undrained**   **3 to 4 sliced bananas**
¼ cup flour   **1 cup chopped pecans**
1¼ cups sugar   **2 graham cracker crusts**

Cook first 4 ingredients until bubbly. Add gelatin and dissolve. Cool. Add bananas and chopped pecans. Put in graham crackers crusts. Top with whipped cream. Chill.

BLUEBERRY PIE   *Serves: 12*

1 (8 ounce) package Cream   **3 bananas, sliced**
**   cheese**   **1 can blueberry pie filling**
1 cup white sugar
9 ounces Cool Whip

Mix softened Cream cheese and sugar until well blended. Add Cool Whip and mix well. Pour mixture into two cooked pie shellls. Next add sliced bananas. Add blueberry pie filling — ½ can for each pie. Refrigerate until ready to serve.

VARIATION: Press pecan halves into unbaked pie shell.

SHREDDED APPLE PIE

1 cup white sugar
½ stick margarine
1 teaspoon nutmeg
1 egg, beaten with fork

3 medium size cooking apples (tart, firm)
Dash of salt
1 teaspoon lemon juice

Melt margarine. Add sugar and other ingredients except apples. Mix well. Grate apples carefully on large size of grater in order to have nice shreds and as little juice as possible. Place apples in unbaked pie crust. Pour above mixture over apples. If using frozen crust, let thaw for about 10 minutes. Preheat oven to 375° and bake for 45 minutes, or until center feels firm. May use top crust if desired.
Preparation time: 10 minutes, plus baking time. May be frozen.

ALMOND 'N ORANGE TART
(From Yorkshire, England)   *Serves: 4*

Pastry:

1 cup flour
½ cup butter
1 tablespoon sugar

Pinch of salt
1 egg yolk
1 to 2 tablespoons water

Mix all ingredients (save water for last). Roll out. Line 12 deep tins or a small flat pan. Prick bottom with fork.

Filling:

1 cup almonds, ground
1 orange (use grated rind and all the juice)

½ cup sugar
2 egg yolks

Mix all together. Fill pastries. Bake in preheated oven 425° for 10 minutes. Lower heat to 350° for additional 25 minutes.

GRAND MARNIER CHEESE PIE *Serves: 8*

Crust:

6 tablespoons butter, melted

8 ounces graham crackers, crushed

2 tablespoons sugar

½ teaspoon cinnamon

Mix all ingredients well, and press evenly into a 9 inch pie pan. Chill in refrigerator until firm.

Filling:

⅓ cup Grand Marnier liqueur

1 tablespoon unflavored gelatin

1 (8 ounce) package Cream cheese, softened to room temperature

⅔ cup sugar

¼ teaspoon salt

2 eggs, separated

⅓ cup milk

3 tablespoons orange juice

1 teaspoon orange rind (less or more to taste)

1 cup heavy cream, whipped into soft peaks.

Pour Grand Marnier into a small cup such as a pyrex custard cup. Sprinkle gelatin over Grand Marnier. Place cup in saucepan with small amount of water. Heat over low heat until gelatin is dissolved. With a wooden spoon, beat Cream cheese in a deep bowl until smooth. Add sugar and salt; beat until well blended. Beat in egg yolks, one at a time; then add milk, orange juice and rind, stirring to blend. In a separate bowl, beat egg whites until soft peaks form. Fold in whipped cream. Beat the dissolved gelatin/Grand Marnier mixture into the Cream cheese mixture. Gently fold in the cream/egg white mixture, as with a souffle. Pour filling into chilled crust. Chill at least 3 hours before serving. Before serving, garnish with whipped cream or orange sections, if desired.

MINIATURE FRUIT TARTLETS   *Yield: 20 tartlets*

Pie pastry, enough for a double crust pie

1 cup vanilla pastry cream (Creme Patissiere)

Dried apricots, wedges of pineapple, pears, or other fruits

⅓ cup warm apricot or raspberry jam

Pie Pastry:

2 cups sifted all purpose flour (Gold Medal)

⅔ cup Crisco or ⅓ cup Crisco and ½ cup unsalted butter (Crisco pastry holds shape better)

½ cup ice cold water

1 teaspoon salt

In liquid measure, measure ½ cup cold water and place in freezer. Sift lots of flour onto waxed paper. Measure 2 cups and sift it again along with the teaspoon of salt into a mixing bowl. Measure ⅓ of this mixture (⅔ cup) and add to the icy water and mix with a fork to make a paste. Put into the refrigerator. Measure ⅔ cup Crisco and cut it into the flour-salt mixture with a pastry blender until the size of peas. With a rubber scraper, scrape the paste (flour and water) into the coarse mixture and quickly combine into a ball. Remove from bowl, wrap in waxed paper and refrigerate at least one hour.

Prepare a board or pastry cloth with lots of flour. Flour rolling pin and be ready to roll out and create pastry shell, pies, or tartlets.

Vanilla Pastry: (Creame or Creme Patissiere)

¼ cup milk

¼ vanilla bean, split in half length

3 egg yolks

⅓ cup granulated sugar

2 tablespoons flour or cornstarch

Boil milk and vanilla bean. Cover, remove and keep hot. With a wire whisk, beat eggs and sugar until mixture whitens and forms a ribbon. Carefully stir in cornstarch or flour with whisk. Pour milk through a strainer to remove vanilla bean and pour hot milk into the egg and sugar, beating constantly. Pour it back into the pan and boil again for one minute, stirring constantly with wire whisk to keep it from sticking. Pour into a container. Rub the cream with a pat of butter to keep a skin from forming. As it cools, refrigerate.

Preparing the tartlets:

Roll out the cold pastry and cut it with a cookie cutter slightly larger than the tartlet pans. Line the pans with the dough and prick with a fork. Refrigerate 20 minutes after filling up a baking sheet with the molds. Bake at 400° 6 to 10 minutes. Watch.

Remove and cool the tartlets. Fill each with the Creme Patissiere. Place on top of each cream a tiny piece of fruit and push it down into the cream slightly.

Melt in a saucepan apricot jam or raspberry jam. Spoon a little over each tartlet to glaze. Refrigerate before serving. Serve same day or next as the pastry shells will become soggy. Put each in tiny paper cups and serve on trays.

A boiled custard recipe might satisfy for the cream:

6 eggs	**4 cups milk**
1 cup sugar	**Heaping tablespoon vanilla**

Scald milk. Beat eggs and sugar. Add milk to eggs. Return to stove and gently simmer until a custard is formed (moderately thick). Do not boil. Add vanilla and refrigerate. It will thicken more after refrigeration.

ALMOND CRESCENTS

½ pound butter	**½ cup sugar**
2 cups flour	**1 cup almonds, ground after measuring**

Mix ingredients. Make crescent shapes. Bake at 350° for 8 to 10 minutes (or until set and only slightly browned). Cool. Roll in confectioners sugar.

HERMITS

¾ cup shortening	**1 egg**
1 cup sugar	**¼ cup molasses**

Beat the above ingredients with mixer. Stir in remaining ingredients:

2 teaspoons soda	**¾ teaspoon ginger**
¼ teaspoon salt	**¾ teaspoon cloves**
2¼ cups flour	**½ cup raisins**
1 teaspoon cinnamon	**½ cup nuts, chopped**

Press in 9 x 13 inch glass pan. Sprinkle with granulated sugar. Bake for 15 minutes at 375°.

POUND CAKE WAFERS

Yield: 5 to 6 dozen

2½ sticks butter
  (do not substitute)
1 cup sugar
2 egg yolks

3 cups sifted flour
1 teaspoon vanilla

Cream butter and add sugar gradually. Add eggs and flour, flavoring last. Drop by spoonfulls on ungreased cookie sheet.
Bake at 350° 12 to 15 minutes.
Decorate with pecan halves or half red or green cheeries.

OLD FASHIONED GINGERBREAD BOYS

Yield: 2 dozen (10 inch) cookies

1⅓ cups margarine
2 cups sugar
2 eggs
½ cup molasses
4 cups flour

2 teaspoons salt
2 teaspoons soda
2 teaspoons cinnamon
2 teaspoons ginger
1½ teaspoons cloves

Cream shortening and sugar thoroughly. Add eggs and molasses and beat well. Add sifted dry ingredients. Mix well.
Roll ⅛ inch thick on a lightly floured surface. Cut with floured cookie cutter. Bake on a greased cookie sheet in a 350° oven for about 10 minutes.
You may decorate with raisin for eyes, nose, and buttons before baking; or you can use icing as a decoration after the baked cookies cool.
Preparation time: 1½ hours.

TOFFEE BARS

Corn oil
Cinnamon graham crackers
2 sticks butter

1 cup light brown sugar
1 cup chopped pecans

Line an oiled 10½ x 15½ inch pan with cinnamon graham crackers. Boil 2 sticks butter and 1 cup brown sugar to soft ball stage (238° on candy thermometer). Remove from heat and add 1 cup chopped pecans. Pour over crackers. Bake at 350° for 10 minutes. Cool and cut into small bars.

CAROLINE'S BROWNIES

2 sticks margarine, melted	1 cup pecan pieces
4 tablespoons cocoa	1 teaspoon vanilla
4 eggs, beaten	Salt to taste
2 cups sugar	Small marshmallows
1½ cups flour	

Blend melted margarine with cocoa. Add to beaten eggs to remaining ingredients and then to cocoa/margarine mixture. Bake 30 minutes at 350° in 13 x 9 x 2¼ inch or 10 x 14 inch pan. While hot, scatter top with marshmallows (after cake is cooked).

Icing:

1 stick margarine	¼ cup cocoa
½ cup milk	1 box powdered sugar

Boil margarine and milk for 1 minute. Add cocoa and powdered sugar and pour over top of marshmallowed cake. Cool in pan.
They do not freeze well.

ORANGE CHOCOLATE CHIP BARS

½ cup brown sugar	½ teaspoon salt
¾ cup sugar (½ cup at first)	1 cup flour
1 cup shortening	½ cup chocolate chips
2 eggs	1 cup dry oatmeal
2 tablespoons vanilla	½ cup orange juice

Cream shortening, add brown sugar, ½ cup sugar, eggs, vanilla and salt. Add flour, oatmeal and chocolate chips. Turn into greased 9 x 9 inch pan. Bake 40 minutes at 350°.
Combine remaining sugar and orange juice. Bring to boil and pour over hot bars.
(Doubled recipe fills 9 x 13 inch pan.)

ALMOND OATMEAL COOKIES *Yield: 4 or 5 dozen*

1 cup white sugar

1 cup brown sugar

1 cup shortening

1 tablespoon almond extract

2 eggs

2 cups flour

½ teaspoon salt

½ teaspoon cream of tartar

1 teaspoon soda

1 cup regular oatmeal

1 cup Corn Flakes or Special K

1 cup chopped pecans or other nuts

1 cup raisins or chopped dates

Cream sugars and shortening. Add flavoring and eggs. Mix flour with salt, cream of tartar and soda; add to mixture. Add oats, Corn Flakes, nuts and raisins. Mix thoroughly. Form pieces of dough into marble-size pieces and put on greased cookie sheet. Space pieces of dough about 1½ inches apart. Bake for 12 to 13 minutes or until light brown at 325° to 350°.

ICE BOX COOKIES

1 cup brown sugar

1 cup granulated sugar

1½ cups melted margarine or Crisco

3 eggs

4 cups all purpose flour

2 teaspoons soda

1 teaspoon each cinnamon, nutmeg and allspice

1 teaspoon salt

2 teaspoons vanilla

1½ cups chopped nuts (floured)

Mix sugar and melted margarine well. Add eggs one at a time, beating well after each addition. Sift dry ingredients together. Add 1 cup of flour mixture, stir in floured nuts, beat well adding remainder of flour. Add vanilla. Divide into 5 portions. Shape into rolls and wrap in foil or wax paper. Refrigerate overnight. Slice in thin rounds and bake in a 325° oven for 10 to 12 minutes or until brown.

Dough can be kept for days in refrigerator and baked as desired.

Cookbook Credits

Mrs. Thomas W. H. Alexander
Mrs. Thomas A. Allison
Mrs. William L. Allsion
Mrs. Frank R. Anderson, Jr.
Mrs. C. W. Arrendell
Mrs. Sissy Ashby
Mrs. Marilee Baker
Mrs. Charles Banner, Jr.
Mrs. Edwin B. Barrett
Mrs. Larry W. Battle
Ms. Martha E. Battle
Ms. Laura G. Beal
Ms. Linda Beatrice-Fuller
Mrs. Samuel Behrends, Jr.
Mrs. Charles E. Bell, Jr.
Ms. Amanda R. Bible
Mrs. William Black
Mrs. Wyatt E. Blake
Mrs. Fred Blount
Mrs. Dan C. Boney
Mrs. Marion Bost
William S. Bost, Jr., M.D.
Mrs. William C. Bowen, Jr.
Mrs. Evelyn J. Brady
Mrs. Frank Bridger
James Bridger
Mrs. Bruce William Bridgfor
Mrs. Margaret M. Broome
Mrs. Alfred M. Brown
Mrs. Bynum Brown
Mrs. W. A. Brown, Jr.
Mrs. Marilyn Bryan
Mrs. Charles P. Bugg
Miss Sarah W. Bunn
Mrs. Bill Burchfield
Ms. Barbara Burton
Mrs. Frank J. Butler
Mrs. Roxanne Buttron

Mrs. Earle G. Caldwell
Mrs. A. P. Carlton
Mrs. Carolyn J. Clark
Mrs. Jane Clark
Mrs. J. Edwin Clement
Mrs. Joseph M. Clement
Mrs. Robert L. Clement
Mrs. Donnell B. Cobb, Jr.
Colonial Inn, Hillsborough, N.C.
Dana Copeland, M.D.
Mrs. Oran J. Cottle
Mrs. David W. Cox
Mrs. D. L. Cozart, Jr.
Mrs. John Crane
Mrs. Stephanie W. Crumpler
Mrs. T. Barker Dameron III
Mrs. Thomas B. Dameron, Jr.
Mrs. Charles Day
Mrs. Fred H. Deaton, Jr.
Mrs. Dean A. DeMasi
Mrs. Russell W. DeMent
Mrs. James W. Dempsey
Mrs. Reba A. Dent
Mrs. Starke S. Dillard
Mrs. Sewell H. Dixon
Mrs. Charles S. Dockery
Mrs. Daniel W. Donovan
Mrs. David W. Donovan
Mrs. Sam P. Douglas
Mrs. Peter St. Pierre DuBose
Mrs. Louisa Duff
Mrs. Thomas L. Dysard
Mrs. Samuel Eberdt
Mrs. Russell B. Edmondson
Mrs. H. Palmer Edwards
Mrs. J. Roger Edwards
Mrs. Paul W. Elam, Jr.
Mrs. James Eller
Mrs. Robert W. Estill
Mrs. J. C. Evans

Family Weekly, pg. 20, 6-7-81
Mrs. William W. Farley
Ms. Becky Farmer
Mrs. Frank T. Farmer
Miss Joan Ferraro
Ms. Barbara Hinton Finch
Mrs. Kenneth J. Finch
Mrs. J. Leland Flanagan
Mrs. Jill Flink
Thomas Fonville
Mrs. Thomas Fonville
Mrs. Vance Forbes
William W. Fore, M.D.
Mrs. Powell G. Fox, Jr.
Mrs. Ellen Fulghum
Mrs. H. Fleming Fuller
Mrs. Charles W. Gaddy
Ms. Gertrude Gardner
T. W. Garner Food Company
William P. Garrabrant
Mrs. John T. Garrison
Ms. Lenora Ann Garrison
Mrs. L. J. Gaskin
Mrs. William Gates
Mrs. Harold W. Glascock, Jr.
Mrs. Elton R. Glover
Ms. Ardath Ann Goldstein
Mrs. Sam L. Grist, Jr.
Mrs. Charles Gryb
Mrs. Douglas Guess
Mrs. Terrie Guin

Mrs. Robert L. Guthrie
Mrs. Richard Haar
Mrs. Thomas Hackney
Mrs. Ladd Hamrick
Mrs. Ted Haigler, Jr.
Mrs. Ira Hardy
Ira M. Hardy II, M.D.
Mrs. Margaret M. Harvey
Mrs. B. Mason Hawfield
Mrs. Robert Hayes
Mrs. Marshall DeLancey
   Haywood, Jr.
Mrs. Hector Henry
Dr. Donald L. Henson
Mrs. Milton Herman
Mrs. Priscilla Hill
Mrs. Carl Hiller
Mrs. Thomas Blair Hines
Norris L. Hodgkins
Mrs. Sara W. Hodgkins
Ms. Marilyn Holder
Mrs. Echols Hollomon
Ms. Kathryn G. Homan
Mrs. Robert Hosea
Ms. Carolyn J. Howard
Mrs. John Howard
Mrs. Graham Hoyle
Mrs. Joe Huntley, Jr.
Mrs. H. Gray Hutchison
Mrs. John Iredale
Mrs. Tanya B. Jackson
Mrs. Ruth D. Janesick
Mrs. Susan Jay
Stuart C. Jenks
Mrs. Joe R. John, Jr.
Mrs. Henry B. Johnson
Mrs. R. Horace Johnson
Mrs. J.W. Johnston, Jr.
Mrs. William R. Johnston
Mrs. Richard A. Jones
Mrs. W. D. Jones, Jr.
Mrs. Clyde Jordan, Jr.
Mrs. Max R. Joyner
Mrs. Walton K. Joyner

Mrs. Luther Kelly, Jr.
Mrs. Benjamin W. Kilgore III
Mrs. Edward B. King
Mrs. Edgar W. Kirby III
Blair Kleitsch
Mrs. Jack Koontz
Mrs. Trish Kirby Lancaster
Mrs. F. C. Lane
Mrs. Robert G. Lang
Mrs. E.M. Langley, Jr.
Ms. Joyce Lawing
Mrs. Thomas S. Lease
William D. Lease
Mrs. William D. Lease
Mrs. Charles E. Lefort
Mrs. Frank R. Liggett III
Ms. Laurie L. Little
Mrs. Roy L. Luckenbach
Mrs. Toddy MacKenzie
Mrs. Roger T. Mann
Henry S. Manning, Jr.
Mrs. Henry S. Manning, Jr.
Mrs. William C. Marlatt
Mrs. Courtney R. Mauzy
Mrs. Robert Mazer
Mrs. Vivian McDonald
Mrs. Ford McGowan
Mrs. Deryl McGuire
Ms. Jane McGuire
Mrs. Lynn McIver
Mrs. Charles C. McKinney
Mrs. Sam McNairy
Ms. Patsy H. McNeill
Mrs. Thomas R. McPherson
Mrs. Arthur C. Menius, Jr.
Mrs. Charles F. Merrill
Miss Sally Merrill
Mrs. Arnold D. Miles
Mrs. Betsy G. Miller
Mrs. W. Stacy Miller
Mrs. William L. Mills, Jr.
Mrs. Henry A. Mitchell
Mrs. Dwight E. Moody
Mrs. Christopher S. Moore
Mrs. Dan K. Moore
Mrs. Kenneth E. Morris
Mrs. William E. Moss
Ms. Bonnie M. Mullen
Mrs. Harris Mullen
Mrs. Allan Murray
Mrs. Marvin D. Musselwhite

Ms. Patty Nealeans
Mrs. Cecil H. Neville, Jr.
Mrs. S.J. Nicholson
Mrs. James R. Nisbet
Mrs. M. Wayne Nixon, Jr.
Mrs. A. Gwynn Nowell, Jr.
Mrs. Verna O'Brien
Mrs. John Odenwelder
Mrs. Kennedy O'Herron
Mrs. Robert J. Page
Mr. and Mrs. Arnold Palmer
Mrs. John C. Palmer
Mrs. Clifton G. Parker
Mrs. D. K. Parker, Jr.
Mrs. Fred P. Parker III
Ms. Joann Parker
Bob Passarelli, Chef,
   Executive Mansion
Mrs. A. M. Paton
Mrs. James M. Peden, Jr.
Mrs. Elbert S. Peel, Jr.
Mrs. Ashton Phillips
Mrs. B. H. Phillips
Marty Pierson
Mrs. F. Shields Pittman, Jr.
Mrs. Worth B. Plyler
Mrs. Jerry W. Powell
Mrs. Larry D. Pressley
Mrs. William I. Procter
Mrs. Lucius Pullen
Mrs. J. Ward Purrington

Cookbook Credits

Mrs. Carl S. Ragsdale
Mrs. George R. Ragsdale
Mrs. J. B. Ramsey
Joseph B. Ramsey, Jr.
Mrs. William G. Rand
Mrs. William G. Rand, Jr.
Ms. June Reichle
Mrs. Walter Reid
Mrs. John L. Rendleman
Mrs. Darrell L. Rhudy
Mrs. John T. Rice
Ms. Winnie Richter
Mrs. J. S. Riggan, Jr.
Mrs. George Patterson
  Ritchie
Mrs. Andrea Ritter
Mrs. Wilbur G. Robbins
Mrs. E. C. Roebuck
Mrs. Allen Rogers
Ms. Jan G. Rogers
Mrs. Virginia B. Rucker
Mrs. Daniel T. Russler

Mrs. Lucille C. Sanders
Mrs. B. Daniel Sapp
Mrs. Emerson Scarborough
Mrs. William Schwartz
Mrs. M. C. Sellers, Jr.
Mrs. Ronnie D. Shavlik
Mrs. Edwina Hardy Shaw
Ms. Katherine Sheerin
Mrs. William G. Shelton
Mrs. Richard Simmons
Mrs. William P. Skinner, Jr.
Mrs. Elizabeth P. Sloan
Mrs. Charles Lee Smith III
Mrs. J. Troy Smith
Mrs. Sherwood H. Smith, Jr.
Mrs. Wade M. Smith
Mrs. S. S. Speedil, Jr.
Mrs. George Speidel, Jr.
Mrs. Howard Sprock, Jr.
Ms. Dixie Stanley
Mrs. Thomas Steed
Mrs. David H. Stevens
Mrs. Scott F. Stidham
Mr. and Mrs. Ed Stone
Edward S. Stovall
Mrs. J. B. Stroud, Jr.
Mrs. William R. Stroud
Mrs. Charles W. Styron
Mrs. Donald F. Sutphen
Mrs. William Taft
Mrs. William H. Taft, Jr.
Mrs. Banks C. Talley, Jr.
Mrs. Natalie Talyor
Mrs. Robert E. Taylor
Mrs. William Grimes
  Thomas II
Ms. Alice Saunders Thorp
Mrs. Rex Tilley, Jr.
Mrs. Hugh H. Tilson
Mrs. Sam Toler
Bill Touchberry
Mrs. W. D. Toussaint
Mrs. Leslie Tremaine

Mrs. William F. Troutman
Mr. and Mrs. Clarence B.
  Tugwell
Mrs. Joseph G. Turner, Jr.
Mrs. Robert Turner
Mrs. Runyon Tyler
Mrs. Harrison A.
  Underwood, Jr.
Durbin H. VanVleck
Mrs. Richard Verrone
Mrs. George Vlk
Wards Produce, Inc.
Mrs. Max G. Warren
Mrs. Robert S. Warren
Mrs. Glen M. Watters
Mrs. Rich Webb
Mrs. M. W. Wester, Jr.
Mrs. Jim Wheatley
Mrs. Frank Leslie White
Ms. Virginia McCrary White
Mrs. Ruth W. Whitley
Mrs. William G. Whitley III
Wildlife in North Carolina,
  Dec. 1981, pg. 14-15
Mrs. Charles F. Williams
Miss Janice Williams
Mrs. Mary W. Williams
Mrs. Max Williams
Mrs. Fred R. Wilson
Mrs. Charles Winston
Mrs. J. Gilliam Wood
Ms. Patricia Wyler
Mrs. C.G. Yarborough, Jr.
Mrs. A. Jones York III
Mrs. Richard L. Young

Listed below are the descriptions of each of the sectional photographs.

MICROWAVE - Chicken in Wine, Blanched Asparagus

SALAD - Star of Sea Salad, Fresh Fruit, Assorted Cheeses

DESSERTS - Cold Strawberry Souffle, Raspberry and Strawberries Romanoff, Mint Chocolate Chip Ice Cream in Chocolate Shells

BRUNCHES - Creamy Eggs and Spinach, Angel Biscuits, Mimosa Cocktail

CAKES & PASTRIES - French Chocolate Silk Cake

MEATS - Crown Roast of Pork with Apple Raisin Dressing

BREADS - Assorted Breads

VEGETABLES - Fresh Vegetables from the Farmer's Market

SEAFOOD - Boiled North Carolina Shrimp and Maine Lobster

POULTRY AND GAME - Roast Duck with Orange Sauce and Apricot Garnish

SOUPS - Gazpacho with Herbed Croutons

HORS D'OEUVRES - Molded Avocado Pinwheel, Feta Cheese Ball

SAUCES - Orange Sauce, Fiery Barbeque Sauce, Spicey Cranberry Chutney

Index

Index